'Companies have arguably never faced such urgency in being able to change as fast as the culture they operate in. Sean Pillot de Chenecey's book is an inspirational and, most importantly, useful map to why and how change is occurring in the world and how businesses are responding – and need to respond. It's a call to arms.'

GARETH KAY, FOUNDING PARTNER, CHAPTER

'It's never been easier to be a disruptor in the business world and it's never been easier to be disrupted. Sean Pillot de Chenecey goes beyond the familiar trends of disruption and writes from the perspective of the new players who are upending traditional business, and the new practices that are shaping change. *Influencers & Revolutionaries* is the field guide to a turbulent time.'

TOM MORTON, CHIEF STRATEGY OFFICER, R/GA

'Perhaps the single most important business skill, today and in the future, is the ability to adapt to changing times and circumstances. This book feels uniquely current and provides a refreshingly idea-provoking roadmap for navigating the business and consumer landscape we're about to enter.'

OLE PETTER NYHAUG, PARTNER, OPINION AS, NORWAY

'*Influencers & Revolutionaries* makes a compelling argument for change, calling for a fundamental rethink about how we do business. This radical, intelligent and much-needed book provides a range of insightful and innovative ideas for those seeking a better way of doing business. Sean Pillot de Chenecey illuminates a way forward, envisioning a world where brands can become a positive force for good.'

HARRIETT POSNER, PROGRAMME DIRECTOR, BA (HONS) FASHION, CONDÉ NAST COLLEGE

DRAWN

'This book explains how and why the business environment is increasingly being shaped by movements such as Extinction Rebellion and B Corps, and by issues such as the Green New Deal and a Contract for the Web. It could not be more timely.'
SARAH RABIA, GLOBAL DIRECTOR OF CULTURAL STUDIES, TBWA\CHIAT\DAY

'Sean Pillot de Chenecey reminds us why research matters – to drive innovation and disrupt thinking. He does both.'
MARTIN RAYMOND, EDITOR-IN-CHIEF AND CO-FOUNDER, THE FUTURE LABORATORY

Influencers & Revolutionaries

How innovative trailblazers, trends and catalysts are transforming business

Sean Pillot de Chenecey

Kogan Page
INSPIRE

First published in Great Britain and the United States in 2020 by Kogan Page Limited

2nd Floor, 45 Gee Street	122 W 27th St, 10th Floor	4737/23 Ansari Road
London	New York, NY 10001	Daryaganj
EC1V 3RS	USA	New Delhi 110002
United Kingdom		India

www.koganpage.com

© Sean Pillot de Chenecey, 2020

The right of Sean Pillot de Chenecey to be identified as the author of this work has been asserted by him in accordance with the Copyright, Designs and Patents Act 1988.

ISBNs

Hardback	978 0 7494 9870 2
Paperback	978 0 7494 9868 9
eBook	978 0 7494 9869 6

British Library Cataloguing-in-Publication Data

A CIP record for this book is available from the British Library.

Library of Congress Cataloging-in-Publication Data

CIP data is available. Library of Congress Cataloging-in-Publication Control Number: 2019052554

Typeset by Integra Software Services, Pondicherry
Print production managed by Jellyfish
Printed and bound by CPI Group (UK) Ltd, Croydon CR0 4YY

Contents

Acknowledgements

I'd like to thank my wife Helen, and children Berry and Thomas, for their love and support during the writing of *Influencers and Revolutionaries*.

I spoke with, and interviewed, many people whilst researching it, but in particular would acknowledge Carsten Beck, Mark Borkowski, Julian Boulding, Joanna Catalano, Guy Cheston, Michael Cohen, Carole Collet, Thomas Coombes, Jonathan Disegi, John Dunleavy, Sabrina Faramarzi, Eki Felt, Geoff Glendenning, Scott Goodson, Lucie Greene, Raja Habre, Jonathan Hall, Teresa Havvas, Ben Hughes, Gareth Kay, Anne Lise Kjaer, Rupert Leigh, Ian McGarrigle, Katie McQuater, Andy Middleton, Tom Morton, Ole Petter Nyhaug, Sarah Rabia, Martin Raymond, Chris Sanderson, Mike Schwarz, Mark Shayler, Timothy Shoup, William Skeaping, Sheela Thandasseri, Thomas Stoeckle, Jen Urich and Nilgin Yusuf.

I must thank the amazing team at Kogan Page for all their help, in particular to my brilliant editor Geraldine Collard, and also to Annette Abel, Matt De Bono, Chris Cudmore, Philippa Fiszzon, Jaini Haria, Caroline Holroyd, Amy Joyner, Helen Kogan, Mary Lince, Christina Lindeholm, Alison Middle, Megan Mondi, Cresta Norris, Paul Raymond, Stephen Stratton, and in the US, Lori Ames, Courtney Dramis, Martin Hill, Kayla Keller, Vanessa Rueda, and Kerri Skarren.

As ever, I'd like to thank the world's best-connected man, my brilliant agent Cosimo Turroturro along with Esther Nelson, Patrick Nelson and Julia Scott at Speakers Associates.

Finally, I must express my gratitude to all those retailers who backed my first title *The Post-Truth Business*. To see it reach No 1 in the business book charts and for it to also be a finalist in the 'Business Book of the Year Awards' was incredibly exciting. Thank you to all concerned.

Introduction

Innovation, on which any organization is so reliant, is about to become more dynamic and challenging than ever.

I believe that hyper-relevance, ultra-personalization, collaboration, ethics and sustainability are the crucial foundations of success. Meanwhile, those tasked with creating that innovation are now faced by two key issues with implications that could not be more profound, nor more disruptive.

The first sees the challenge of the environmental crisis mean that society and business alike are confronted with an existential dilemma. It's one that has, in the majority of cases, effectively been ignored. That crisis has in fact become a 'climate and biodiversity emergency' and major action is needed, with businesses in every industry having a role to play.

The second sees technology, and particularly artificial intelligence, having game-changing impacts across all sectors. From product development to service provision, from smart cities to connected homes, and from future jobs to next-generation education, the effects will be deeply felt at all levels, across society and business, around the world.

Throughout this book, therefore, I illustrate the effect of these issues across a wide variety of areas. The first being a global problem that has to be addressed with the utmost urgency, and where innovation has a crucial role to play; while the second is set to be the ultimate 'innovation enabler' as we also finally move into the second phase of the internet, where the Internet of Things enables ever more ubiquitous connectivity.

In each case, creative thinking and collaborative approaches show the way forward.

For companies that are seen, by their behaviour, to be meeting these challenges in an effective and inventive manner, then on purely consumer-engagement and brand-differentiation levels, this will enable them to achieve greater business success.

In the book, I take note of renowned innovative 'thinkers and doers' (from philosophers to entrepreneurs) and reference international agencies, consultants, think tanks, brands, movements and organizations that illuminate, in my opinion, best-case examples of 'how to do it'.

In a consumer context, I portray a major overall shift from passive to active consumption.

In a consumer context, I portray a major overall shift from passive to active consumption. The implications are that businesses must reflect new lifestyles, behaviours and attitudes from people who are both more demanding in their desires from brands, and less satisfied with current branded offerings. Meanwhile, a key ongoing trend in innovation circles sees product development being recast as 'service renovation' or 'experience creation' and this move shows not the slightest sign of abating.

From a business strategy perspective, being customer centric via agile responses to attitudinal trends and behavioural change is a more vital approach than ever. This is why, for instance, the role of the designer is of such importance. And it's also why the influence of the educational establishment is so significant, as their ongoing promotion of 'design thinking' benefits organizations around the world.

In addition, an absolutely vital point is that of 'social innovation', this being a core issue reflected everywhere from debates at the World Economic Forum to global activist group protests. What is fascinating is that both combine some similar demands. These include that organizations of all types now demonstrate a proactive social purpose, which requires ever more open-minded thinking in order to achieve the required results.

So, how do innovators answer the variety of demands with which businesses are confronted? I believe that relevance, personalization and sustainability are the key issues on which to base strategic and tactical approaches, and that a simple formula for enabling successful innovation, and then proving the results of it, is 'Insight + Ideas + Impact'.

I've worked on innovation projects, on an international basis, for a very wide range of clients and agencies over the years. It still amazes me how much confusion there is about this subject. For me, the innovator quite simply 'seeks problems to solve when confronted with a challenge'.

On a practical level, how do they do it? I believe that the sign of genuine innovators is that they look for inspiration, consider ideas, products or services that may already be relevant, and then either utilize these to solve the dilemma they face, or move from incremental innovation to genuine invention, and create a new answer to that problem.

Meanwhile, all too many organizations seem to remain in a wilful state of inertia when it comes to understanding the disruptive changes taking place across their sector or industry. To them, I would merely repeat the well-known advice of Henry Ford, who so memorably said 'Whenever you get the idea that you are fixed or that anything is fixed for life, you'd better get ready for a sudden change'.

Chapter guide

To illustrate how I've approached the variety of innovation areas covered in this book, this is a brief guide to the chapters within it:

Chapter 1 Classic innovation theory and current leading-edge thinking

I begin the book by providing a brief overview of a selection of renowned innovative thinkers, highlighting an eclectic mix of philosophers and business visionaries including René Descartes, Joseph Schumpeter, John Locke, Karl Popper, Theodore Levitt, Rebecca Henderson, Peter Drucker, Rita McGrath, Philip Kotler, Mariana Mazzucato and Amy Webb.

In doing so, I identify what I believe are some crucial routes to innovative thinking, regarding the need to challenge established thinking, being aware of cultural signals, leveraging organizational assets, and conducting research into tension points, prior to concept evaluation.

Chapter 2 The disruptors disrupted. What next for adland?

In this chapter, I discuss innovative actions that are revitalizing communication strategies and the agency world that creates that brand communication. In setting the overall picture, I highlight a sector still reeling from a decade of unparalleled disruption, a situation to which there is absolutely no end in sight.

I also look into a key fault line running through much of the agency world, which impacts their output – a continuing lack of diversity. Hence suggesting that the make-up of their teams is well overdue regarding issues based around gender, ethnicity, sexuality, age, religion, lifestyle and background.

Chapter 3 The future of retail and the future home

In Chapter 3, I focus on the future of retail and the future home; subjects that are joined, like so many others in this book, within the overall context of smart technology, environmental issues and changing consumer behaviour.

Yet, somehow, many businesses appear to be ignoring these new realities despite the implications of smart stores, smart homes and informed consumers being so important. From a retail perspective, the pace of change has never been faster, and the pressure on retail margins has never been greater. It is crucial that businesses reflect new lifestyles, behaviours and attitudes. Meanwhile, the overall impact of retailing is infiltrating our domestic environments as never before. I therefore focus on the implications of the connected home and, within it for example, the future kitchen, where technology 'knows us and assists us' as never before. The issue of the staggering amount of consumer data being gathered in our living environment is discussed in depth relating to both the positive implications, ie personalized services, and the negative, ie increased privacy intrusion.

Chapter 4 How the food and drink industries leverage catalytic trends

This chapter describes a series of catalytic trends being utilized by organizations ranging from multinational corporations to local start-ups, alongside the highlighting of a variety of category-changing products and packaging that have resulted from leveraging those issues.

Throughout the chapter I therefore outline a range of dynamic actions focusing on global consumer behaviour and sector trends that have issues such as ethics, sustainability, individual health benefits, and user experience as foundational considerations. Specific activity connected to these areas reference factors such as localism, provenance, mindfulness, transparency, traceability, bioengineering, premium convenience and hyper-personalization.

Chapter 5 The wellness economy meets the lifestyle industry

In Chapter 5 I examine the health and wellness market, where the amount of innovation taking place is staggering. Hence, I cover a wide spectrum of areas undergoing transformational change. In doing so, I illustrate an increasingly holistic and multi-sector approach to mental and physical health. This has led to a 'multiplier-effect' where traditional notions of health products, services and organizations are being leveraged by individual and collaborative activity across sectors such as beauty, fashion, hospitality, sports, food, architecture and retail. In addition, this dynamic situation is being continuously impacted by catalytic start-ups, alongside progressive action from legacy brands, on a global basis.

Chapter 6 Smart cities, the IoT and connected living

This chapter looks into a range of dynamic issues and trends affecting 'cities of today and tomorrow' and highlights a variety of catalytic innovations impacting the people living and working in, and visiting, them. This is happening at a time when serious questions are being asked of those tasked with creating progressive answers to the problems facing citizens, businesses and governments alike.

The approach I've chosen to take focuses on the 'chaotic realities' of urban life, alongside some extraordinarily innovative ways in which these realities are being addressed, regarding plans being developed and actions being taken relating to the here and now, in addition to insights gained from leading-edge trend forecasters and scenario planners.

Chapter 7 Intelligent and sustainable: a new era of tourism and mobility

In Chapter 7, I cover a range of trends and innovative activity taking place across the tourism and mobility sectors. I've joined these areas together from the perspective of similar cultural and social trends linking to product development and service provision, from both legacy brands and start-up operations.

The two issues that I focus on most in these sectors (in all their guises) are environmentalism, from the perspective of 'conscious consumption' where sustainability is a central concern, alongside ongoing digitization, particularly relating to artificial intelligence and the anticipated impacts of other forms of next-generation technology.

Chapter 8 The transformation of entertainment by technology, experiences and personalization

In this chapter, I look into the overall entertainment industry, and a range of specific areas within it, including the gaming, sports, television, radio, film, music and festival sectors. These areas all have key areas in common: relating to the effect of technological innovation and a demand for ever-greater levels of consumer experience.

I highlight issues such as the gaming sector being impacted by a new generation of consoles and streaming technology. Regarding sports, I look into how augmented and virtual reality will offer fans a 'full-immersion' experience. In the television sector, I note that, despite all rumours to the contrary, broadcast TV is alive and well. Meanwhile, customer online-viewing behaviour has transformed content consumption and, with it, the film industry. I also look into the music business where consumer experiences are becoming ever more rewarding, and then cover the festivals sector, where the number and variety of these catering to niche audiences has multiplied massively.

Chapter 9 The future of work: goodbye to certainty and stability. Hello to Industry 4.0

In Chapter 9 I outline how a range of trends are impacting the future of work from a range of perspectives including future workforce desires, the catalytic impact of technology, the enablement of autonomy and the broadening remit of creativity. I illuminate why the future workplace will become a more emotional, diverse, inclusive and responsive 'exchange space' and why issues ranging from wellness to flexibility to virtuality are becoming ever more key considerations.

I therefore look into specific areas such as leadership, 'conscious coworking', multi-generational teams, lifelong learning, the search for meaning and value creation, and how we're witnessing a move from 'talent owning' to 'talent attraction'. I also explain how we need to fundamentally reappraise work by taking a fresh look at the impact of social and cultural trends regarding the 'who, how, why and where'.

Chapter 10 Fintech and insurtech, and the battle of choice vs privacy

This chapter looks into the dynamic areas of the banking and insurance markets, where the level of disruptive innovation, particularly in Western markets, is at long last catching up with those in the East.

The supercharging of the financial services industry (in all its guises) by Big Tech provides them with a dynamic challenge, or a 'perfect storm' problem. The implications of ever-increasing technological progress, the impact of stricter regulations and the effect of increasingly demanding consumers, set against a broader backdrop of changing social expectations, mean that both these sectors are set for a turbulent ride over the next few years. Common denominators include innovation based around increased consumer choice while safeguarding consumer privacy.

The Influencers and Revolutionaries Innovation Manifesto

I believe it's virtually impossible to imagine any type of business that won't be affected by the issues I describe as being set to impact the sector, or sectors, within which they operate. (And yes, I'm well aware of that being a big claim.) In a context set by the global crisis of climate change and the disruptive impact of technological developments, governments, businesses and society alike require levels of change that see innovation, in all its forms, being highlighted as 'the answer' as never before.

But while many view these issues with a sense of resignation, even fear, I believe the future is one to look forward to with a positive mindset and a progressive attitude.

In the final chapter, I therefore summarize my thinking around the way ahead for innovation, by providing an 'Influencers and Revolutionaries Innovation Manifesto' for readers to use as an easy reference guide to some of the key points discussed and examined throughout my book.

Set as a backdrop to my thinking is the belief that the catalytic times in which we live have profound implications for organizations of all varieties, meaning that it's no longer 'business as usual'. The levels of imagination and creativity required to successfully deal with the challenges that affect us were indicated in the starkest terms by, for instance, Greta Thunberg's speech at the UN when she called for systematic change. They continue to be highlighted via the ongoing activities organized around the world by Extinction Rebellion and via the ethos of those such as the B Corp movement, who advocate for a radically different approach to capitalism.

A well-known industry saying has it that the most successful companies achieve their ongoing success by preparing for change, rather than simply attempting to adapt to that change when it appears.

I therefore hope that the wide range of innovative approaches and actions that I've illuminated in this book assist readers in their own preparations for the ever more disruptive changes that are appearing around us, and the unknown ones that must surely come.

CHAPTER ONE

Classic innovation theory and current leading-edge thinking

B efore we go into the series of chapters covering a wide range of specific business sectors, I hope you'll find it beneficial if I provide a brief overview of some classic 'thinkers and doers' held in immensely high regard in the innovation world.

For those of you well-versed in this area, most – possibly even all – of the people highlighted will be familiar to you, although perhaps not in the context of innovation. But for others, I hope this approach provides a useful guide.

Regarding a common question 'where does innovation come from?' I interviewed an exceptional thinker, Martin Raymond of the Future Laboratory, who outlined how 'innovation – the product of knowledge and insight – happens in clusters, and shifts in culture come in peaks, or movements, or periods in history. Knowledge, once unleashed, acts like a catalyst firing and flinging other ideas together. Thus "bridge moments" are created that enable new levels for new but associated ideas to grow'.

As for those 'peaks, movements or periods in history' obvious examples are the Dark Ages, the Renaissance, the Enlightenment, the Modernist Movement, the Consumer Society, the Information Age, the New Economy, the Knowledge Economy and the Creative Economy.

I really like his thinking, and the issue of catalysts and bridge moments are ones that I frequently reference when discussing classic industry examples of innovation, where the equation goes: Insight + Ideas + Impact = Innovation.

As for the importance of this area, the industry legend Peter Drucker aka the 'founder of modern management' famously said that 'the two most important functions of a business are innovation and marketing, as they are the only two functions that contribute to profit, while all others are costs' (Drucker, 2002).

> *The whole raison d'être of innovation is that the person or team responsible 'seeks problems to solve'.*

The whole raison d'être of innovation is, to put it even more simply, that the person or team responsible 'seeks problems to solve'.

And to provide a simple guide to doing that, I think that *Forbes* magazine put it neatly when stating that 'the key route is to seek inspiration, combine similar ideas, then solve the problem.' For them, and for so many tasked with innovation, the issue is facing a dilemma of 'confronting chaos, with the aim of creating order' (Denning, 2015).

So, as you'll find when reading this book, the themes of insights leading to ideas, which when successfully put into practice prove themselves via the genuine impact they deliver, are referred to time and again across multiple business sectors and areas of life, be they cultural, social, economic or political.

I'll focus on some of my favourite business innovators in a while, but first would like to highlight a collection of philosophers and visionary thinkers who, I think, provided an array of 'influential and revolutionary' thinking that is entirely relevant, indeed deeply inspirational, to the world of business.

From a marketing perspective, René Descartes might be viewed as the 'founding father' of innovation, due to his independent stance and a core belief that when seeking the truth one starts by questioning accepted thinking and established practices.

He essentially asked us to pose the question 'how can we know this for certain?' This is a question that everyone tasked with managing a brand should ask themselves on a regular basis. (As in 'you may believe this, but does the consumer?') One could argue that good marketers, and particularly researchers, take a 'Descartian approach' to business problems by directly challenging the core beliefs around the 'consumer reality' of a brand, which are very often based on either outmoded, unrealistic or simply wishful thinking.

The amount of senior company personnel who see things as they'd like them to be, rather than as they really are, is quite extraordinary.

One of the business buzzwords that any reader of this book will be only too familiar with is 'disruption' as it's one of those terms that, while being 'correct' has also become deeply irritating due to its almost continual use.

However, something that never ceases to amaze me is how rarely the 'Godfather of Disruption' is mentioned. Joseph Schumpeter is, or rather was, a genuinely revolutionary thinker in business terms, with his thinking being as relevant today as it was when he was one of the leading business intellects of his era, and who believed that true innovation is effectively never-ending, and therefore disruption can be an ongoing issue, not a 'one-off'. This is because once an idea has been created, someone else may create a better iteration of it.

He also warned us that innovation is the market introduction of an idea, not just its invention, and this is a vital point that many innovators seem to forget, when assuming that just thinking of a new idea or concept is enough.

And, of course, when one talks about 'never-ending' innovation, one has to also acknowledge the famous take on that issue highlighted by Clayton Christensen in his book *The Innovator's Dilemma*. In it, he focused on the inbuilt problem that faces a successful company that is doing the 'right thing' by obsessing over their loyal customers to the exclusion of others. The inbuilt problem, or Catch-22 situation if you prefer, is essentially one where companies try simultaneously to both look after their core customers while also trying to be innovative, and yet not be so innovative as to disrupt their own business. Yet if companies don't do this, they can quickly become stale in the eyes of those very consumers or customers. Hence constant iteration, if nothing else, is required.

Another philosopher that I'll reference is John Locke, who was a great believer in empiricism and observation, ie where knowledge derives from experience. That standpoint is a bastion of the market research world. I'm a strong believer in his thinking, and believe that Locke might have said, regarding the current context of endless brands proclaiming their (often tenuous) 'brand purpose' that brand credibility is based on brand experience, not brand stories. That, by the way, is an issue which I explore in more detail, in the chapter on marketing.

The word 'tenuous' is one often used when referring to the world of trend forecasting, where a personal favourite perspective comes from the futurist William Gibson, who noted that 'we have no genuine idea of what the future may hold because our present is too volatile. We have only risk management and the spinning of the given moment's scenarios' (Gibson, 2003). Like many people working in research, I've long been an admirer of Gibson. This led me to interview him for *Dazed and Confused* magazine many years ago, regarding his just-published book *Pattern Recognition*, where that quote arose.

Since then, I've seen that title used in so many trend presentations around the world (including mine, I must admit) that it's become an utter cliché. But what Gibson had to say was genuinely interesting and entirely relevant, and had clear links with the Karl Popper school of thought regarding there being no such thing as a certain, predictable future (with the exception of scientific/mathematical prediction) due to events being out of our control in a chaotic world.

Defining innovation and the innovative organization

From the point of view of how we're currently defining innovation, how to approach it, and what the desired skills are from the perspective of a 'perfect innovation team', I'll now provide a range of examples.

My overall aim is for the reader to be able to swiftly identify a viewpoint or process that they can use on their own 'innovation problem'.

I believe that one of the most vital things to do is to be crystal clear in recognizing that invention (the creation of a process or device) is markedly different from innovation, which is a process of transforming via iteration, styling or alteration.

That's a crucial distinction and an important one to make clear at the outset of a project, or the laying down of a strategy or indeed job description, as most people tend to say 'innovate' when they actually mean 'invent'.

So, once we're clear that we mean 'innovation' and not 'invention' it clarifies the parameters for the resulting task from the outset.

When it comes to those parameters, Rebecca Henderson (from MIT) and Kim Clark (from Harvard) devised their 'radical innovation' theory back in the late 1980s, and published a ground-breaking paper in which they described four types of innovation: 'Incremental, Modular, Architectural and Radical'. Each related to setting out a practical way forward, and the clarity of their thinking was amazingly influential, ie for product development.

Meanwhile, once we're agreed on an appropriate 'innovation, not invention' route, we then need to answer a series of straightforward questions, and must be brutally simple when answering them.

These include: what's the insight behind the potential innovation need, what concept does this thinking inspire, what can be expected to alter due to this innovation, what actually could it be, via which route to market can the most powerful effect be made, and how – and when – will a return on investment be proven? With regard to that point, the words of Barry Nalebuff from the Yale School of Management 'people tend to overestimate the impact of innovation in the short run and underestimate it in the long run' have echoed down the years. Now, while those are a set of staggeringly obvious questions, unless each one is answered with absolute clarity, then the chances of success weaken.

The first of those questions, about defining the insight behind the innovation, goes right to the heart of producing an innovation that is actually useful and/or desired. That's something that the renowned Philip Kotler focused on when stating that 'companies last as long as they continue to provide superior customer value. They must be market-driven and customer-driven. In the best cases, they are market driving, by innovation' (Kotler, 2003).

Being 'customer-driven' means, in my eyes, getting out from the comfort of an office and seeking those customer insights by conducting ethnographic research, ie research conducted in the real-life context of the consumer and the product or service in question.

That was the approach espoused by Douglas Holt (a Professor of Marketing at Harvard Business School) and Douglas Cameron, from the amazing creative outfit CF&P. They suggested that most conventional innovation and strategy models aren't fit for purpose, and that a large number of legacy brands find themselves behaving in a stereotypically orthodox way of doing business, conducting a sort of 'cultural mimicry'.

This is where the cultural researcher comes into their own, and crucially, it helps legacy brands, start-ups and social entrepreneurs to leapfrog competitors into new areas of dynamic growth, or to simply reconnect with existing customers by showing that they both understand and empathize with their 'cultural realities'.

A classic example of this is youth culture, and you only have to spend a few minutes subjecting yourself to an array of TV commercials aimed at young people to see some exasperating examples of how not to do it, from a communications-engagement perspective.

But what about the need for, vs the reliability of, trend forecasting? After all, I've already highlighted Karl Popper and his 'chaos theory' regarding the uncertainty of a 'predictable future', along with William Gibson and his thinking about current volatility and pattern recognition.

Surely the answer, or at least a vital element of it, is to take heed of all those 'signals and noises' that trend researchers aim to highlight. This point is referenced by Peter Schwartz of the Global Business Network, who talks about companies putting themselves at risk by not giving credence to these events, from a forecasting and scenario planning perspective. He maintains that 'we can't stop disruptions from happening, but we can cope with them far better than we have in the past, if we watch and listen constantly' (Schwartz, 2004).

As to the approach researchers should take and the problems that face them, the much-admired futurist Amy Webb is renowned for her viewpoint that 'trends are signposts'. In her book *The Signals are Talking*, she says that 'novelty is the new normal. It's about tracking trends across sectors, not just one vertical. If an organization can see over the horizon, it'll be positioned as a first mover'.

That point about being a 'first mover' was identified by Richard Foster from McKinsey, who wrote the highly acclaimed book *Innovation: The attacker's advantage* way back in the 1980s.

This, he believed, was the strategy needed in order to gain competitive advantage.

He thought there was an endless battle going on in business life between the innovators (or attackers) and those who wanted to maintain their existing advantage (the defenders). He was therefore a real believer in companies changing their mindset from being defence-orientated (ie complacently managing the current situation) to being attack minded (ie focusing on innovation) with research being a key element.

Anyone who's had to deal with the deeply frustrating inertia of companies that move at a glacial pace will, no doubt, recognize exactly what that McKinsey viewpoint illuminated. It holds so many organizations back, and is a terrible hindrance to future success, in a fast-moving competitive environment.

The very first thing to do, I believe, is to go right back to the thinking that went into the foundations of a brand, and to then trace its development to the present day, while taking note of changing market conditions and the competitive set.

Link this thinking with detailed trend research using a 'bricolage' technique of gathering a wide range of interesting data from both within and outside the brand's sector, alongside expert interviews and ethnographic research with consumers reflecting the extremes of the market.

That ethnographic research needs to establish, from a 'genuine' consumer perspective, what the actual attitudinal and behavioural realities of the sector within which the brand operates are, and the deep-seated emotional connections, motivations and constrictions that underpin those beliefs and actions. It's remarkable how few brands and agencies make the effort to get out and meet people 'on their own turf' but the results always pay dividends.

One can then build an actionable picture of where the brand sits in the marketplace, and where a potential future may lead. In addition, via scenario planning, the implications and opportunities indicated by some 'logical or chaotic' possibilities from a combination of relevant cultural, social, industry-sector, economic and political perspectives can be developed.

The fundamental point, from an innovation perspective, is that ideas are implemented, as opposed to being endlessly discussed. In having that point of view, I'm in great company, as according to that endlessly quoted business figure Theodore Levitt 'ideas are useless unless used.'

So where do you actually start on day one of a project? A great, if incredibly wide-reaching, example is given by Rita McGrath of Columbia Business School, who's one of the world's most influential business thinkers and who recommends key strategies to drive growth, such as 'change the customer's total experience'. Which may sound obvious, but you must surely agree that if you're going to go big, that's a great way to start.

Meanwhile, the issue of brand experiences, be they either purely practical (of the product type) or indeed deeply immersive (of the experiential type) are discussed in detail throughout this book, and I hope you'll find the examples as fascinating as I did, when researching them.

And when you do begin to formulate a concept around a new, or indeed iterative, variation of something, then it's worth mentioning *Leap* by Howard Yu, who is the IMD Business School Professor of Innovation. I noted earlier that a lot of what people term as 'innovation' is actually just a version of somebody else's original invention. (Or more probably, innovation, but let's not go there again.)

This is key for Howard Yu, who in his book, says that 'succeeding in today's marketplace is no longer just a matter of mastering copycat tactics; companies also need to leap across knowledge disciplines, and to reimagine how a product is made or a service is delivered' (Yu, 2018).

Finally, I must mention a crucial part of any successful innovation team: the 'Exit Champion' who is the person briefed with injecting a dose of scepticism into the innovation process.

The individual tasked with exhibiting this 'healthy scepticism' was highlighted in a highly influential article published in the *Harvard Business Review* years ago, and I have to say, I've been quoting it ever since.

Crucially, this person has to be as equally positive and progressive as others in innovation teams (a vital thing to remember here is that 'cynics' are very different from 'sceptics') but who plays a 'voice of reality' role. As the *HBR* stated in that article, these types of people need to have the 'temperament and credibility to question prevailing beliefs, and if necessary, forcefully make the case that it should be killed' (Royer, 2003).

We can hopefully agree that innovation is 'something different that has impact'.

We can hopefully agree that innovation is 'something different that has impact'.

Examples are all around us, as they include some of the biggest brands in the world. Classic examples include Airbnb and Uber (neither of whom invented the idea of sleeping or taxis) who, by taking an iterative and collaborative approach, utilized a ubiquitous form of technology to offer a useful new service where there was a 'tension point'.

That key 'tension point' was trust (followed by cost and convenience) but by leveraging 'digitally empowered trust' they were able to satisfy consumers in both markets, along with homeowners and drivers. What those companies therefore leveraged with enormous success, were clear consumer needs that were going unsatisfied.

There was nothing 'secret' in what they did, and neither invented anything, and yet each were absolutely revolutionary in their respective sectors.

Building a culture of innovation

Let's move on to identifying some other 'big thinkers' from the perspective of building a business culture, and a team within it, to develop innovation. I'll start by highlighting some mavericks, change agents and hard-headed strategists who shine a spotlight on those who take a dynamic approach to innovation.

Regarding the different types of intellect that innovation teams require, the famous psychologist Robert Sternberg, author of numerous books including *Perspectives on Thinking, Learning and Cognitive Styles* categorized intelligence via his 'Tri-archic theory'. This saw intelligence being viewed from three perspectives, which he termed:

- *Componential* (analytical, critical, evaluation or judgemental skills; or what's commonly termed being 'book smart').
- *Experiential* (creativity, discovery, imagination, inventiveness, prediction).
- *Practical* (contextual, practical or implementation skills) or what you or I might term being 'street-smart' (Sternberg, 2001).

Taking this point about the different types of thinkers required in a business context, John Adair, who is an expert on leadership, wrote in his best-selling book *Effective Innovation* that the 'unbeatable business' would have key personnel in their innovation team who would be tasked with specific roles, ie the *Creative Thinker* (who produces new ideas), the *Innovator* (who brings new products/services to market or changes existing ones), the *Inventor* (who produces commercial ideas), the *Entrepreneur* (who translates ideas into business reality), the *Intrapreneur* (regarding internal company innovation), the *Champion* (tasked with implements ideas) and the *Sponsor* (who backs ideas and removes obstacles) (Adair, 2015).

I mentioned at the beginning of this chapter that the foundation of innovation is that the person or team responsible 'seeks problems to solve'. The key route to doing so is to seek inspiration from both inside and outside the organization, combine relevant ideas and concepts, and then work your way forward to solving the problem.

But how exactly do teams approach problem solving? Whenever this subject is mentioned in innovation circles, the name of Genrich Altshuller is naturally mentioned, as he achieved fame as a result of his acclaimed book that was, somewhat unusually, titled *And Suddenly the Inventor Appeared: TRIZ, the theory of inventive problem solving.* (Try saying that after the office party.)

According to him, universal principles of creativity form the basis of innovation. In the book, he utilizes his TRIZ theory to identify and codify these principles and uses them to make the creative process more predictable. It follows four basic steps:

- Define your specific problem.
- Find the TRIZ generalized problem that matches it.
- Find the generalized solution that solves the generalized problem.
- Adapt the generalized solution to solve your specific problem.

MindTools (nd)

Another great problem-solving method is the CPS framework of creative problem solving and brainstorming. A key element of this is that it requires the would-be problem solver to divide their 'divergent' and 'convergent' thinking. Divergent thinking is the process of generating lots of potential solutions and possibilities, otherwise known as brainstorming. Convergent thinking involves evaluating those options and choosing the most promising one. For those of you wanting a quick DIY guide to the framework (invented by Alex Osborn) it goes like this: *Clarify* (set out the key project goal/data/questions); *Ideate* (research the area and brainstorm the resulting ideas); *Develop* (develop solutions to the issues identified); and *Implement* (build a plan of action) (Creative Education Foundation, 2016).

But what about management's role? Peter Drucker focused on the discussion around how much of innovation is inspiration vs how much is genuinely hard work, from the angle of appropriate management. As he stated 'if it's mainly the former, then management's role is limited: hire the right people and get out of their way. If it's largely the latter, management plays a more vigorous role: establishing roles and processes, setting goals and measures, and reviewing progress at every step.' But above everything else, he pointed out that innovation 'is work rather than genius' (Drucker, 2002).

As for the culture that's needed in a corporate setting, a key thing is that 'rebels and mavericks' have to feel respected, in a welcoming, collaborative and supporting environment. That's something that the hugely influential thinker and all-round innovation expert Don Tapscott suggests, and I absolutely agree with his views around collaboration, this being one of the issues that runs through my book and is reflected by numerous examples of multi-sector international business activity.

In a corporate setting, a key thing is that 'rebels and mavericks' have to feel respected, in a welcoming, collaborative and supporting environment.

As he says 'the world is deeply divided, too unequal, unstable and unsustainable. But the spirit of collaboration is penetrating every institution and all of our lives. It's part of problem solving, innovation and life-long learning in an ever-changing networked economy. More and more society will create wealth through networks of collaborators' (Tapscott, 2018).

Summary

To begin to finish a chapter that I have deliberately filled with references and quotes that focus purely on innovation, there also has to be one that illuminates the pressing question of the genuine impact of business, in its wider social context.

In order to do that, I'll turn to the astonishingly successful Tom Siebel, who sold his company to Oracle for approximately US $6 billion.

I'm very envious, to put it mildly.

When asked for his advice on 'how to do it' he responded in a much-repeated remark that 'what creates great companies is to focus on satisfying your customers, become a market leader, be known as a good corporate citizen and a good place to work. Everything else follows' (Wharton College, 2001).

I think that's a really admirable point of view, and the sort of advice that every business leader should reference.

I must also mention the brilliant thinker Mariana Mazzucato, and her dynamic economic viewpoints which are rightly lauded for their catalytic impact on international governmental policy. By this I allude to, for example, her perspective of state investment being a critical driver of 'original' innovation, in order to create economic value. This sees the state itself being viewed as an entrepreneurial entity, using its extraordinary powers to turbocharge innovation by taking a collectivist 'moonshot' approach to tackle major issues. This also sees governments increasingly leveraging internal tech-driven innovation, in the form of 'Govtech'.

Which brings us neatly to the summary.

I do hope that this brief guide to some 'influential and revolutionary' thinkers on innovation has been useful. There are obviously many more, but in the meantime, I'd encourage you to read the various books and articles I've highlighted, if you haven't already done so.

As for my 'top-line interpretation' of all of the great thinking that I've identified, here's what I'd suggest from the perspective of five key routes to innovation:

- **Question and confront.** Be sceptical, and challenge established thinking. So... think like René Descartes.
- **Look and listen.** Be aware of cultural signals and market dynamics. So... think like William Gibson.
- **Collaborate and utilize.** Leverage a range of team abilities and organizational assets. So... think like Don Tapscott. (Or on a genuinely macro, eg governmental, level, Mariana Mazzucato.)

- **Research and develop.** Conduct consumer research of needs, desires and tension points, then test innovative concepts. So… think like Peter Drucker.
- **Be a good corporate citizen.** Take note of, and try to help fix, social and environmental problems. So… think like Tom Siebel.

A final point I want to emphasize is that, while those creating 'the next big thing' do indeed occasionally 'get lucky' and therefore appear to have some sort of secret methodology, in the vast majority of cases they've purely worked hard, have followed a proven formula and put in the effort.

Thus proving that there is no 'secret methodology' and we can all give ourselves the best chance of achieving innovation success, if we simply follow that approach.

However, it needs a spirit of being open-minded, collaborative, intuitive, agile and honest with those around us.

To finish, in a business world featuring increasingly intense competition, and where innovation has never been more vital, perhaps the last word should go to that great management thinker Tom Peters, who so notably said 'relentless experimentation was probably important in the past. Now it's do or die' (McKinsey Quarterly, 2014).

CHAPTER TWO

The disruptors disrupted.
What next for adland?

Throughout this book, I look into innovation across a wide variety of areas, either from the perspective of product and service innovation impacting a specific sector, or in the context of a social or cultural subject.

In this chapter however, I look into innovative actions that are revitalizing communication and the agency world that creates that communication. I've done so by highlighting what I consider to be some of the most dynamic thinking and best-practice activity taking place. Not from the angle of 'which campaigns are winning most awards' as that would merely mean repeating information widely available elsewhere, but by highlighting some genuinely influential and indeed revolutionary activity.

To set the overall picture, the communications sector is reeling from a decade of unparalleled disruption, a situation to which there is absolutely no end in sight. I also highlight a profound question confronting adland: what is that sector (aka the 'billion-dollar persuasion machine') to do regarding their ongoing role in causing the climate crisis? One thing is clear for an industry that, just like the fashion sector, is massively implicated in this horrendous problem – moral neutrality is an unacceptable position.

On a macro level, a seemingly bottomless lack of trust has resulted in a 'reputation building' advertising industry, in particular, having a reputation itself that seems to sink only downwards, albeit with a few shining and inspirational exceptions.

This issue has seen the president of the Advertising Association say that 'while advertising does good through things like providing a free press and building great brands, ever-declining trust is a major problem'. The cause of this has been what he termed the 'seven deadly sins', these being 'the reduced quality of advertising; the challenge around influencer marketing; concerns over data; brands funding bad activity including online fraud; fake news; personalization; and bombardment' (Vizard, 2019).

I wrote a book (*The Post-Truth Business*) about those issues, and one of the key points I noted about the titans of Silicon Valley was the way they've smashed everything in their path, utterly dominating the agency world in a reversal of the David vs Goliath battle, which in this case sees Goliath winning over and over again. I also detailed the knock-on effects of data breaches in further reducing the public's trust in a brand-communications industry so utterly intertwined with social media platforms, via links to issues such as tracking technology.

A central part of that situation is the issue of AI-driven personalization, which has found itself clashing with an ever more important one of privacy. On one side of that debate we have fans of personalization, who point to its impressive abilities (in the context of this chapter) in creating 'just-for-you communications'. They do so via machine learning software that, for instance, can utilize psychographic modelling technology (which divides people into ever-smaller cluster consumer groups based on their beliefs, motivations and priorities) to predict and then fine-tune exactly the type of communication that the recipient may find interesting and motivating.

Which may sound great if we're talking about holiday ads that tell you all about your favourite destination, but sound less palatable if you then mention the words 'Cambridge Analytica' from the perspective of dubious and divisive political messaging. And if the intrusions of Cambridge Analytica scraping all your personal Facebook data sounded horrendous all the way back in 2016, then just wait until eye-tracking technology, care of smart glasses, really takes off. The key problem being that eye tracking represents an unconscious 'like' button for everything, and that your stylish new smart glasses will effectively have you under surveillance from approximately one inch from your face.

I really apologize for what I'm about to say, but just can't think of a better time to use that worn-out saying 'what could possibly go wrong?'

Back to the hyper-targeted personalization side of the debate, and for fairness' sake it needs pointing out that this is matched by an alternative view, that agencies should be 'fame factories' creating activity that resonates deeply on a cultural level. That type of approach sees people turned into slightly alarming sounding 'weaponized consumers' who are so enamoured by the communication with which they're confronted, that they pass on this information themselves via word of mouth, thereby often creating fresh content about that original piece of creative activity, either face to face or via social media. The overall effect being that they're doing the creative and media agencies' storytelling jobs for them, at zero cost to the brand owner. What's not to like? As they say in agency boardrooms.

The attack of the consultancies, and future agency roles

Meanwhile, the likes of Accenture, BCG, Bain and McKinsey are all taking away ever juicier parts of the marketing, innovation and strategy elements of clients' business needs. Add to this that brands are reducing agency fees, bringing a lot of marketing services in-house and, in addition, also buying directly from the technology platforms themselves, and this all leaves a dwindling amount of revenue for the weakened agency holding groups to fight over. Hence serious existential questions about the nature, role and indeed long-term future of agencies. As for the holding groups that seemed ever-powerful until recently, well they look seriously down on their luck.

And yet it would be unfair to deny that some of the old legacy agencies are still holding their own, and indeed a few that are more associated with the *Mad Men* era of the analogue past, rather than the digital present, have been re-energized and found a new lease of life.

But while many dated and dinosaur-like agencies are fighting each other over a dwindling supply of 'business as they used to know it' there are some staggeringly dynamic independent outfits pushing their way to the front of the industry's attention. And while an array of European (usually English) agencies, continue to fight well above their weight, many of these new and exciting outfits are from, for instance, South America or Africa.

But what's fundamentally changing the traditional (Western) agency landscape, is the rise and rise of Asian, and usually Chinese, companies that are often way ahead of their Western counterparts in ambition and innovation.

Meanwhile, for an industry that prides itself on connecting brands with consumers, it's amazing just how out of touch its leaders are with the wider world and the lives of those not working in advertising, and indeed how increasingly outdated its work-practices are.

This all comes at a time when agency roles are changing dramatically. I cover the 'future of work' in depth later in this book, in a chapter devoted specifically to that subject. But when it comes to adland in particular, there are numerous future jobs that agencies should be preparing for in an increasingly automated world. These, quite naturally, need to reflect the blizzard of social, cultural, political, economic and technology trends that are impacting the sectors relevant to their clients' businesses.

A key question therefore is where is the next generation of talent coming from? Or rather, where are they going to, if it isn't into the world of advertising that until recently, seemed so attractive for would-be employees?

I asked a leading industry figure, Julian Boulding of The Network One, about this, and indeed where he would advise someone to look for a really exciting role in the 'agency of the future'. As he told me 'where I would point to now are data and analytics, behavioural economics, neuro-linguistic programming, neuroscience, etc. Because we're now taking a quantum leap with understanding what people actually do and are able to observe what people do and why they do it. All the things that actually impact behaviour, teaching us "why different people do things differently". If you understand human behaviour and then learn how to influence it... well there can't be many more interesting things to do in the marketing world'.

So what's holding the old guard back, particularly in the Western world? If I had to choose one word it would be 'diversity'. A serious rethink regarding the types of people employed by agencies is well overdue, including issues around gender, ethnicity, sexuality, age, religion, lifestyle and background.

A trend-driven and scenario-aware approach would mimic one of the agency sector's all-time heroes, William Gibson, famed for superb books such as *Pattern Recognition*, as mentioned in the previous chapter. His endlessly quoted point that 'the future is already here, it's just not very evenly distributed' is entirely relevant in this context, as in so many others, for instance when we see other industries clearly demonstrating that they have understood where future job specifications are headed. Meanwhile, most of adland is appearing to be staggeringly slow in catching up with numerous other sectors.

That's why agencies should be considering job titles such as 'Head of Bot Creative/Data Ethnographers/Mood Managers/ Neuro A–B Tester/Sixth Sense Analyst/Purpose Planner'.

Furthermore, when thinking about a raison d'être for the future CMO (chief marketing officer) in a hyper-connected landscape, the foundation for that person's role would be 'resonance: making meaning for the consumer and building brand experiences that last' (Davis, 2019).

Agencies should be considering job titles such as 'Head of Bot Creative / Data Ethnographers / Mood Managers / Neuro A-B Tester / Sixth Sense Analyst / Purpose Planner'.

But what is the central role of the agency these days? For me, it's not only advertising but the whole consumer experience that matters to brands. As for Brian Whipple, Global Chief Executive of Accenture Interactive, 'the fundamental premise we operate under is that a brand is not built from advertising anymore. It's built from a collection of touchpoints, increasingly digital, that customers go through when interacting with your brand. The sum of these touchpoints forms an experience. So we transform stale experiences for human good' (Rogers, 2019).

Brand purpose or 'toxic pomposity'?

I'll now focus on an approach that was originally based on a well-meaning and progressive point of view, but has become so bland and overdone as to be almost meaningless when done by most organizations: brand purpose.

Bluntly put, perhaps a great deal of the enthusiasm for this in adland goes down to a sense of collective self-loathing. The last few years have seen an onslaught of reports illuminating the utter pointlessness of the vast majority of advertising, ie that most is never noticed, and when it is, is neither liked, remembered, nor leads to a positive outcome.

Adding to those reports, I'll also highlight a point made in the best-selling book *Utopia for Realists*. In it, reference is made to research carried out by the renowned UK think tank, the New Economics Foundation. Their research, which was conducted a few years ago but is still entirely relevant, uncovered a profound insight: 'estimating that for every pound earned by advertising executives, they destroy an equivalent of £7 in the form of stress, overconsumption, pollution and debt. Conversely, each pound paid to a trash collector creates an equivalent of £12 in terms of health and sustainability' (Bregman, 2018).

The actual think tank report obviously goes much further, also stating, for instance, that 'for every £1 of value created by an agency executive, £11.50 is destroyed'. In addition, the report highlights the much-repeated critique that 'economists such as JK Galbraith argue that advertising has very negative effects on society. It does this by creating socially and environmentally wasteful "wants" where needs have already been satisfied.'

Bringing this up to today, one almost feels sorry for those in the agency world suffering an ongoing torrent of criticism both of what they do and why they do it. (You can see why they all have copies of Simon Sinek's book *Start with Why* hidden under their beds, which they read while sobbing.) Hence, perhaps, adland's recent obsession with being seen to be 'nice', which may indeed be a progressive move, but it's neither always convincing, nor effective.

In fact, far from it. Indeed, as Saurabh Varma, CEO of Publicis South Asia said of the biggest agency awards event on the planet 'the Cannes Lions has become too causey. This is not advertising anymore' (Dams, 2019).

Taking that point forward, and regarding brand purpose being an example of a well-meaning but delusional element of virtue signalling on behalf of those working in the elitist world of agencies, a more accurate description would be 'social virtue' marketing strategies. However, and to be fair, this sits at odds with reports from the likes of Accenture, who in their 'To affinity and beyond: from me to we' report stated that '62% of customers want brands to "take a stand" on sustainability or fair employment, and 50% are attracted to brands supporting and acting upon causes. Consumers champion brands they believe in and reject those they don't; with price, product quality and customer experience seen as important but table stakes'.

When it comes to 'taking a stand' as Accenture state, I find the thinking of Charles Vallance of the agency VCCP to be fascinating. But as he says, regarding the trend for brands to put themselves at the heart of a polarizing issue 'it seldom works as well as being a unifying force. The strongest brands focus on feeling, fluency and fame. The best communicators all understand feeling and they also understand that feel-good is feeling at its most persuasive. This is something we forget at our peril' (Vallance, 2019).

But why are brands doing this at all, and is this behaviour genuine? To clarify this point, I asked Julian Boulding of The Network One for his point of view. He told me that 'companies and corporates are taking on more of a genuine commitment to social responsibility. This is not unprecedented – if you go back to the beginnings of the 19th century you think, in England, of Lever and Cadbury. I think there's an interesting start of a trend there, it's no longer just "greenwash and avoid the negative" but there's a really positive feeling which is maybe coming out of a vacuum created by governments abdicating long-term social responsibility'.

So in order to do that credibly, does the somewhat saccharine notion of 'brand purpose' need a rethink? For an answer on that, I went to Tom Morton, from one of the industry's leading agencies, R/GA. He told me that 'Purpose was in danger of becoming a cliché at the Cannes Lions Award. We saw so many branded crusades on behalf of borrowed causes. Now we're seeing an evolution of purpose: higher than a dramatized benefit, lower than a crusade, closer to a focus on what's the best thing the brand does for the world and why people should care about it. It's more a brand ambition than a moral purpose'.

He went to on to explain some fascinating examples of brands such as Volvo reflecting their purpose in their products or services; eg their open-source sharing of research into why women were being injured more than men in road accidents.

Another that I found particularly interesting, because it's so practical, is IKEA. As explained by Tom 'they have an initiative called "Thisables" because something like 10% of IKEA customers have some form of disability, and people with disabilities feel more disabled inside their own home. So IKEA provide little add-ons that are disabled-friendly, such as handles you can put on doors to make opening them easier if you don't have a lot of arm-strength. That's close to the business and expresses IKEA's values through the design of the product and service innovation.

Once we get to a place where "purpose" becomes "the impact you have in the world and why people should care" and brands reflect that through useful innovation rather than "cry your eyes out" long-form films, then we'll see how much growth a purpose can unlock for a brand. What we find at R/GA is that a purpose or an ambition is vital when you're designing a business, or an eco-system or service. Just as the traditional advertising business has started asking whether films about causes are the right form of advertising, we're finding that services built on values and purpose are the new bedrock of how you build a brand'.

I find that sort of thinking incredibly inspiring. But meanwhile, what about NGO brands that were founded on a 'social purpose cause' but who find themselves competing for attention against others who are creating powerfully emotive communication?

Amnesty International is an organization that really does have 'genuine purpose' running through its DNA. I spoke with Thomas Coombes, their Head of Brand, who explained how 'from the angle of people's hopes and fears we realized that just focusing on "all the bad things" and what we were against, as opposed to what we're for, was becoming less effective. Particularly in a populist environment full of negative stories.

Essentially, we needed to respond to harmful populist narratives by promoting one based on kindness and belonging.'

So when it comes to specific cause-related campaigns, what did they actually do? 'We want to talk about "the world people want to see" rather than reinforcing negative stereotypes. We want them to think about "what does it look like when you act on your values?" So, for instance, we indicated how individuals had stood up for victims of oppression, showing "how to do Human Rights" and how people can act on their own sense of humanity. When it comes to communicating an anti-racism message, for instance, now we also talk of positive realities of non-racist actions and behaviour. We also wanted to look at things from the point of view of innovation and creativity. We want brands and organizations to promote that vision; to articulate their values via a storytelling strategy based on empathy'.

Which is an amazingly inspiring message.

The rebels

Equally inspiring, and amidst all this talk of 'the next big thing' in advertising, there's one genuinely 'really next big thing' that is, quite literally, a matter of life or death for humanity – that of the environment in general, but specifically climate change.

This issue is one where, at long last, the advertising industry, or rather should I say 'the communications industry' has a crucial role to play, for the benefit of all humanity.

And that, as they say, is the start of quite a brief.

Why this is an issue that has the advertising industry at the epicentre of its debate is because the industry, like no other, is all about combining the ability to leverage behavioural change with its primary task of promoting consumption.

The first skill is vitally needed by a planet that is in a downward spiral due to unsustainable carbon-based lifestyles, which are destroying the living environment on which we all depend.

The 'always-on' expertise learnt by a global industry regarding the secondary point, leads us to the issue of ethics and responsibility from brand owners, media and agency staff, and consumers alike. All have to make better choices for all and taking a neutral position is no longer acceptable.

Because as the old political saying goes 'we're all in this together' and this happens to be (finally) resonating with a society that is 'woke' to the issue.

I discussed the actions taken by those including the deeply impressive B Corp in my last book *The Post-Truth Business* and the actions exhibited by them are now being reflected in an advertising industry that for years has been accused of leaving its morals at home when it goes to work, ie happily advising clients to commission more ice-cream ads when the weather gets ever hotter as opposed to suggesting that something more serious might be advisable.

This might even be the clarion call that changes behaviour within it to the benefit of the rest of society. I fully realize that some have already taken, and continue to take, inspiring action, and indeed have written of numerous examples in the past. Those are the types of influencers (and occasionally revolutionaries, ie when it comes to superb campaigns like #TrashIsles) that I so admire.

But vastly more needs to be done by the remaining 99 per cent of an advertising world (in all its many varieties) that have done little or nothing to address this issue.

William Skeaping of the incredibly 'influential and revolutionary' pressure group Extinction Rebellion said of adland 'You don't have to be on the wrong side of history. Tell the truth about this emergency. Collaborate as an industry: refuse to work for toxic brands. If not for the planet then do it for yourself because there won't be any pop-ups or human rights when the crops fail' (Kemp, 2019). When I interviewed him, he explained the way they take their message out to the world is, and needs to be, revolutionary. As a starting point, the use of the word 'extinction' in their name doesn't purely relate to the dangers towards environment in all its forms. It categorically and directly means us.

Therefore it's encouraging to note groupings such as #CreativesForClimate are taking real action about this most crucial of issues.

As for the key manifesto demands of Extinction Rebellion, these are to:

- **Tell the truth** Government must tell the truth by declaring a climate and ecological emergency, working with other institutions to communicate the urgency for change.
- **Act now** Government must act now to halt biodiversity loss and reduce greenhouse gas emissions to net zero by 2025.
- **Beyond politics** Government must create and be led by the decisions of a Citizens' Assembly on climate and ecological justice.

Among many demonstrations around the world, the Extinction Rebellion activists also made their viewpoints heard at the Cannes Lions event. Skeaping, himself an ex-advertising agency strategist, explained in an interview that 'this is the meeting of the global advertising industry, so we organized a non-violent act of civil disobedience. We need to wake people up as the consumption driven by the advertising industry is immense' (Arrigo, 2019).

So how do those activists 'promote' their causes in an effective manner? I asked the cultural strategist Thomas Stoeckle about the implications for both protestors and, for instance, the publicizing of their causes. As he explained 'recent political events call for new and different models of activist, protest and dissent PR theory and practice. The new models and concepts will help overcome activists' struggles with the role and function of PR, as it will be re-imagined, if not reformed to meet the challenges of an ever more uncertain world where fundamental principles such as trust, informed dialogue, a shared sense of reality are being put to the test'.

But what about adland, ie can that part of the agency world genuinely step up and make a vital difference? I asked William Skeaping about this, but as he told me 'the strange thing is that they're completely missing a trick – reflecting the present rather than creatively visioning or even considering the future. There's an opportunity and due diligence for agencies to explain the nature of the climate ecology and climate emergency to brands; it's the single biggest issue of our age. They spend so much of their time talking about Gen Z, but have somehow not understood that this audience are deeply concerned about climate change'.

Regarding the Extinction Rebellion challenge to the advertising industry, and that protest at Cannes Lions 'we got there and found a festival calendar packed with panels on "Brand Purpose" and "Brand Activism". Meanwhile there were a load of genuine activists outside being manhandled and arrested and cuffed by police who'd been told that Cannes Lions would be "shamed" by their presence. I think that's what we'd call cognitive dissonance isn't it?'

Influencer marketing and false authenticity

For a little light relief, let's turn to the increasingly inane/much maligned (take your pick) world of influencer marketing.

There is so much controversy about this apparently lawless area that it's difficult to know which of the seemingly endless examples of malpractice and dubious behaviour (that's a great name for ad agency by the way) to choose from.

So I'll go with a couple of hopefully interesting examples, regarding a world where brand owners are fighting back against a communications route inundated by widespread fraud.

That fraud is costing US advertisers alone at least US$200 million a year, in a sector embodied by platforms like Snapchat, TikTok and, of course, Instagram.

Now the very foundation of the sector is that the influencers in question are actually 'influential'. Which in this context has tended to simply equate to the amount of the following that they claim to have, 'claim' being the operative word.

Those followers enable them to charge large amounts for 'being influential' via their social media posts/real-life endorsements. Yet, to state a fact that will surprise no one on the planet, many of these supposed examples of brand engagement are largely made up by automated bots, often generated by 'bot farms' in South America or Asia.

In just one infamous case, when Instagram (which bans them in order to protect its own integrity) deleted millions of false accounts on their platform, numerous celebrities found that, as an instant result, they'd lost over 50 per cent of their followers.

How fascinating it would have been to be a fly on the wall in the next meeting their agents had with their brand-sponsor clients.

Yet the appeal remains for brands, where 'using influencers to market products means that they can put out low cost content that is technically advertising – but looks and feels far more authentic, at a time when ad blocking is becoming increasingly common' (Murphy, 2019).

As for another example, and again there are seemingly endless numbers to choose from, I'll start by referring to another statistic: which is '0.00001'. That being the figure highlighted by industry sage Dave Trott, when he wrote of the (perhaps not overly influential) influencer Arianna Renee and her attempted leverage of her apparently 2.6 million Instagram followers, whom she tried to 'influence' in order to buy some of her new clothing line. The result of her influencer campaign was the sale of 36 items of clothing, ie 0.00001 per cent.

To be fair, Dave Trott pointed out that the use (or attempted use) of celebrity influence has been used as far back as anyone in the advertising world can remember, or indeed as far back as any advertising publications record.

Not that it always, or even usually, works as intended. For when it comes to the brand association from those campaigns, as he points out 'Steve McQueen for Breitling (or maybe it was Omega). John Travolta for Rolex (or maybe it was Breitling). David Beckham for Nike (or maybe it was Adidas).... Have you seen the new Robert De Niro/Harvey Keitel ad for insurance/bread, or the Elton John ad for Snickers/John Lewis?' (Trott, 2019).

The general idea is that, when chosen well, they can be a great route to take, from the perspective of creative engaging communications. The reason being they are 'relatable to the consumer and relevant for the brand'. The problems set in if they're either badly chosen or over-used i.e. everyone else has exactly the same idea, particularly when the celebrity of choice has such mass appeal, often coupled with a lack of 'constricted-interests', that they can therefore be associated with just about anything. The results being a lack of linking with the very specific values of an individual brand means that the brand association is weakened, often to the point of invisibility.

Either that, or the stereotypical type of content means that achieving differentiation via communication (and a lot of brands essentially only achieve that due to an often mirror-image similarity of product features within categories among competitor brands) is thwarted.

An example was highlighted by the ubiquitous fashion influencer Victoria Magrath, who pointed out how 'there's been a million makeup tutorials and a million fashion hauls. People are a bit done with it.'

As for where influencer marketing is heading, the head of her talent agency Gleam says that it's all about authenticity, and Magrath doesn't disagree, talking about that as 'honesty is in', this means a trend for 'more honest portrayals of people's lives. I want to move that way as well'. Which is probably a good thing, as in that same article, the head of Unilever's marketing efforts explained how 'the influencer ecosystem had to rebuild trust before it's gone for ever' (Elmhirst, 2019).

The other really serious problem is (and say this quietly if you find yourself in the company of agency types) this route has very often just been used when no one in the agency concerned has any idea of anything better to do when trying to promote a branded product or service.

When it comes to 'how to do it properly' then the current received wisdom spoken about at industry events seems to focus around an acceptance that four broad approaches seem to indicate the most effective strategic way of utilizing this methodology. These are:

- **'Micro-influencers'** who by having a great deal of knowledge about a very niche area, gain considerable kudos as a result.
- **'Associated'** influencers who are known for their obsession with, and loyalty to, a particular brand.
- **'Covert'** influencers, who by using methods like dark social (as in communicating via non-trackable messaging platforms) gain a cult following for the clandestine nature of their activity.
- **'Campaigner'** influencers, who are often activists and who link with and influence others via their passion about values that attract a like-minded audience.

And it's not just fashion or games brands doing this of course, the techniques of consumer – or voter – influence and manipulation are being used by political propagandists. Indeed, and according to the communications expert Julian Boulding 'the mass scale of this is at a government level, where governments plant influencers, and it's becoming increasingly apparent that that is a strategy of Trump. Influencers can now be the difference between who is in government – and in some countries that is a major difference. Those people have learnt how commercial marketers lead and set trends for society'.

Charlatans and rogue managers

So where's it all really going? To be bluntly honest, anyone's viewpoint is equally valid; the reason being that the sector, in its digital and social-media format, is so new that no one exists who can give us a long-term perspective on dealing with the change and disruption that will surely follow, at some point after tomorrow. All the sector can seem to agree on, from the angle of the agency heads at the many conferences dealing with the matter, is that to connect with consumers, you neither need to 'go big' (as in leveraging a megastar like PewDiePie or Kendall Jenner) or 'go small' via a trusted voice relating to things such as a specific area of health, type of travel or approach to parenting.

The killer point about influencer marketing is that it's all about authenticity, hence influencers being completely obsessed with being 'the real thing'.

The absolutely killer point about influencer marketing though, is that it's all about authenticity, hence influencers being completely obsessed with being 'the real thing'.

This presents the influencer sector with something of an existential problem, when seemingly no one involved in it appears to have any idea if vital things such as the claimed audiences of most influencers actually exist. Nor do they have any coherent forecasting viewpoints, regarding strategic planning.

Which sounds like 'an issue' for those desperately seeking to portray their authenticity, although they might take comfort from a true influencer with proven long-term, international, and cross-demographic appeal. Yes, it's a philosopher, and no I don't mean Kim Kardashian. For as Jean-Paul Sartre pointed out 'to try to be authentic is to fail, as any attempt to grasp it within a conscious experience is doomed'.

For a final example in this section, I'll look to the opposite end of the spectrum from the admirable Extinction Rebellion activists that I mentioned earlier in this chapter, who are perfect examples of being 'ultimate influencers with a campaign of ultimate importance'.

I therefore can't resist turning to an example that didn't go so well, when the whole point of 'influencers' is that they're supposed to be one thing above all else: credible. Or to put it another, 'trusted'.

And if it's a group of people who probably consider themselves to be a great deal more important than something as mere as the global environment, then you have to look no further than the spectacularly inward looking worlds of fashion and music, and to a disastrous event that gave the rest of us an immense amount of pleasure to observe.

I'm referring, of course, to the almost surreally-ridiculous spectacle called the Fyre Festival, a Bahamas-located event organized by the deeply unpleasant Billy McFarland and the not entirely un-Ali G like rapper Ja Rule.

The event seemed to promise the opportunity for vast numbers of festival goers to party with models including Bella Hadid, at a luxurious music event on an island in the Bahamas. The whole thing still sounds so oddly surreal that it's reminiscent of something straight out of a J G Ballard novel.

As the *Guardian* put it 'scandal sells, but few have captured the zeitgeist with quite the velocity as the rise and fall of Fyre. The luxury music festival – a Bahamas-set Coachella with villas and supermodels – collapsed into financial fraud and memes of drunk twentysomethings scrambling for Fema tents and styrofoam tray meals' (Horton, 2019).

The resulting documentary broadcast via Netflix, and another produced via Hulu about the ensuing catastrophe, showed overprivileged attendees viewing the lack of boutique tents and artisan catering as something akin to the carnage of the D-Day landings.

That whole nuclear-level fiasco can be viewed in many ways. One of them, in cold business terms, may be used for future reference by those wanting examples of 'how not to do leadership'. Indeed, according to *Forbes* magazine, the 'amazingly cringe-worthy documentary about the Fyre Festival could also be seen as a masterclass in bad leadership. While the festival was a bust for the party-goers, it turned out to be a great lesson for the rest of us on how to spot a charlatan and rogue manager' (Kelly, 2019).

The many lessons that *Forbes* spoke of included areas varying from charisma not equalling trust, consistently exaggerated claims needing to be viewed with suspicion, bullying bosses being treated with the contempt they deserve, and others such as when the team start to be asked to do something illegal, then it's probably time to think about finding another job. To which we can hopefully agree.

The documentaries also acted as great examples of calling-out the highly questionable 'Wild West' world of influencer marketing, where a lack of rigorously enforced and transparent standards mean basic issues such as brand safety apparently either don't exist, or in the very least are in great danger.

What's needed of course is third-party verification, rigorously enforced international standards, total accountability from the influencers themselves, and transparency from the advertising and PR agencies involved. To which, all I can say is good luck to whoever has to be in charge of all that.

Summary

So what do these examples of 'the good, the bad and the ugly' indicate?

On a purely technical level, the predictability element given to advertisers via data-fuelled, machine-read, algorithmically fine-tuned and artificial intelligence powered technology (and yes, that is quite a sentence) will mean ever more personalized behavioural tracking, automated targeting and individualized messaging is a given.

Meanwhile, anxieties over privacy will push back against a lot of this, from the perspective of suspicions over intrusion and mass surveillance.

Elsewhere, what I find inspiring is that increasing numbers of rebels in adland are standing up to be counted, as noted earlier in this chapter. They've realized the consequences of the industry's actions in endlessly promoting hyper-consumption and high-carbon lifestyles. To them, moral neutrality is a non-excuse for inaction when it comes to the climate emergency, and they have realized that they're confronted with a simple choice – are they on the side of creating solutions or generating more problems?

To me, the situation has close parallels with, for instance, the way that agencies and their personnel choose whether or not to work with tobacco companies, or how they use their creativity on behalf of anti-tobacco activity. In my previous book *The Post-Truth Business*, I wrote about how the amazing US anti-tobacco 'Truth' campaign, which remains one of the most successful marketing campaigns of all time and has saved many thousands of lives along the way, came into being. (A campaign in which, by an amazing coincidence, I played a very small role.) I also wrote about this David vs Goliath battle for *Contagious* magazine, noting the role that researchers and planners acted in its creation.

But if those of us working on that anti-tobacco activity thought we had a real battle on our hands, then the challenge that climate activists have chosen to accept is of a far higher order. They're using their commitment, passion and creativity for the global common good.

That's why I'll end this chapter by referencing the work being done by everyone linked to Extinction Rebellion, who in this instance are utilizing the techniques of PR and advertising to raise awareness about climate and biosphere facts, impact political policy and change behaviour.

To do so I'll borrow that wonderful quote from the social anthropologist Margaret Mead, who so memorably said 'never doubt that a small group of thoughtful, committed citizens can change the world; indeed, it's the only thing that ever has.'

CHAPTER THREE

The future of retail and the future home

I n this chapter, I focus on two connected areas: the retail sector and the home.

Each of these are set within the overall context of the macro trends framing this book regarding smart technology, environmental issues and changing consumer behaviour.

Yet, somehow, many businesses appear to be ignoring these new realities for consumers living in a world where the retail implications of 'smart cities, smart homes and informed consumers' are going to be profound.

From a retail perspective, the pace of change has never been faster, and for brands in the sector, the pressure on retail margins has never been greater.

The retail war is an unforgiving one, and it's clear that the winners will be those who both understand and then act on the overwhelming need to enhance customer experiences, adding genuine value through innovation in their personalized service offerings and product development activity. The overall effect will be, as Jack Ma stated at the AI conference in Shanghai 'the new retail'.

That's why we're seeing the ever more mainstream impact of issues such as in-store technology leveraging virtual and augmented reality, alongside inventory-scanning bots to ensure 'the right stock is in the right location, all the time' and algorithmic recommendations meaning fine-tuned advice for individual customers.

When it comes to e-commerce, innovations include ongoing platform-based social shopping, while the convenience of home-based voice-activated hubs and the efficiency of ever faster delivery will only become more beneficial, from a shopper perspective.

An issue (or perhaps 'the issue') that will become ever greater, is the one of those 'informed-consumers' making decisions based on a growing awareness of environmental and ethical issues linked to decisions around their consumption behaviour.

Therefore, in this chapter I take a specific look at one sector in particular (the fashion industry) and the challenges it faces from this perspective. The implications for innovation, across areas ranging from manufacturing to entire business models, are profound.

The overall shift is one from passive to active retailing, where businesses must reflect new lifestyles, behaviours and attitudes from consumers who are both more demanding and less satisfied.

The overall shift is one from passive to active retailing, where businesses must reflect new lifestyles, behaviours and attitudes from consumers who are both more demanding and less satisfied.

It also means that the use of predictive analytics will become ever more prevalent, moving on to far more innovative results than the current situation that sees weather forecasts impacting specific types of products being stocked and staffing levels required.

Innovative actions with regard to all of the above are being shown by leading-edge 'innovators and outsiders' from the local to the multinational, across a wide range of areas. These operators are transforming the way retailing is done in an omnichannel environment where 'constant evolution' is a new reality that all brands must face.

A fascinating element of that evolution relates to payment innovation, which will see us increasingly paying via our face (in store) or by voice (in home).

That issue of convenience-based facial recognition will, however, be another area highlighted in this book, where legislation around privacy will see retailers involved in the battle over civil rights. This means retailers offering payment services will need to ensure that, for instance, they offer this type of 'personalized convenience' via innovative brands like Facenote, with its 'opt-in' service offering that ensures the business in question is on the right side of this ethical debate.

Meanwhile, with homes increasingly becoming a central location in the battleground for brands, and with so much consumption across a staggering array of products and service areas taking place within them, the world of retailing is infiltrating our domestic environments as never before.

Developments in the 'home of tomorrow' centre around, from my perspective, the issues of the 'smart home' as a connected place (particularly in a 5G world) where conscientious living and informed consumption are enabled to take place.

The epicentre of the home, in technology terms, will be the kitchen, as opposed to the more usually highlighted main living space, where most traditional (as in late 20th century) television-based entertainment took place. Those old mental images of a fixed-location television being watched by an entire 'traditional' family seem ever more distant, having shifted into a more nodal and modular approach, with reference to the home being utilized in more flexible, useful and imaginative ways, which also means the concept of 'what is a family?' reflecting changing social mores.

The idea of 'enablement' is absolutely key in technology terms across a wide range of areas, as so many people still massively underutilize the smart technology available to them. There are, therefore, huge opportunities for brands to simplify the products and services they bring to market, with the aim of helping people to live healthier, less stressful and more enjoyable lives. And with regard to this, the home is pivotal.

And, just as I mentioned with regard to retail, an ever-present tension point in the home, just as it is outside of it, will be that of privacy.

The debates will be founded on the agreed area where our technology 'knowing-us and assisting us' will bump up against privacy intrusion and technology failures, as they relate to problems such as data breaches and the dubious leverage of tracking software.

An ever-present tension point in the home, just as it is outside of it, will be that of privacy.

This issue is vital in the 'truly connected' home of tomorrow, where a smart meter will be at the centre of operations, with cost and energy efficiency as its core function, enabling us to be more efficient and lead more sustainable lives.

Hence a crucial element of the home being the integrity and safety of the operating systems used to run it, and therefore the avoidance of 'tech-hubs' being hacked and malicious software used to deny the resident access to the utilities on which we all rely.

So, having highlighted that range of trends, let's take a deeper look at some specific ones that I find fascinating within the retail environment, along with some best-case examples of innovation throughout that sector, before moving on to looking into the future home, from a similar range of viewpoints regarding dynamic and disruptive innovation. For all of them, the implications of a world that is ever more connected via the 'Internet of Things' are extraordinary.

The consumer and the environment

When it comes to retail, a renowned expert in the area is Ian McGarrigle, chairman of the World Retail Congress. He set up the WRC over a decade ago and is a well-known figure in the sector, for his specialist knowledge.

According to him 'the unifying issue in retail, the single most common factor, is that it's all about the consumer, who has to literally be at the heart of everything now. This is because consumers are acting in ways that we haven't seen before: they're less loyal, more fickle and want to shop 24/7. A classic example of this is the incredible statistic that, whereas before we may have shopped locally or just out of town, now consumers in Europe have access to around 800,000 choices of retailers online from which to choose.'

I asked him about the 'New Retail' comments made by Jack Ma in his discussions at the futures event in Shanghai, and if there was an opposite danger, ie about the total market dominance of a major player like Alibaba or Amazon.

He didn't think this was necessarily where things are headed, but instead pointed to four business models that really interest him, 'platforms, brands, value champions or customer solutions', while the common factor among successful retailers 'is that there's a dynamism about their leadership teams, they are "influencers or revolutionaries" and have really "got it" in terms of genuinely understanding issues around speed and direction. They're anarchic and like to rip up the rulebook. Start-ups have a similar sense of anarchy'.

But away from the start-ups, what about the major legacy brands, such as Walmart? Ian thought that you had to admire them. 'Just five years ago they looked as though they were going to get taken apart by Amazon. But they've totally transformed themselves via a complete change of culture. They're unafraid of innovation in all shapes and guises, and their "Store No 8" innovation lab concept, where they hothouse ideas is incredibly powerful. To be able to turn around the world's biggest retailer is pretty impressive!' Another 'pretty impressive' reinvention is the legendary La Samaritaine in Paris.

Meanwhile, and as covered in detail in the chapter devoted specifically to marketing, the debate over the current validity, and future strategies and portrayals, of 'brand purpose' is a central one for marketers across virtually every sector, retail very much included.

I've given speeches about that issue for years, including at the World Retail Congress, and as Ian mentioned, it was a key theme again at the event. As he explained 'I was really struck by the power and focus of it this year. The biggest interpretation for me is hearing of a real wake-up call from retailers around the world with reference to sustainability, climate change and the overall environment. Retail sits right in the middle of all of that, because it is the ultimate consumption model. A specific example are the questions now being asked about the sustainability of fast fashion. For me, that's the really big take-away when you talk about business purpose and social purpose. And retailers have to be increasingly aware of Millennial and Generation Z views on all of this, who are very aware of ethical and environmental considerations'.

An example of circular-economy action in this area is the 'Worn Wear' pop-up stores from Patagonia, featuring their 'ReCrafted' collection.

Ethics and innovation

That issue of ethical consumption was illuminated by Alan Jope, the CEO of Unilever, who was widely reported as saying that 'it's no longer enough for consumer goods companies to sell washing powders that made shirts whiter or shampoos that made hair shinier, because consumers want to buy brands that have a "purpose" too.' Illuminating the Unilever approach further, he went on to state that Unilever brand teams were challenged with having to work out how the brands they worked on 'could make society or the planet better in a way that lasts for decades' (Wood, 2019). Unilever then announced that it is to sell off brands that do not deliver a positive impact to society.

And the issue of ethical consumption also has a direct link with the so-called 'sharing economy' the size of which is reflected by the staggering statistic that globally, more than two-thirds of people want to share or rent out personal assets for financial gain. Similar numbers want to use products and services care of other people.

But while the sharing economy has long been associated with certain attitudinal typologies and demographic indicators, for instance 'young, urban, middle class', the issue today is that it's time to revisit and reframe those stereotypes.

In fact, a Nielsen survey in 60 countries revealed broad support for collaborative consumption across a wide array of age groups, incomes and geographical locations. This illustrates that we're seeing fundamental shifts in consumption patterns where now, as a popular saying has it, 'access trumps ownership'.

A key interpretation of this is that total ownership of a product has become less valid than 'product utilization' which, furthermore, is linked to the circular economy where 'reuse and recycle' is an alternative to a traditional linear economy of 'make, use, dispose'.

This approach has also reframed accepted notions of consumer purchase behaviour, eg a potential Uber driver may choose to go up in the class of potential vehicle, regarding the return on their investment. The same approach may go for a potential home-owner, where the number of bedrooms they desire may reference potential Airbnb guests, contributing towards their mortgage payments. On the other hand, a potential car or fashion buyer may opt out of that purchase completely, in favour of potentially sharing or renting an existing product from the ultimate owner.

A crucial issue here, from the perspective of the manufacturer, is that quality is becoming less heavily judged against purchase price. As the saying goes, 'Welcome to Sharing 2.0', where renting a power tool or parking space used to be a hassle, but now is easy.

While one implication could be lower overall volume negativity, it could also mean increased product sales at higher price points. Or in soundbite terms 'consumers may buy fewer cheap products but more expensive ones'.

According to Deloitte 'we can no longer afford to, or indeed want to, own our own assets in the way we've always done. I may not own a car but might borrow my friend's for three hours.' The implications for a range of sectors, including for example the insurance one, are profound. As that report goes on to note 'why buy an annual insurance policy when you only want it for a short time?' (Deloitte, 2019).

The impact of the sharing economy therefore has profound, and thankfully positive, implications for the environment.

An example, as mentioned by the chairperson of the World Retail Congress, is the fashion sector, which is always under a media spotlight with regard to the environmental impact of that industry. So let's take a closer look at that industry.

Environmentalism meets fashion and luxury

The issue of environmentalism is now being seen as, quite literally, a centre-stage issue at Fashion Week events around the world.

I've given lectures at universities including the University of the Arts London (ie London College of Fashion and Central St Martins) for over 20 years, and an issue that the students often discuss in depth, is that the knock-on environmental effects of the fashion industry are staggering from the perspective of both environmental sustainability and ethical 'humane capitalism' production.

The resulting action from these debates often sees these leading-edge fashion students moving straight into upcycling initiatives, or developing concepts where, for example, shared or exchanged clothes are then customized or adapted to the new user's benefit.

Meanwhile, the international Fashion Week events, led by London, Milan, New York and Paris are effectively purely in existence, with very few exceptions, to encourage yet more consumption and thus more environmental damage.

So it's been fascinating to observe the climate change and environmental pressure group Extinction Rebellion taking on this most visible of industries.

In the UK alone, they've demanded that London Fashion Week be called off and that the BFC (British Fashion Council) declare a 'climate emergency' as the group does when targeting other areas. And during the Fashion Week, activists from the group who demonstrated at fashion show venues, highlighted some shocking facts about the level of carbon linked to the fashion sector.

The fashion industry has long been one promoted (by itself) as being 'utterly wonderful' and has somehow managed to swerve most long-term impacts of criticism aimed at it. A reason for this is presumably that 'people like looking nice' and most appear happy to wilfully ignore the depressing realities about production methodologies, be they innovation-related or not.

But this situation simply can't go on, as manufacturing intensifies for growing populations. The blunt reality is that the overall sector is getting worse, not better, from the angle of being a net contributor to climate change.

During a recent discussion I attended at the London College of Fashion about the textiles sector, it was made starkly clear that within 30 years, without genuinely radical action, that industry will be accountable for about 25 per cent of all global carbon emissions.

That's a terrible statistic to be associated with, for an industry that prides itself on being 'fun and fabulous'. Which means that, innovation or no innovation, the activists from Extinction Rebellion now have that sector firmly within their sights.

Or to put it in terms that might make a fashion brand CEO choke on their Bollinger, because they've grown used to talking about 'putting the consumer in control' this debate is now framed by the notion that 'the fashion business now belongs to the activists'.

A key problem with the approach taken by the fashion industry is, as noted by the *Observer* with regard to the existing Fashion Week situation, that 'these display all the pitfalls of late-stage capitalism, reflecting a reluctance to admit the need for systematic change. That complacency is deep-rooted and happens in every sector. Basically, we want things a bit like now, but less bad. Extinction Rebellion's stance shakes this assumption to the core' (Siegle, 2019).

This doesn't mean that there's been no action at all. Indeed, an early mover on this was shown by the cancellation of fashion week in Stockholm, until it could be reformulated in a more sustainable manner.

Meanwhile, and according to Tamsin Ormond, one of the founders of Extinction Rebellion, the next London Fashion Week 'should be a declaration of emergency, not a celebration. It should "be the death of fashion", after which there will be rebirth' (Bramley, 2019).

That 'rebirth' also has links to successful ideas like the one developed by the app Depop, which enables people to buy and sell second-hand (or should I say 'pre-loved') clothes and accessories. It has carved out a highly significant niche in the market, in a space that someone from Central St Martins described to me as being somewhere between Instagram and eBay.

Crocodiles and supply chains

For a different take on some 'positive innovation' being demonstrated by the fashion sector, in Chapter 2 about marketing, I name-checked a selection of brands that have conducted ethics-based activity.

To explain further, and in the context of this chapter, Lacoste involved itself in a brand-relevant manner by engaging with a campaign (launched at Paris Fashion Week) to save some of the planet's most endangered species. It did this in the incredibly simple, but exquisitely relevant way, by replacing its famous crocodile logo.

In its place went a collection of various animals threatened by extinction.

The brand had never removed the famous croc logo in its nearly 100-year history, but did so on this occasion on behalf of the International Union for Conservation of Nature.

In doing so, they illustrated the danger that each threatened species was in, by directly linking the limited-edition numbers of items produced for this campaign, to the exact number of each remaining animal. Very clever, and very poignant.

The concept of supply chain transparency was virtually unknown a decade ago, yet today it's moving ever more centre stage.

That issue of playing around with logos and brand codes is one that must, by the way, only be done by brands with a rock-solid foundation of saliency, who are clear about the strategic reasons for playing with their visual identity and have strict tactical guidelines. The few that do it well, such as Google, Absolut and in this instance Lacoste, do it very well. But it's a dangerous path for those who are just 'trying to be creative'.

Meanwhile, the concept of supply chain transparency was virtually unknown a decade ago, particularly from a mainstream consumer perspective, yet today it's moving ever more centre stage.

In retail terms, the reasons for, and implications about, this are crystal clear: just as we've seen with Fashion Week events being targeted by environmental campaigners regarding production methodologies, there are additional issues at stake.

This sees governmental pressure being applied to corporates, alongside that requested by 'informed consumers' with reference to demands for more information about the realities of production and distribution.

As I explained in detail in my previous book *The Post-Truth Business*, the dangers for brands in terms of their 'reputation capital' (this being made up of demands relating to whether a brand is 'trustworthy, reliable and competent') are huge. The key reason here is that, with brand differentiation generally being so minimal, it is in the 'actual' behaviour of brands, ie that exhibited by their actions as opposed to just that of their communication, where consumer decisions around brand adoption or rejection are increasingly being made.

The implications in terms of innovation in supply-chain transparency are immense, with the resulting cost of failing to meet those demands being substantial. This is shown by, for instance, food and beverage companies being confronted with increased demands for supply-chain data relating to factors including child workers, animal welfare, specific ingredients and transport practices.

Examples of brands that prove the credibility of their marketing claims include the renowned Patagonia, who illuminate the integrity of their supply chain via their 'footprint chronicles' guide, which illustrates where and how they source and produce their products with reference to the various textile mills, factories and farms involved in their business.

For 'informed consumers' wishing to know about the implications of their consumption, the Patagonia website will soon bring them up to date with regard to issues relating to recycling, fair trade certification, organic cotton and wool sourcing, synthetic microfibre pollution, and their overall approach to corporate social responsibility, along with other vital considerations towards living wages, the climate crisis and the impact of their business practices on the environment.

This approach sees that admirable business taking an innovative approach across its entire business, where the levels of innovation are both strategic and tactical, and utterly transparent.

Meanwhile, and continuing to highlight the issue of supply-chain transparency, brands such as the Canadian family-owned company, One Degree Organic Foods, operate a 'farm to spoon' transparent traceable operation. Hence the 'one degree of separation' ethos that gives the company its name.

Elsewhere, companies such as Red's Best offer their traceability via on-pack QR codes that link the consumer straight to the specific boat from which their fish was caught. They believe that their 'brand plus logistical approach' equates to trustworthiness and that an intelligently minimized carbon footprint 'adds only value and zero transactions cost' between fisherman and seafood buyer. That easily checkable and innovative approach delivers the vital issue of trust that's so important for consumers for whom marketing claims are not enough.

As for future innovation in this area, creating a culture of continual improvement throughout businesses in vital, as the current consumer demands for transparency will only grow. Let's be realistic, only a few years ago, the idea of having 'ethical supply chain manager' on a business card may have been novel, even unusual. But not any more.

Luxury brands and the ultimate luxury store

When it comes to the fashion sectors links with environmentally friendly production and manufacture, the luxury sector is one not immediately associated with this approach.

So it was fascinating to see Prada reformulating old fishing nets and discarded plastics that had been collected from the sea, into a sustainable collection of beautiful bags titled 'Re-Nylon'. The name is a play on their partial association with bags made of nylon, but in this case Prada utilized a closed-loop, eco-friendly form of the material called Econyl, where ocean waste and textile waste are mixed and upcycled into the type of ultra-high-quality products associated with the brand.

According to the global luxury industry journal, the *Robb Report* 'when Prada makes a meaningful step to reduce a negative impact on the environment, it makes a statement, and a very real impact. Prada has announced that it plans to move from using virgin nylon to Econyl across all of its product categories by the end of 2021' (Fenner, 2019).

We're seeing brands developing new approaches based around an awareness of cultural differences and aesthetic perspectives.

Meanwhile the couture sector is clearly changing, and it's a change that sees this somewhat 'analogue' area being completely revitalized, via the utilization of digital technology. This makes sense of course, as the 'luxury consumer of tomorrow' is today's Millennial or indeed Generation Z individual.

We're seeing brands developing new approaches based around an awareness of cultural differences and aesthetic perspectives. These being what these consumers have come to expect as a matter of course from the brands to which they are already loyal and with whom they've built an emotional bond.

As for trends impacting 'the ultimate luxury store' I interviewed Guy Cheston, the Partnerships Director of Harrods, who told me that 'we can confidently showcase Harrods as the "store of the future", which is ironic as we've been around since 1849. How have we achieved this? By working hard to become both a destination and an experience'.

He also explained how 'the whole digital revolution is changing people's shopping habits and has created the perfect moment for Harrods. Online exposure has made consumers more visually literate, sophisticated and discerning. No one wants to just "go shopping" any more. What they want is a more involving and ultimately rewarding experience. The sensory experience within a physical store has an obvious advantage over shopping online. Sound and smell are becoming more and more important'.

As for their Millennial and Generation X customers 'investment is of course key to remaining cutting edge, while retaining our brand values of luxury, heritage and history. Harrods is undergoing the biggest multi-million-pound development in its history to be at the forefront of cutting-edge innovation in luxury retailing. Our latest investment is the stunning beauty hall, an exceptional retail space fitted with the absolute latest technology'. At the other end of the scale, it'll be fascinating to watch the development of the 'mainstream' grocery stores from Amazon.

Now that we've taken a look at a range of innovative approaches taken by both the retail sector in general, and specific industries and brands within it, let's turn our attention to a location where more and more retail is taking place: the home.

The future home and the Internet of Things

When it comes to the 'future home' a good place to start when looking into the area is to consider that, throughout the last century, the home (and within it the kitchen in particular) has been a place witnessing staggering technological innovation and social development.

It's often said that while our lifestyles are ever more mobile ones, empowered by technology, the idea of 'home' remains an intrinsic psychological foundation for us all. The concept of what a home actually means is bound up in cultural norms that often reflect a stereotypical past and indeed a utopian future that bear little connection to everyday reality.

What is clear is that the key trends impacting today's and tomorrow's product and service innovation revolve around key issues such as smart technology, flexible spaces, IoT-connected environments and informed consumption.

The trends that impact a lot of the innovation in this context are discussed endlessly at tech shows like the Consumer Electronics Show in Las Vegas. At the last event, it was clear that, with smartphone sales flatlining, and with automated cars still being years away from mainstream use, it was items such as smart speakers and virtual assistants that were the obvious winners in terms of home-based sales.

In fact, voice-activated retailing has been a serious game changer for the interlinking of retail and the home, in the form of voice-assistant products from Amazon, Google, Apple and Microsoft; hence reports of the 'AI-powered voice economy'.

This technology is, essentially, still in its early form, but for the future implications of these, I spoke with Chris Sanderson who co-founded The Future Laboratory. He explained how 'the "ability to recognize" utterly transforms the way we then interact using "phygital" – which is a term The Future Laboratory came up with – the physical and the digital and what happens when you put the two together. So you think about retail as being separate from online shopping, but the two coexist extremely happily and actually all the research today has shown that the customer who has a phygital relationship with a brand is likely to be more loyal and also shop more deeply with that brand'.

We also spoke about the rise and rise of voice activated software. As he pointed out 'voice totally changes our relationship with the technology that we use, especially within home. Today the majority of our relationship with technology is tactile so we have to touch it in order to make it work; broadly speaking it's a mechanical iterative process, interacting via your hands. The moment you are able to talk to a machine and not have to iteratively touch it to make it work is hugely important. We are hard wired as human beings to start to think of that machine in a very different way because it no longer becomes a machine, we anthropomorphize it and it actually becomes something we have a relationship with'.

So why is this so important, and is it as big a deal as the media portrays? Chris explained that 'an object doesn't have to be intelligent, doesn't have to be sentient in order for us to believe that we can have a relationship with it. That's a very important fact to remember because the next step is that increasingly we will have a relationship with our Alexa or the more complex next-generation phone systems that we will see coming up on the market, because they will have conversations with us, they will be minded to do certain things for us'.

And a next-generation issue with huge implications for brands was also noted by the *Financial Times*. They report that as we're also seeing 'machine learning and real-time graphics evolve, we're going to get to the point where Siri and Alexa take on a visible form.' (This adds to the point I make about 'virtual influencers' in the chapter on marketing trends.) A fundamental point about brand differentiation is also mentioned by the *FT* as 'if I can see Alexa or Siri, and the way that those characters speak to me is emotional, then I'll feel a deeper loyalty to those brands' (Bradshaw, 2019).

Elsewhere, and a key aim for the future home, as technology is absorbed into every part of our lives, will be to ensure that the multitude of innovative developments in our living spaces focus around specific goals. These include ensuring that the individuals within them are mentally and physically enabled; with safety, contentment, health, relaxation and joy being among the most desired outcomes.

Indeed, according to the technology futures magazine *The Verge*, 'the home of the future is always listening and always watching, yet still secures your privacy as well as your belongings. It's adaptable but comfortable, a respite from the urban jungle and a place to savour those face-to-face encounters that have largely been supplanted by the virtual unrealities of modern life' (Ricker, 2018).

The design of these homes will take, just as I note in the chapter (9) on 'best-practice' office design, a biophilic approach. This features plants and natural materials, and aims for as much sunlight and fresh air as possible, for their obvious beneficial results regarding our physical and mental health.

In specific product terms, innovations around the future home will see incremental developments in existing offerings, where gadgets combine with analytic technology, to keep, for instance, the 'healthier you' via the leveraging of everyday human behaviour.

When it comes to products operating in this space, these range from next-generation air purifiers providing a cleaner home environment, to brand portfolios from those like Philips offering us a range of products and services including, for instance, bathroom mirrors that offer top-line health checks, toothbrushes that automatically inform your dentist of any dental issues, and scales that analyse body fat.

Meanwhile, our smartphones will check heart rates, activity rates, monitor blood pressure and observe our sleep patterns. As for the lavatory, suffice to say that the readings enabled here will give vital information relating to our levels of nutrition and internal health.

The area of sleep is where I also see huge opportunities for innovation. I first looked into that sector about 20 years ago, via interviewing a wide range of experts in the US, Asia and Europe, and it was a fascinating subject to research.

Fast-forward to today, and as reported by *The Economist* in a report into sleep technology and the quantified self, 'the market for sleep technology is expected to grow to over $80bn this year. Many tech entrepreneurs regard sleep hygiene as an effective way to maintain mental health, boost cognition and enhance productivity. For tech tycoons it seems, sleep is the new fitness' (Schumpeter, 2019).

The market has grown markedly since I first researched it, and indeed I looked into it again only recently, but despite there being an array of products from which to choose, including sound machines to smart sleep masks, and from app monitors to tech-enabled pillows, there is clearly a massive amount of innovation to come, from the very basic issue that in a stress-filled society, we all need to get better sleep.

Another area where products will deliver directly targeted benefits include designing products for elderly people, who often live alone and who need assistance to enable their independence to continue. This is where robots, which are often spoken of in terms of the perceived detrimental effect they'll have on the jobs market due to automation, being welcomed as an innovative answer to a widespread need.

Examples are increasingly being shown at tech trade shows, where the lack of mobility that is often associated with older people means an innovative means of helping them to simply get out of bed or move around their homes is required.

Hence 'carebots' that resemble friendly-looking robots offer the ability to lift elderly people or assist them when walking or carrying items around the home. Meanwhile, the product design students at Central St Martins in London presented concepts at a show I attended, which included household furniture that, transformer-like, reconstructs itself from being a wheelchair to becoming a bed or a standing support.

A country at the leading edge of this technology is Japan, where, as explained by the journalist Gillian Tett, 'the media tend to view robots as a source of pride, not terror, since they highlight the country's ability to innovate. Indeed, with 300-plus robots per 10,000 employees, Japan has one of the highest take-ups of robots in the world. "We just like robots!" a Japanese friend explained' (Tett, 2019).

And with reference to home-based services aimed at those with disabilities, as an illustration of just how private and secure the issue of voice-based consumption must be, in an environment where voice-activated software is becoming ever more ubiquitous, it was announced back in 2019 that in the UK, the NatWest bank was to enable voice-based financial services. This would enable customers to, for instance, have direct access to check their bank accounts just by talking with their home-based Google technology.

Based on successful trials, plans are for the technology to swiftly move on to other services such as paying bills or transferring money to other accounts. The benefits offered are obvious, according to the bank, with particular regard to blind or disabled customers for whom this service could be highly beneficial. But the pitfalls, in terms of data breaches or hacking, are obvious.

The kitchen of the future

It's the kitchen where a great deal of the most exciting innovation is taking place. Endless trend reports talk of IoT- (Internet of Things) enabled homes, focusing on kitchens that offer 'smart fridges', which enable us to remotely monitor the range and quality of products stored within them, and to set automatic re-stocks of various items when needed, via barcode scanning and internal cameras.

It's the kitchen where a great deal of the most exciting innovation is taking place.

Elsewhere, from personalized recommendations that relate to health or occasion, or empathetic tutorials that guide us in our cooking skills, to hydroponic kitchens and those that assist in recycling and composting, are all areas that are well covered in trend reports.

But for a really 'over the horizon' look at where innovation may be leading us, I again spoke with Chris Sanderson at The Future Laboratory. As he told me 'One of the things that we've noticed over the last couple of years is the shift in the technology focus of the home, in terms of where the digital hub sits. For us, it's interesting how it's moved from being based around where the old-fashioned telly would have been. Everything that was tech-related in your home really sat around this idea of television and that form of late 20th century screen-based entertainment'.

I've conducted research into future homes and future kitchens for numerous brands over the years. So it was fascinating to hear Chris talk about a major shift that the agency's observed, with regard to the way in which products and services are now being created, and then promoted at major tech-trade events like CES. 'Suddenly the kitchen seems to have become the technical heart of the home – the hub – and home assistant devices naturally play into that. While their geographic location could be anywhere, it seems increasingly that they are actually located in and around the kitchen. So suddenly our Alexa or our Google Home is increasingly about the technology shifts that we see going on around our cookers and our refrigerators and our home organization and home assistant opportunities, which moves our technological focus in our home environment away from this idea of 'flat screen entertainment' and towards 'lifestyle management'.

This all points to a combination of a range of social, cultural and brand trends, such as wellness, which I cover in detail in a specific chapter devoted to the subject. And as Chris also pointed out 'it also relates to lifestyle, which is how we manage our time – what we are doing, what we are doing together as a social unit, as a family, what each of us is doing individually, what we are doing privately, professionally and as part of the community'.

Entertainment

Finally, and linking to the point made by Chris about 'home-based digital entertainment hubs' let's take a very swift look at the entertainment sector. I say 'very swift' because the specific markets included with the overall entertainment sector (ie gaming, sports, television, radio, film, music and festivals) are covered in a separate chapter devoted to those areas.

So in this context, I'll simply point towards the aspect and implications of one issue that may not be readily associated with the area: home-based tracking technology. The reason for this is that it relates to our behaviour around, and use of, entertainment, ie the type of content we access and for how long we use it.

That links to a point I alluded to earlier, regarding home technology enabling 'contentment and happiness' as it links directly to an emerging area of innovation called 'emotional AI'. This is most obviously seen in things like the Netflix 'recomoji' that, essentially, enables the better functionality of our entertainment systems via empathetic media personalization.

Or to put it in a simpler way, when it comes to tracking entertainment content, and both the perceived motivation and result of it, crucially, our technology will monitor how music, film or other entertainment affects our emotional well-being. Thus, entertainment systems will analyse our moods, enquire how we want to feel and then suggest an appropriate piece of content based on the instructions we give.

Indeed, as Chris Sanderson pointed out, 'Alexa Hunch is the perfect example of next-generation software that suggests actions based on your behaviour. As this evolves we predict that it will have hunches about the mood that you're in when you walk through the door and so will set the ambient light accordingly or put on the most suitable music, or say something to you as you walk through the door in recognition of the fact that you've either just had a great day, or you've just had an argument with your children in the car. So there's a sense of recognition of behaviour and sentiment, which means the machine responds accordingly'.

This issue, about smart technology getting ever smarter, and by doing so understanding and genuinely interacting with us, has enormous implications across a wide range of areas, and in the context of this book, particularly with reference to ongoing innovation.

For, as Chris also explained, 'voice utterly changes the way that we interact with technology and the way that we will personalize it in the home environment. That again will have a hugely important impact on the way that businesses and brands will be able to innovate in that space'.

Summary

To summarize this chapter, when it comes to both the future of retailing and the future home, it's clear that smart stores and connected homes are at the forefront of innovation being provided for tomorrow's consumer.

We've grown used to hearing of 'experiences' being the next big thing, but it now seems as if the abilities of VR and AR technology are combining to provide truly stunning examples of this. Meanwhile, the issue of hyper-personalization, which again has been a hot topic of debate at industry events for years, is evidently being delivered at scale, with AI enabled services being a prime example.

Voice-activated hubs and the efficiency of ever faster delivery will, as I noted, become ever more user-friendly, and beneficial from a shopper perspective.

But it's in the macro issue of the environmental crisis where I see 'informed-consumers' making brand adoption or brand rejection decisions at a far greater level than we've seen in the past, linking these consumption choices directly to a growing awareness of environmental and ethical issues.

The implications for innovation and indeed entire business operations across a wide range of areas are, as I noted in this chapter, profound. It's crucial, therefore, that companies note the 'revolutionary' significance of the circular economy, which is not a passing trend, but a movement that is here to stay.

Elsewhere, the dynamic 'tech-led' innovation associated with those such as Alibaba (early utilizers of 5G, pioneers of 6G and who aim, for instance, to be able to deliver to anywhere in China within 24 hours and anywhere in the world within three days) is being matched by the 'ethical-led' innovation shown by 'rebel stores' like Hisbe, who are reinventing the way shops do business. Appropriately enough, the Hisbe name stands for 'How it should be', regarding their mission to break the mould by putting customers, suppliers and employees first.

The major overall shift we're witnessing is from passive to active retailing and from passive to active consumption, and this is where businesses must reflect new lifestyles, behaviours and attitudes from consumers who are both more demanding and less satisfied.

In each case, it's in the area of dynamic innovation that answers can be provided to these most pressing issues, meaning brands can achieve powerful differentiation while remaining true to their core purpose and gaining stronger consumer engagement.

CHAPTER FOUR

How the food and drink industries leverage catalytic trends

This chapter describes a series of catalytic trends being utilized by organizations ranging from multinational corporations to local start-ups in their innovation activity, alongside the highlighting of a variety of category-changing products and packaging that have resulted from leveraging those issues.

Throughout the chapter I'll outline a range of dynamic actions focusing on global consumer behaviour and sector trends that have issues such as wellness, ethics, environmentalism and user experience as foundational considerations.

Specific product and packaging activity connected to these areas references factors such as localism, sustainability, provenance, mindfulness, transparency, traceability, bioengineering, premium convenience and hyper-personalization.

The food and drink sectors have always been renowned for their extraordinary levels of innovation, but what we're seeing now are sharp-thinking concept development teams within agile organizations taking their own approaches to utilizing cultural trend information, cutting-edge digital tools and concept development research to create the next big thing. Some of those 'next big things' such as vertical farming, or 'plant factories' have actually been with us for a long time in theory, but are finally having their day in practice.

What I'll focus on are some of the leading-edge iterations of macro and micro trends, to hopefully illuminate current best practice and to therefore show a way forward for more mainstream sector offerings. A classic example (of innovation disrupting a sector) has been demonstrated by e-commerce, where what was seen as 'emerging' only a few years ago has completely reconfigured food and drink retail.

Meanwhile, increasing concerns about the impact of the dairy sector, for instance, in terms of the associated environmental damage and ecological consequences, are causes for major strategic innovation within that industry.

This all comes at a time when, for example, gene-edited foods (which have nothing to do with GMOs) are sneaking into our lives. These potentially change the foods we eat every day, whether it be dealing with gluten allergies, improving flavour or growing crops that are more resilient, to innovative health improvements and indeed in the fight against the climate emergency. Additional implications include altering land use, better water conservation, less food waste and specific consumer benefits such as 'better for you' fats.

Deciding where to start is always a difficult thing to do when writing about food and drink trends, due to the sheer amount of them. So I took the easy option and had a cortado, while considering catalytic activity in the restaurant sector...

Radical restaurants and truth machines

At industry conferences, we're endlessly told that innovation is the most dynamic force in business, and therefore something we just have to get right. And an accepted way to kick-start that process is to indulge in a bout of creative destruction regarding current industry norms. Or, at the very least, to reject past sector offerings.

But truly dynamic innovation can be created just as effectively by seeking inspiration from the past as opposed to purely dismissing it.

Indeed, according to the *New York Times* 'true innovation isn't some magic invention, like a Steve Jobs keynote with a toy at the end, but a process of gradual improvement and assessment. Often that means adopting already existing ideas or returning to past methodologies. Rearview, or reflective, innovations have proved to be as transformative as novel technologies' (Sax, 2018).

Truly dynamic innovation can be created just as effectively by seeking inspiration from the past as opposed to purely dismissing it.

Some fantastic examples of this approach to innovation are found in restaurants and cafés in cities around the world.

A brilliant case history is Silo, a place that was genuinely groundbreaking when it opened, featuring a very strong environmental agenda. A café that has as its raison d'être an absolute commitment to closed loop systems and an open supply chain, it still feels leading-edge, and both 'influential and revolutionary'. Yet the ethical views of its owners would be entirely familiar to anyone born many years ago, with its 'pre-industrial food system' ethos.

Silo received a great deal of attention when they launched with their 'zero-waste' take on sustainability and the circular economy. The owner, Doug McMaster says that he doesn't have a bin in his kitchen, and that nothing at all is thrown away, which totally alters how a kitchen works and also forces the staff to be seriously creative. The amount of food waste generated by restaurants is a serious fault line within the food industry, and a number of operators have been set up with this issue as a core element of their business model. For instance, WastED pop-ups in New York have 'menus with a mission' and are a great example of a community of designers and retailers, farmers, fishermen, distributors, processors and chefs, working together to reconceive waste that occurs at every link in the food chain.

An overall 'conscious dining' ethos entails looking out for our health, planet and community as one.

This all links to an overall 'conscious dining' ethos, which entails looking out for our health, planet and community as one.

A holistic stance, with one eye on the future and the other to the past, revolves around everything being done for the greater good, and where the preserving of botanicals and authentic traditional cuisine is catalysed by cutting-edge technology. It goes as much for drinks as it does for food of course, indeed, according to The Future Laboratory, 'narratives about drinks such as whisky and wine are often strongly linked with provenance, but environmental and geopolitical turmoil means that we may not have the same access to these goods in the future. As climate change affects where ingredients are grown and consumers demand more local products, brands are challenging what provenance and sense of place mean for wines and spirits'.

So, a celebration and championing of the hyper-local and hyper-seasonal shows a sustainable way forward, and combined with hyper-creativity, is an inspiration for those interested in where the world of gastronomy is heading.

Silo churns its own butter, makes its own bread and has its own composter, with an approach to food that sits between paleo, vegan and 'nose-to-tail'. These trends, alongside those including 'root-to-stem' and 'pollen to petal' and the overall 'conscious dining' movements will soon move from their current links to 'specific issue' restaurants, to have a higher impact on the wider international restaurant sector.

And, to state the stunningly obvious, this directly links to health. As Doug McMaster puts it 'if it comes in a packet, there's probably something wrong with it. In nature there's no waste, so being zero waste is as close to nature as possible.' He also notes the health implications of this approach to eating, saying 'If we all ate ecologically and environmentally, how much ill health would be avoided?' (Wilson-Powell, 2017).

Indeed, according to *Forbes* magazine 'In the US, the unfortunate reality is that the foods we eat are the No.1 cause of preventable death and disease. Harvard's School of Public Health just reported that by the time today's kids are 35, half will be obese' (Lempert, 2017).

Another 'unfortunate reality' is the issue of illegal behaviour in the food sector. A clear example being 'food fraud'. This issue, according to the World Health Organization, results in almost one in ten people becoming ill every year from eating contaminated food, and with 420,000 dying as a result.

The increasing 'crisis in trust' that I focused on in my last book *The Post-Truth Business* sees a desire for truth and transparency now becoming a demand. The good news for 'good brands' is that proving the truth of their 'good story' leads to massively improved consumer–brand engagement and loyalty.

A key element of the decline in trust has forced brands to highlight open and honest stories about the realities of not only their supply chains, but also how their products are manufactured and exactly what ingredients are used. Mintel note sharply increasing demands 'that require honest disclosures about how, where, when, and by whom food and drink is grown, harvested, made, and/or sold'.

The ever-growing demands for transparent, and by that I mean crystal clear, supply chains are evidenced by countless consumer research studies that report consumer interest is becoming ever more specific, ie not just 'is this dairy produce from a grass fed cow?' but 'where is the actual farm, and what was the breed of cattle?'

And something genuinely catalytic that's delivered precisely the results required is a technology that has generated seemingly endless media reports, yet still retains an aura of mystery: blockchain. This 'truth machine' is already transforming levels of trust on a B2B and B2C basis across the world.

Indeed, *Forbes* magazine states that 'blockchain technology could transform the entire food industry, by increasing efficiency, transparency and collaboration throughout the food system. When leveraging the "Internet of Things", blockchain can be used to gather a wealth of data'. It's not the complete answer of course, for that article also notes that blockchain 'can't verify that a chicken is truly cage-free or what that whole location really looks like' (Lempert, 2017). So there's clearly a need for additional context regarding the realities of animal welfare, production materials, etc.

From local foraging to global traditions

On that theme of 'reality' it is fascinating to observe the increasing interest in wild foods, with foraging being rediscovered and reinvigorated for the modern day. Our interest in eating wild edibles is seeing extraordinary growth, with seemingly 'forgotten foods' appearing on menus around the world, and hence being picked up by product development teams, among for instance, healthy snacks.

Health-focused drinks with botanical extracts are also increasing in popularity. In the UK, the Midnight Apothecary in Rotherhithe serves Douglas-fir-infused vodka martinis, while forager Andy Hamilton runs a 'wild booze' course in Bristol. Another product example that, quite literally, grew out of the foraging trend is shown by the brand Forager's Gin, who as their site says, use flavours that are 'derived from the finest freshly foraged botanicals and cut with the purest waters that flow from the mountains to our copper distillery in the foothills of North Wales.' And when it comes to uniqueness, another really intriguing operator is Growing Underground, who grow microgreens deep below London's streets.

'Localism' also plays a very strong role in the luxury dining sector, where menus clearly evidence the links between restaurant and items sourced from their immediate locality, along with a cuisine that intimately references a wider regional heritage. A key benefit of this, for chefs, is that it enables them to create truly unique dishes.

Meanwhile, the concept of restaurants growing their own food is not new, and those that do it, such as the legendary Le Manoir aux Quat'Saisons have often been based in big country house locations, which benefit from their own extensive gardens.

But the new crop of hyper-local restaurants tend to be smaller, DIY and cultivate their own supplies even in, or indeed particularly in, urban locations. A decade ago, when molecular gastronomy was at its height, chefs were budding scientists. Now, as the industry saying goes, 'they're studying nature'. Why this obsessional interest in nature? I think it's because botanical ingredients and extracts are only available for a limited time and are therefore also 'hyper-seasonal' when utilized by chefs.

An excellent example of this is the restaurant Where the Light Gets In, part of a new wave of gourmets swapping gastro-science for gardening and sourcing produce from within a few miles, or indeed metres, of their restaurants.

And a central part of the locality issue is that of the local community. When it comes to that angle, a sense of integrity and authenticity are generated as a result of this approach. The hugely successful Street Feast food market was set up nearly ten years ago by a collective of volunteers who liked the idea of strengthening communities through food. Every one of the products sold by the independent traders who sell at their locations comes with a story. Why is this of interest? Because, around the world, people are looking for, and need, a compelling narrative.

Another example of a 'community brand' who have integrity built into their DNA is the company Trawler Trash. They work with local fishermen to source alternative breeds – such as grey mullet, sprat, and coley – instead of the 'standard' cod and haddock to which consumers have become accustomed.

Looking to the opposite extreme, ie the global or 'glocal' as opposed to a local-sourcing ethos that's interpreted purely by physical proximity, a recent trend report from Whole Foods stated that 'things like hummus, pita, and falafel were tasty entry points. But now consumers are ready to explore deep traditions, regional nuances, and classic ingredients of Middle Eastern cultures'.

Meanwhile, the 'rediscovery' of traditional items from regions around the world like sauerkraut, kefir, miso, kombucha and kimchi are a highly visible demonstration of the glocal impact of these global influences.

And when it comes to both global and local community issues, from an activism and empathy perspective, this is where a very wide range of socially responsible activity is taking place around the world. Typical examples that benefit society include Action Against Hunger whose teams work in nearly 50 countries, with an aim to save the lives of malnourished children; while the Cook for Syria campaign raises funds and awareness of the appalling humanitarian catastrophe due to the conflict in that country.

We have to change what we eat and drink

Back to the world of innovation and… we're also seeing more and more 'eat yourself clean' concepts with brands positioning superfoods as immunity boosters, as well as others championing their pure sourcing from unpolluted areas, which is standard for bottled waters but beginning to emerge in sectors like fish and meat. Another emerging issue that's witnessing dynamic innovation is, according to JWT Intelligence, 'Prescription Nutrition'. Their report outlines the subscription service Plantable, which bills itself as 'a health company whose prescription is food'. Their meals are plant-based, vegan, and come with nutrition coaching.

Elsewhere, the multi-sector trend for personalization or customization is seen in a food and drink context as also linking to special needs such as allergies and specific cultural food habits. The health angle here is also seeing more and more fascinating activity focusing on the gut (or the 'second brain'), and via fermented food and drinks, which have a very high level of probiotics, this area is rapidly gaining more and more attention.

While the concept of gut health is nothing new, when it comes to innovation, consumers are increasingly looking for ways to help their gut health. Hence a move on from probiotic yoghurts to fermented foods, this being an area where, for instance, the benefits of Asian cuisine are proven. Interestingly, it's also a scene that is seeing a lot of activity via leading-edge (and highly influential) independent innovators such as the Little Duck Picklery in London.

And, while the trend for healthy living is shown by consumers demonstrating a more holistic approach to wellness, which encompasses both spiritual and mental well-being, *Euromonitor* notes the implications for brands of a group they term as 'Clean Lifers' who demonstrate strong beliefs and ideals. For them 'it's no to unhealthy habits, no to animal-based products. Their attitudes and preferences are a major disruptor for businesses.' The agency also note that 'concerns over obesity, food sensitivity and people affected from disease continues to rise' (Angus, 2018).

And the catalysts for all this activity? Look no further than informed consumers who are becoming ever more aware of and indeed angered by the ethical and environmental impact of the meat industry.

The attitudes and behavioural preferences shown by people around environmental concerns are therefore having a huge impact on the food sector. The issue of 'educated and intentional consumption' means that more and more people are increasingly moving towards plant-based and locally produced eating, demanding detailed information about food provenance and ethical production. The first of those points being illustrated by the extraordinary rise in veganism, which became the fastest-growing consumer lifestyle trend in the UK in 2018.

What's becoming resoundingly clear is that the 'vegan revolution' is transforming eating habits. What was until only recently a niche lifestyle choice that, for many, was based upon their beliefs in animal rights and sustainability, has become truly mainstream, particularly for Millennial and Gen Z consumers. And, of course, where the leading-edge start, big business soon follows, hence an explosion in the amount of vegan choices now being presented to consumers.

I asked food trends expert Mark Shayler about this, who told me that 'the interesting thing to me is that as soon as you look at what eating is doing to you – as soon as you perceive that the taste of what is on your lips being less important than the years of life it takes off, then suddenly you change what you eat. And it speaks of that health/wealth shift but it's really about giving yourself a fighting chance of living longer.

We've suddenly realized that we are what we eat. It's taken a long time to realize this. And so, veganism is purely an extension or the logical conclusion of saying "it's bigger than my health, it's actually the health of all... the animals that are producing the food we eat and secondly the planet." And it's the second one of those that fires me up. I don't want to eat my way to extinction, and you can take that in two ways! I don't want to eat my way to planetary extinction, and I don't want to eat my way to obesity extinction. I think people are looking at what they're eating and saying "I'm part of the problem, not of the solution". And the obvious and first step to take is the extreme route, which is to say "You know what, I can eat less harm – less harm for the planet, less harm for the animals, etc".'

He went on to point out that 'as soon as you get a couple of high-profile vegans, or high-profile macrobiotic celebrities, then the world falls in line. But being vegan is not enough – it's got to be about a whole food diet. A diet that is regenerative for the planet. But the lazy vegan is causing as many problems as the lazy meat eater.

This is a really interesting staging post on the way to looking at things like full bodily health. That whole "diversity = strength" is driving the gut agenda, as it's driving the whole foods agenda. It's an anti-commercial, anti-production agenda'.

And at this point I'd like to highlight that, on a genuinely mass level, of course meat isn't being rejected entirely, indeed very far from it, but instead it's increasingly being seen as a treat, with a 'quality up, quantity down' ethos becoming ever more prevalent. But the bad press for meat will continue, with it being positioned in the public's eye as a pollutant vs the need for more greenery.

This will in turn bring more championing of vegetarian diets, and indeed more plant-based and edible packaging from groups like Wikifood. We'll also see more plant fabrics and the recycling of plant waste, ie coffee grains being used as biofuel.

Meanwhile, the benefits of plant-based foods still need more clarity, due to the amount of confusion that makes this area so difficult for many consumers to understand. A key issue is to focus on 'positive benefits' as opposed to 'beneficial deletions' in the foods offered. Essentially, just as I discuss in Chapter 2, positive messages beat negative ones. Hence, brands should promote affirmational nutritional information about exactly why it is that we should consume specific vegetables and grains, etc. Basically, it seems the plant-based food sector requires an ongoing reframing of its overall positioning, in order for it to be seen by mainstream consumers as having an eco-friendly 'healthy halo' as opposed to being a niche area aimed primarily at vegans and vegetarians.

So how to do this? An answer is highlighted by JWT Intelligence who noted that vegan food 'is often not marketed as vegan and by targeting all foodies with its flavour and healthy ingredients has crossed into the mainstream like never before. As consumers realize the effects of meat on their health, as well as its carbon and water footprints, they're adapting their diets and seeking these plant-based alternatives'.

An affirmational approach is also increasingly being taken, with powerful brand stories communicating the provable benefits of plant-based products, for consumers who view an eating regime as part of their 'self-care' routine.

Elsewhere, and from the point of view of another 'influential operator' an increasing amount of attention is being given to seaweeds as a source of nutrients and energy. Hence, brands like the Dutch start-up Seamore, which makes whole and unprocessed seaweed-based products such as 'pasta' and 'bacon' out of what is renowned as being one of the most sustainable foods on the planet.

An equally interesting approach is being taken by 'healthy junk food' café chain Pure Filth, which aims to provide healthy food for hedonists via dishes and juices packed with flavour, using nutritional science to target different areas of well-being, while a cult-brand in the restaurant and pop-up scenes is the vegan fast-food business 'Temple of Seitan', which sells plant-based burgers, wraps and wings to a growing following.

And as for plant milk, that ongoing boom is a genuine part of the emerging shift towards a more conscious, sustainable way of living, with a respect for the 'natural and ecologically sustainable' being core beliefs. There's a huge variety in this highly innovative 'mylk' sector of course, with walnut, cashew, hazelnut, peanut, almond, tiger nut, coconut, spelt, quinoa, hemp, pea, etc. A brand that I really admire in this sector is Oatly, who have a truly superb approach to communication, used to promote their oat-based products.

There's also the 'elephant in the room' of course: an aura of suspicion directed at BigAg, where consumers are not only sceptical of the 'accepted' benefits of the dairy industry's products, but are increasingly alarmed by reports of the massive ecological damage caused as a direct consequence of the sector.

From impossible foods to experience dining to snackification

Yet, while eco-conscious consumers are a highly important and influential consumer base, when it comes to innovation, their environmental and purity concerns are also being met increasingly by scientifically engineered foodstuffs.

Interestingly, Mintel report that the technology is 'enabling enterprising manufacturers to replace farms and factories with laboratories. A key aim will be for products to provide acceptable substitutions to their harvested counterparts, similar in taste, texture, and/or appearance to real meat'. Technology is also increasingly being utilized to create food and drink that are more nutritious as a result.

One of the next generation of companies in this area are Silicon Valley based Impossible Foods, who are on a mission to make the global food system more sustainable. For instance, they make a plant-based burger that bleeds, and tastes, smells and looks like ground beef. In addition, it uses 95 per cent less land, 74 per cent less water, and creates 87 per cent less greenhouse gas emissions than the current meat supply chain. They say 'we're working to transform the global food system by inventing ways to make the foods we love without compromise. Our brilliant team of curious, creative and collaborative scientists take a fresh look at food and invent new ways to make the meat we crave, directly from plants'.

One innovative example of how the search for more healthy and sustainable diets is being realized is in the use of an 'original superfood' that has appeared in trend reports around the world: insects. These are highlighted as a healthy, ethical and sustainable source, a key issue being they contain nearly 70 per cent protein. According to the UN, millions of people eat insects, particularly in Asia. The West is just starting to catch on to eating them, for instance the Crické brand sells cricket flour, the Finnish baker Fazer make insect bread, and there are also insect snack brand Eat Grub and HOP! a premium craft beer.

Elsewhere, food halls and specialist food offerings at festivals are becoming ever more popular. Bologna, for example, has a food market, 20-acre park and culinary hub featuring four acres of farms showcasing local crops, classroom and event spaces.

From a different perspective, one of the key trends that's seen truly explosive growth, has been the healthy snacking sector, where a sector that had essentially started as home-made oat bars has witnessed amazing growth via seemingly unstoppable innovation, where the annual global market value is approximately US $5 billion.

I remember working on this sector when I first worked in advertising, way back in the late 1990s, when the products were highly utilitarian, and, quite frankly, inedible. How anyone finished a race after consuming 'athlete fuel' that looked, weighed and tasted like a small brick escaped me.

Fast-forward to today, and there's an extraordinary range of innovation in the sector, via brands such as ProBar, Taos Mountain, Clif, Kind, RX, Luna, Zing and Picky, which of course all have specific target markets and are differentiated accordingly via paleo, gluten-free, vitality, gender-specific or protein offerings, etc. Meanwhile, the growth of other innovative product lines like gelatin blocks and gels shows that this sector has a huge amount of latent concept and product development to come.

From Public Enemy No 1 to customized sustainable design

Moving on from product – what about the packaging? This is an area that witnesses an incredible amount of almost continual innovation.

A genuine shift is now well under way, from the perspective of consumers' attitudes finally impacting the way they behave around packaging, as an important part of sustainable lifestyles.

The implications for brands are huge, from the perspective of either 'zero packaging', which is an approach that is, at long last, finally being seen in retailers around the world, to packaging that, when it has to be used, is being designed and produced in a truly dynamic, and sustainable, way.

In doing so, it brings to life the industry saying that 'OK packaging protects a product, brilliant packaging protects and promotes a brand'.

Arguably the most key contemporary product focus of this, plastic, demonstrates the power of mass media, with packaging being an issue thrust into the spotlight following the stunning social impact of the BBC's programme *Blue Planet*, which has been viewed around the world. The programme reinvigorated the public's awareness of the negative impact of plastics and has accelerated a demand for environmentally progressive action from packaging manufacturers.

Fortunately, this coincided with strong leadership at a governmental level and, following the World Economic Forum, global companies stating that they'd work towards using 100 per cent reusable, recyclable or compostable packaging by 2025. These organizations include a host of household names including PepsiCo, Mars and Unilever, while McDonald's has pledged to use sustainable sources for all its packaging worldwide and to recycle 100 per cent of its customers' packaging by 2025.

At the same event, P&G announced that they'd joined the Loop circular e-commerce platform, and were to launch refillable and reusable packaging. According to Virginie Helias, their chief sustainability officer, this was just one example of how P&G are delivering on their 'Ambition 2030' goals. As she explained, these are all about 'accelerating sustainable innovation and driving circular solutions. The time to act is now. We're passionate about harnessing the power of our global reach and transformative partnerships are key to achieving this mission as no one can succeed alone' (Qureshi, 2019).

Plastic waste is choking the seas, and has fast become perceived as Public Enemy No1. Cardboard and paper options will increasingly be seen as a positive and sustainable choice. The drinks brand BrewDog replaced non-recyclable plastic can holders with cardboard boxes. Exciting initiatives have also been seen from those like the Dutch organic supermarket Ekoplaza going entirely plastic-free. Meanwhile, the supermarket Iceland committed to eliminating plastic from all their own-label packaging, switching to paper pulp alternatives.

Companies in all sectors that utilize packaging have to do their part, and Coca-Cola, which uses 120 billion bottles a year, has pledged to tackle this global issue.

James Quincey, their CEO, was quoted in the *Financial Times* as saying that Coca-Cola 'will collect and recycle the equivalent of all its packaging by 2030; by which date it also aims to make all of its packaging with an average of 50 per cent recycled content.' The company will also trial different collection techniques, including networks of 'scavengers' in some markets (Nicolaou, 2018).

This whole area needs more contextualizing, so I also spoke with the trends expert Mark Shayler, who pointed out that 'Packaging is fascinating because everyone has an opinion. That opinion is often not rooted in fact, but in perception. One is that man-made, ie plastic is bad and that natural materials are good, but that's not always the case. Don't get me wrong, there's no place in the ocean for plastic and single-use plastics are a curse. But, in many situations, plastics have done more benefit than harm, and fundamentally, it's not plastic's fault that it gets put in the ocean, it's the person's fault'.

As he went on to tell me '90 per cent of ocean plastic comes from eight rivers, and those rivers are in the emerging world, and the reason that plastic ends up there is that they don't have a waste collection system. So consequently, there's a lot that can be done about introducing waste systems into emerging nations'.

Many people are also entirely confused about how to understand the problem, and indeed if there is just 'one problem'. But as Mark explained 'there are three major threats to the oceans. The first two are significantly bigger than the third one. The first one is climate change, and the resulting acidification and warming of the ocean. The second threat is overfishing. And the third that comes quite a way back is marine pollution, ie plastic. But as individuals we like to blame everyone else: the packaging manufacturers, the soft drink producers, the ready-meal producers, rather than ourselves.

Interestingly, the way we eat is becoming the frontline on taking some of that responsibility internally. It builds on provenance, knowing where your food comes from. The consumer is confused, so the challenge we have in packaging is that everyone touches it, and everyone has an opinion, but hardly anybody understands it. A bit like politics!'

To deal with some of the issues that Mark highlights, packaging is therefore witnessing an ever-greater use of recyclable and biodegradable materials, lighter packaging and a visible commitment to eco-design within the settings of the circular economy. At the same time, of course, it must continue to deliver against the 'always-on' demands of consumer convenience.

When it comes to trend forecasting in the area, we'll be witnessing a lot more product-packaging interaction, including smart packaging that prolongs contents' life and provides more useful information to the customer.

Another key area hugely impacting packaging trends is, as mentioned in the introduction to this chapter, e-commerce. In an omnichannel environment, when traditional notions of shopping channels have become blurred, packaging clearly has to work in both physical 'bricks and mortar' stores along with being viewed and ordered purely online. That is where brand identity has to have maximum impact, particularly for new consumers, or for brands operating a 'direct to consumer' model, or indeed purchased via voice-commerce apps and then delivered to us. This vital 'touchpoint' issue means that packaging has become ever more important as a means of engaging with consumers, and communicating branded messages with them and those around them regarding 'shareable experiences'.

For an example of that, look no further than scent, this being a sensory experience not traditionally associated with packaging. Special inks can now deliver, for instance, the scent of 'freshly cut grass', as the consumer opens their shoe box, reflecting a brand's outdoor messaging. Alternatively, gender-neutral minimalist packaging (reflecting a gender-fluid young generation) is another exciting area to watch.

Elsewhere, the growth of convenience solutions for busy consumers has seen a huge rise in meal kits, gourmet ready-meals and grocery box subscription services as a specific area where brands are championing cardboard packaging as a sustainable and attractive packaging solution. The practicality of easily returnable resealable packaging is also a fundamental issue, and one in which the adaptability and flexibility of 'roundtrip-designed' cardboard means that consumers who find it simple to return items are far more likely to reorder replacements from the same brand.

Despite this, the world's most widely recycled packaging material (corrugated cardboard) still seems to have an aura of dullness about it, despite it being renewable, recyclable, reusable and biodegradable. It will, quite frankly, be an essential material as we move towards a regenerative, circular economy. It's also 'consumer friendly' in practical day-to-day terms relating to storage convenience, ease of use, safety and ease of recycling.

And as if that isn't enough, the protective and preserving qualities of this environmentally friendly packaging format can help to reduce food waste via its superior abilities to keep food fresher.

The idea of being 'functional and aesthetically pleasing' is particularly vital when aiming to appeal to those informed consumers who desire both individuality (which can be offered through personalized digital printing technology and limited edition offerings) alongside wanting brands that communicate provenance or 'good for the planet' values and aspirations.

Smart packaging and holistic thinking

Meanwhile, the development of blockchain technology means that physical products can now have 'digital passports', which underline their authentic credentials and full production and delivery histories, things in which consumers who make 'intentional buying choices' are ever more interested.

Smart packaging offers additional embedded security features that will facilitate traceability, anti-counterfeiting and offer both brand and consumer the possibility to ascertain a product's authenticity and origin. Added layers of technology such as QR codes, VR and AI allow brands to create a greater level of engagement with consumers, linking to matters discussed throughout this book, including brand stories, product origins, tutorials, etc. In addition, branded content can be updated in real time, enabling brands to gather data from consumers, and as a result delivering special offers in return for their information. This being another area where innovative packaging will facilitate new revenue streams.

Elsewhere, reactive inks can inform customers if, for instance, there's been a break in the 'cold-chain', which can indicate problems for products that require a steady temperature from the production line to the hand of the consumer. Scientists are also creating colour-changing smart labels to detect when food may have gone off, with these types of indicators also enabling the combating of significant food wastage.

The overarching issue being, as highlighted earlier, that the circular economy is shifting from being a niche issue to one that is centre stage. This means the absolute minimalizing of raw materials, the reduction of waste and a huge increase in either the reuse or the recycling of them back into that circular, sustainable system.

The most immediate implications range from the way in which the overall issues around packaging are discussed on a global basis, how materials are sourced and manufactured, and the delivering of powerful initiatives from brands/retailers relating to repurposing or recycling. And this is where innovation has a huge role to play.

A paradigm shift in consumer behaviour is clearly beginning to match their attitudes towards sustainability, with the growing rejection of single-use plastic and 'over-packaging' being core concerns. We will see brands that don't show leadership in the area of sustainability, or are perceived as ignoring it, being punished by consumers who, when faced with a viable alternative, will increasingly choose the 'better for the planet' option.

Core issues to watch therefore, are trust, creativity and sustainability. It's now socially unacceptable not to care about the environment, so consumer-centric packaging that reflects customer environmental concerns is the way forward. The end result will be a stronger emotional consumer connection with 'betterness' at its core. A result that is all about 'good business', which is 'better for me, better for us, and better for the planet'.

Summary

If we accept that the food and drink sectors, from a product and packaging perspective, are prime examples of a sector faced with increasingly demanding customers, ever stricter regulation and an extraordinary amount of competitive innovation, then the old maxim that brands must 'innovate or fail' is an absolute truism.

And that innovation, can, of course, simply be a case of re-evaluating and rethinking existing ideas and processes. I mentioned earlier, for example, that the 'old' idea of vertical farming is currently being seen as the next big thing. While the results certainly won't feed the planet, it will be an additional way of enabling more of us to eat freshly produced healthy food, grown on a hyper-local basis utilizing a hydroponic methodology.

I'll go into more depth on a whole range of innovative activity impacting the health and well-being sectors in another chapter, but from a specific food and drink perspective, I'll turn to my interview with Mark Shayler.

We talked about the incredible growth in functional foods, and brands positioning themselves as being very much 'on our side' when it comes to looking after consumer health. As he said, 'fundamentally, companies can't continue to make a profit by having a customer base that's fat and ill. Brands have to change that, with brand teams thinking "how do we help these people live longer, live better and how do we charge for that?" So, it won't be long before many food companies reclassify themselves as "health companies". We're on the brink of it now. I'd happily pay a food company to keep me healthier.'

That sounds a lot like combining an activist angle with a 'demanding consumer' one to me, and that takes us towards the increasing politicization of the food and drink sectors.

In this chapter, and indeed throughout this book, I've noted the implications for innovation as a result of a societal context of 'fear, uncertainty and doubt' and it's clear that, around the world, consumers are aware of the significance of what they eat and drink, taking into account where it was produced, who was involved and how it was transported, and are making brand adoption or rejection choices as a result.

Hence the concept of 'informed consumers' has moved from a trend forecasting issue to one that is being witnessed as a key part of mainstream daily consumption.

If supply chains and production methodologies were 'ignored issues' in the past, those days are gone. The beneficiaries include animal and workers' rights, along with the environment and ecosphere in general; and of course, those 'good brands' that innovate and profit accordingly.

As for the results of long-term trend research into change, from the perspective of where our food starts its journey, ie farming, then according to the influential 'Future of Food in 2040' report, there are already 'technologies being developed that can care for crops on a plant-by-plant basis or control the grazing of cattle without physical fences, and by 2040 this technology will be commonplace in farming, while new biotech production techniques will not only help preserve crops but also make them more nutritious' (Doward, 2019). This clearly points towards perhaps not the definite, but certainly a potential, way forward.

And on that note, I'll now move on to the following chapter, which looks at how a wide range of innovations, including next-generation technological developments, are impacting the health and wellness sector. These often reflect straight back onto the food and drink industry, and so you'll therefore note how a lot of the issues highlighted in this chapter link directly to the next.

This illuminates the 'golden thread' that runs through my book, that a great many examples of leading-edge innovation have multi-sector implications, linked as they are to trends that weave their way through a wide variety of consumer attitudes and behaviour.

CHAPTER FIVE

The wellness economy meets the lifestyle industry

This chapter examines the health and wellness market, where the amount of innovation taking place is staggering. Hence, I cover a wide spectrum of catalytic issues, eg biotech and nanomedicine.

In doing so, I'll illustrate an increasingly holistic and multi-sector approach to mental and physical health. This has led to a 'multiplier effect' where traditional notions of health products, services and organizations are being leveraged by individual and collaborative activity across sectors such as beauty, fashion, hospitality, sports, food, architecture and retail. In addition, this dynamic situation is being continuously impacted by catalytic start-ups alongside progressive action from legacy brands, on a global basis. The overall effect is profound.

What all of those individuals and companies know is that a route to guaranteeing business success is to gain a strong relationship between brand and consumer. And I can't think of a better way of doing that than to help someone genuinely feel better. This sure-fire way of building loyalty also has strong links to 'mindful consumption and conscious consumerism' where informed individuals manage and control their own healthcare.

So how should companies approach the health sector in its many forms? *The Economist* states 'there are two broad routes in: the first is doing business in the existing system. A second is for tech firms to use their platforms to create entirely new channels though which care can be delivered.' Two statistics illustrate why the amount of innovation taking place via those particular routes is so vast: on average, healthcare costs make up about a tenth of any country's GDP (*The Economist*, 2018). Meanwhile, Reuters reports that the global digital health market is expected to reach US$665 billion by 2026 (Reuters Editorial, 2018).

The 'new normal' for this activity is driven by key structural shifts: from cure to prevention, where 'powerless masses' are being remodelled as 'empowered individuals' and from technological progress in areas such as artificial intelligence (AI), machine learning (ML) and augmented reality (AR). Not to ignore the present, the last of those, AR, actually appears to offer equal amounts of augmenting current knowledge as it does future R&D opportunities. This illustrates once again that innovation generally comes in two broad forms, the incremental/iterative and the disruptive/revolutionary.

Of course, amidst all the flurry of product innovation and service initiatives, the focus has to be firmly on the recipient rather than the product, ie not just 'innovation for the sake of innovation'. That's a complaint often directed at those involved in new product and concept development across a multitude of sectors, where obsessing over the next big thing rather than simply sorting out a needed improvement to the current situation is a systemic problem, and a cause of endless consumer dissatisfaction.

This 'order of priority' issue is summed up by the Centre for the Advancement of Sustainable Medical Innovation, which states 'such is the pace of scientific advancement, rising R&D costs, and limited budgets, that ensuring early patient access to more affordable, transformative, safe and effective products in a sustainable way is paramount' (Gottlieb, 2018).

And that point is key, as just as in any sector where the impact of innovation can be life changing, or indeed life threatening, there are two key questions that have to be asked: 'does the innovation work as intended, and if there any side effects, what are they?'

But when based on an ethos of purpose, relevance and value, the 'influencers and revolutionaries' in the health market are taking positive steps for us all, underlining the saying that 'good business is good business'.

This all comes at a time when, worldwide, the consumer landscape is developing and evolving to an incredible extent. Key trends driving the overall sector include ones that are also reflected across an array of others highlighted elsewhere in this book, such as personalization, convenience, privacy, connectivity and, of course, well-being.

And with individuals being viewed ever more as 'informed consumers' the health sector is confronted, as are so many others, with people who are demanding that their specific needs and desires be met, and met at a reasonable price. These needs and desires extend, on a holistic basis, across the mental and physical well-being landscape.

So whether it's a yearning for better sleep, a desire for glowing skin, an antidote to anxiety, advice on the best recipes for your specific health issues, a search for happiness, health being viewed 'as the new wealth', the need to find the most relevant doctor in the right location to deal with a specific health need, or simply the unavoidable realization that we're all going to die at some point and that we want to 'die well', innovation in the health sector via the brands and organizations serving it is spectacularly exciting to observe.

I have taken a 'here, now and next' approach that I hope provides the type of innovation content that this book was written to deliver.

Health is everything

In an era where the basic definition of 'health' is rapidly evolving, it's worth setting the scene by considering just how far we've come over the last few years. Unusually, simply defining what the sector actually includes is an existential question in this context. Indeed, the more that we learn about health, says the JWT 'Well Economy' report 'the more it seems to include everything. The definition is expanding as consumers begin to include health as a factor in everyday decisions and purchases. At the same time, technology is driving unparalleled changes, creating a storm of disruption in the $3 trillion US healthcare industry alone'.

The implications for a wide array of sectors and indeed local and national government are immense, because if health can include everything, then everything (within reason) can include health. That point, and the implications of it, are hugely important, for instance with reference to wellness communities in future cities, and consumer lifestyle behaviour in future homes, are points that I reference in the chapter devoted to those specific subjects.

This link to communities and architecture is summed up by Katherine Johnston of the Global Wellness Institute 'we're at the beginning of a new movement in home and community design that tackles our uniquely modern problems: sedentary lives, unhealthy diets, stress, social isolation, pollution and nature deprivation' (Global Wellness Institute, 2017).

The subject of modern lifestyles is, quite naturally, a key element of any 'next big thing' presentation at health conferences, where a seemingly endless array of consumer trends are discussed alongside product and service concepts referencing them, which are intended to help soothe unstable, constantly connected lifestyles. 'Brands are also evolving' according to JWT Intelligence, providing much more than traditional notions of product development. As the agency reports 'they're becoming civic leaders, advocates, even therapists. They're driving dialogue change by reinventing how we address taboos in everyday life, tackling everything from sexual health to menopause to hair loss – and are empowering refreshing, open new dialogues' (JWT Intelligence, 2018).

A situation I find fascinating is that traditional cures are combining with next-generation AI, AR and ML technology to deliver a stunning array of personalized options for people who are rightly taking advantage of their new-found power as 'unreasonable consumers' and are demanding to be treated better than previous generations.

This, particularly in hospital environments, sees the rejection of an outmoded quantitative or 'volume' approach where care is allocated and evaluated according to numbers of people treated. That's as opposed to a qualitative or 'value-based' model, which is based on more humane sounding 'positive outcomes' where care is structured around the holistic needs of both the individual person and the society in which they live.

Indeed, and in the context of this book, I believe that we're witnessing a fascinating redrawing of the relationship between brands and individuals, which is moving from one that was almost entirely based on a coldly functional 'supplier–buyer' relationship, to one where that relationship is becoming more of a partnership, and that sees brands working alongside citizens in a spirit of collaboration, where prevention rather than cure is the aim. The result being that we, as individuals, are actively empowered to be 'the best version of ourselves'.

The empowerment of taking personal responsibility for one's own health will continue to be given a turbo-boost by technological developments.

This empowerment of and drive towards taking personal responsibility for one's own health becoming an easier prospect has, is and will continue to be given a turbo-boost by technological developments.

Meanwhile, emerging ideas such as crowdsourcing techniques are being utilized and leveraged by doctors as they link, and share valuable information, with other specialists around the globe. Added to this, the latest iterative developments in virtual reality (VR) mean that specialists can improve their ongoing education about best practice and next-generation equipment and medical techniques.

Trust and transparency

In terms of the overarching issues concerning consumers, I'd suggest the importance of trust and transparency can hardly be exaggerated.

A highly visible example is a regrettably long line of ongoing organizational failures of those tasked with safeguarding our personal information. It's a fault line impacting the health sector on a deeply worrying scale.

Around the world, disastrous experiences of data breaches have led to people being worried, to put it mildly, about the safety and security of their data. In a famous instance, 'hackers breached 1.5m Singapore patient records, including the prime minister's, and data breaches in the US in 2018 alone took place from Florida to New York State to California' (Davis, 2018).

I illuminated the issue of trust in my book *The Post-Truth Business*, where I stressed a belief that, in this context, in order to gain trust, brands must be transparent in their business behaviour and respect their customers' privacy, be ethical and have empathy. All these would go towards building their reputation capital, by answering that crucial question of whether a company or brand is 'competent, reliable and trustworthy'. I found it fascinating that, when I gave a speech at one of Europe's biggest tech fairs 'Tech BBQ' in Copenhagen, the talk among delegates and an array of start-ups presenting their ideas was of one-to-one healthcare services being provided on a long-term 'trusted guardian' basis.

But while discussions around transparency are usually along the lines of 'if it can be provided, that's a brilliant and beneficial idea', another angle is a hot topic of concern in, for instance, health insurance circles, particularly when it comes to citizens' rights. That angle relates to questions regarding those who may unfortunately be flagged up as being 'high-risk' cases, due to their test results indicating a high proclivity to future health needs. Being 'high-exposure' customers, regarding the implied costs that they may bring to the company concerned, poses obvious ethical questions over the amount of access health insurance companies should have to our health records, and how they can use that information.

Another issue that is causing serious concern among health insurers is how to entice those potential customers who, perhaps having taken advantage of highly accurate diagnostic tests, realize that they are at low risk of actually needing the 'worst-case scenario' services often offered via expensive and potentially irrelevant health insurance. Those people may instead commit to leading a suitably healthy lifestyle that hopefully negates the relevance of a wide range of 'pointless' healthcare coverage offered by standard insurance policies.

Join these two issues together, and the very foundation of many insurance business models is called into question. This being where the insurance risk is spread widely, therefore exposing the insurance company to the 'needle in a haystack' risk, while covering all those in that haystack equally, when none of them can know which of them will unfortunately have to call on that insurance policy, and to what extent. That is an existential question for the industry in an era where technological advances clash with ethical privacy agendas.

Meanwhile, one answer was given loud and clear by John Hancock (one of the biggest health insurance companies in the US) when they announced they'd decided to stop selling traditional life insurance in favour of 'interactive policies' that track health data through wearables and smartphones. According to

Forbes, 'policies of this type are sold as an advantage for users, who are incentivized to be healthier, and for insurers, who get clients with healthier habits who tend to live longer, making fewer claims. Detractors argue that insurers may try to offer less attractive conditions to higher risk individuals' (Dans, 2018).

Not to be outdone, the world's leading retailer, Amazon, has been enabled by its enormous infrastructure to make inroads into healthcare services, ie distribution and insurance. And their vast data analytics and AI abilities mean they're able to develop enhanced pricing and more accurate underwriting decisions than insurers have been able to achieve in the past. Reuters note that 'policyholders score premium discounts for hitting exercise targets and get gift cards by logging their workouts and healthy food purchases in an app. In theory, everybody wins, but privacy and consumer advocates have raised questions about whether insurers may eventually use data to select only the most profitable customers' (Barlyn, 2018).

This all goes to show that, to build trust, transparency is absolutely vital and indeed is a key driver of innovations in the well-being arena, with two particularly beneficial outcomes of this relating to better quality of services and a reduction in costs.

But what about innovation with regard to the use of that data (eg the astonishing amount held by Google in the US)? Artificial intelligence is obviously at the absolute forefront of developments.

Algorithmic interpretations and personal control

Not long ago, the idea that individuals could benefit from being put firmly in control of their own healthcare would have seemed ludicrous in all but the most progressive and tech-savvy cultures. But the idea that we're rapidly moving towards a near future that sees physicians being recast as our 'health partners' and where the 'management structure' of that relationship has morphed from being vertical to horizontal, means we're living in dynamic times. Times when, for instance, genomics are helping to develop personalized medicines for individuals. This idea of the adoption of 'precision medicine' was referenced by the National Human Genome Research Institute, which 'noted calls for genomics, epigenomics, environmental exposure, and other data being used to more accurately guide individual diagnosis' (NHGRI, nd).

Patients' data will increasingly be algorithmically interpreted and clinicians will be augmented progressively in terms of accuracy, speed and workload efficiency via artificial intelligence. According to *Wired* magazine 'that is the big challenge – and opportunity – of future healthcare'. AI, ML, data and computing power can help us try to figure out how to reduce mortality rates for progressive diseases, or rare early childhood diseases. *Wired* magazine goes on to say 'If the intention is putting the patient at the centre and providing more personalized care, it all boils down to leveraging data better. Patients will be empowered, and doctors will be able to take better care of them' (*Wired*, 2019).

A key source of that information is due to more and more of us tracking our own data, using smart technology to gather it. This adds to the knowledge that we and our healthcare providers, including physicians and insurers, already have.

Traditionally, all but the wealthiest patients were at the back of a long queue when it came to swiftly accessing personalized, high-quality medical attention. But in a 'smartphone diagnosis era' the consumer is most definitely in charge, due to health monitoring being just a wearable-enabled app away, eg giving constant blood pressure readings or skin-friendly glucose sensor data, etc. A really clever idea that reimagines how we might interact with our personal smart technology is an app developed by Sage Bionetworks, which measures how users interact with and hold their devices, ie via tapping speed and tremor activity that reflect the severity of motor symptoms in those with Parkinson's disease, in addition to their gait and balance while walking.

Other 'unexpected' uses of wearable technology that have grabbed media attention have ranged from phobia treatments being delivered via VR and smart insulin patches that can eliminate the endless requirement for blood testing by assisting those with diabetes to keep a consistent level of glucose, to wearable micropatch needles that could revolutionize treatment. According to Professor Owen Guy at the Centre for NanoHealth at Swansea University, 'combining the smart patch and the injection would be the ultimate aim' in an interview he gave for the BBC (BBC, 2018). Alternatively, innovators like Proteus Discover have created ingestible sensors (the size of a grain of sand) that link with wearable devices. As a report on these sensors says, 'once it reaches the stomach, it transmits a signal to the patch worn on the torso. A digital record is sent to the patient's mobile device and then to the Proteus cloud where with the patient's permission, healthcare providers and caregivers can access it via their portal' (Proteus Digital Health, nd).

As an aside, and in terms of links between health and the obvious 'wearable' sector, ie fashion, that sector is now witnessing a move towards 'well fashion', which is the next iteration beyond that of the most irritating term in the world, 'athleisure'. This, essentially, sees clothes that are quite literally 'better for you'.

When it comes to all things fashionable and indeed rebellious, and in a bid to improve current wearables, a collaboration between MIT, the University of Illinois and Harvard has seen the creation of 'smart tattoos'. According to a Penn State blog 'Dermal Abyss tattoo ink is capable of keeping track of athletes vitalities. It can track your heartbeat, water level, and blood sugar in realtime, notifying the person if something is wrong in a second, by changing its colour, making it perfect for athletes or people with diabetic problems' (Pursel, 2018).

Meanwhile, by having secure access to one's own medical records along with the ability to share them securely with the medical practitioner of one's choice, means that what had been the preserve of the wealthy is now truly in sight as being in the realm of the masses.

In terms of efficiency, blockchain activity from companies such as SimplyVital with their 'Connecting Care' platform is really exciting. I outline the sector-specific benefits of blockchain throughout this book, as it relates to the various chapter subjects, but in this context it does one key thing: keeps an 'unlosable' ledger of patients' health records, which solves a problem impacting patients around the world.

Why is this so important, indeed why is it a situation that most readers of this book will readily recognize? According to *Forbes*, 'There is much inefficiency in the healthcare and medical space. It is further complicated with privacy laws, regulations and stakeholders who may have conflicting interests. This has hampered the ability for healthcare data to be safely shared and efficiently moved by providers, hospitals and individuals. Blockchain can change that' (Moy, 2018).

We're now entering an age when 'the doctor will see you when-ever you like', and that doctor may be a virtual one, when technology from brands like Apple means their 'Health Records' app gives citizens 'digital management' of their medical records, by enabling them to inspect, control and share their medical information. Until recently, for mainstream consumers, all they saw from Silicon Valley companies was fitness trackers (including the Google-owned Fitbit) or virtual hosting of health-tech data.

But all this dynamism functions only when the data stream on which it's based flows smoothly; healthcare systems on a national or even local level, indeed even within hospitals themselves where different departments and specialists may be involved, are notorious for being anything but smooth and unruffled.

That's why I say 'in sight', as the frustration of waiting for 'serious' healthcare is, as ever, at crisis point for most people. In an age of omnichannel retailing, instant ordering and high-speed delivery, healthcare has traditionally been in the slow lane. The issue of time was put into focus by *The Economist*, who pointed out that 'no wonder they are called "patients". When people enter healthcare systems today, they know what they will get: prodding doctors, endless tests, baffling jargon, rising costs and, above all, long waits.

Some stoicism will always be needed, because healthcare is complex and diligence matters. But frustration is boiling over' (*The Economist*, 2018).

Product and service innovation – back to the future

But, moving away from the retail problems of today and focusing on the future, let's look at an area receiving a huge amount of attention at trend shows and trade events around the world: 'nootropics'. This being the overall name for a selection of drugs, adaptogens and synthetic compounds, ie products aiding or improving mental performance such as focus or memory. The potential areas that may benefit from a 'mental boost' range from simple relaxation to creative enhancement, memory strengthening and personal motivation.

The drinks industry media company BevNet note that consumers desire beverages 'that can provide both physical and mental fuel throughout the day. Nootropics or "smart drugs" are a niche but a rising segment of the supplements industry promising boosted brain function. It's helped inspire a growing subculture of consumers who experiment with different compounds and "stacks," ie combinations of different nootropics' (Avery, 2018).

We're already seeing 'niche' beverage products currently in market, including TruBrain shots made with all-natural active amino acids, Brain Booster gel-based supplements, Alpha Brain 'memory focus' drink mixes, Brain Toniq with blends consisting of eleuthero, choline, rhodiola rosea, sunflower lecithin, bacopa monnieri and centella asiatica, etc; so it was interesting to see a major move in this area when *Marketing Week* announced the launch in Hungary and Spain of Coca-Cola Energy, which combines caffeine, guarana extracts and B vitamins.

When a company the size of Coke gets in on a trend like this, you know it's gone, or is soon to go, seriously mainstream on an international basis. That issue of 'naturally derived sources' to which their launch material referenced, is a fascinating one, as we see more and more products coming to market utilizing remedies ancient and new, but always 'natural'. Hence ingredients such as yerba mate, St John's wort, L-theanine, ginseng and lemon balm being seen in more and more consumer beverages around the world.

In terms of innovations that may point us to future healthcare, developments in issues such as brain–computer interfaces and 3D-printed organs are receiving media attention. And as John McNamara from IBM's R&D Lab suggests, 'within 20 years we may see AI nano-machines being injected into our bodies, providing huge medical benefits, such as repairing damage to cells, muscles and bones – perhaps even augment them'. He also believes that we're moving into the Second Machine Age 'which will see human mental capabilities reproduced and bettered and it will have a huge impact on medicine and healthcare' (Armstrong, 2018).

Another cutting-edge device that could provide guidance to doctors right inside the operating theatre: HoloLens, Microsoft's holographic computer. This allows, for instance, surgeons to produce multiple types of images of a patient's organs and, potentially, to access a patient's scans while operating on them.

Mixed-reality headsets such as HoloLens could also revolutionize the way diagnoses are carried out and treatment is administered. That is according to Professor Neil Sebire, of the UCL Great Ormond Street Institute of Child Health. 'We have seen demos where you've got someone wearing HoloLens in one country and someone in another country, looking at the same thing', he says. 'So, you can imagine having an X-ray that I'm looking at here, while another doctor somewhere else is looking at the same thing at the same time, and we can communicate and interact with the object at the same time'. That is potentially huge for healthcare, and was a point referenced at the Cannes

Lions health event, regarding the highlighting of 55,000 people having watched the world's first virtual reality operation by Dr Shafi Ahmed (Cannes Lions, 2017).

Mental health, and combating anxiety

To state the stunningly obvious, mental health, particularly from the perspectives of anxiety and depression, is a hugely important issue that has risen up the public agenda in recent years. However, it's one with very different levels of being seen as either a 'socially acceptable' or a 'taboo' subject, depending in which part of the world you live.

While a great deal of the blame for increased levels of anxiety is being aimed, quite rightly, at the social media platforms, and at the combined impact of the mainstream media, fashion industry and celebrity culture in general, innovation will have a hopefully positive role to play, to the benefit of people's mental health.

This is because the 'anxiety economy' (which, I have to say, is a depressing concept) is thriving, often as result of public health services failing to offer or efficiently deliver the required levels of therapeutic or counselling support. That's due, I have to add, as a result of a lack of funding, not a lack of empathy on the part of those involved in the various health services concerned.

The array of services and products that are linked to this 'economy' are phenomenal, regarding options catering for mood, (lack of) sleep and overall stress, etc. What's really acted as a catalyst in this category (which is sub-divided into around 30 different ones) is that we're now self-diagnosing and self-caring. Alongside this, alternative therapies and increasing variations of holistic services are playing a huge role. Thus the basic issue of us 'becoming our own doctors', where social media, mindfulness apps and health-specific websites play a vital role, has become something of immense significance.

The overall health context within which this sits is defined by the World Health Organization as 'a state of well-being in which every individual realizes their own potential, can cope with the normal stresses of life, work productively and fruitfully, and is able to make a contribution to their community.' Regarding a specific viewpoint on mental health, this is highlighted in the constitution of the WHO as health being 'a state of complete physical, mental and social well-being, not merely the absence of disease or infirmity' (WHO, 2014).

Meanwhile, the Consumer Electronics Show in Las Vegas always provides a vast array of future concepts. The latest one featured a staggering number of products and services that, for instance, encourage mindfulness, combat anxiety, boost sleep, aid nutrition and interact with users to create vital observational data.

In terms of individual products, *Forbes* magazine highlighted the neuroscientific 'TouchPoint' wearable that turns down your stress switch to restore calm, rational thinking and thus better performance, Harman's in-car 'Neurosense' tech that uses cognitive analysis to detect your emotional state and assists you in driving more carefully, and Sleep Robots that help relax you by simulating human breathing (Bell, 2019).

Other stress-busting products included a headband from Interaxon – Muse, which claims to help users improve their focus, reduce their stress and have better sleep, along with stress-related products like the HeartGuide blood pressure monitor from Omron.

Acting as an overarching view of all of this, is the ever-growing awareness that we need to view ourselves as part of the larger communities that surround us (and social inclusion), and indeed of the well-being of the planet itself. Which, once again, links us right back to the issue of, and our responsibilities with regard to, climate change.

Play and community

And of course, when discussing 'anxiety busting' one must highlight a vital link to the world of play. Usually associated purely with childhood, and where, to quote the famous Jean Piaget, 'Play is the work of childhood', we now see a complete reappraisal of this for all the personal and societal benefits that it brings. From an emotional and mental health aspect as an antidote to anxiety and stress, it knows no bounds.

I discuss the 'play' topic in more detail in the chapter on entertainment and sports, but in the context of this chapter, I'll refer to psychiatrist Stuart Brown of the US National Institute for Play, who says that 'what all play has in common is that it offers a sense of engagement and pleasure, takes the player out of a sense of time and place, and the experience of doing it is more important than the outcome'.

As for encouraging 'positive change' at an individual and community level, examples obviously exist around the world, but, to take one example about as far away from my desk as one could go, the South Australian Government states, 'to make our state the healthiest state, we need to make healthy choices easy for all. Whether you are a council, community group or centre, service club, sporting club, hospitality business, food outlet, large or small business, there are plenty of ways you can boost your community's health and vibrancy through healthy eating and physical activity' (Government of South Australia, nd).

Meanwhile, the Healthy London Partnership have a strategic aim of enabling London's diverse communities to thrive and a policy of social integration; this is a proven method of making communities healthier, more engaged and better connected.

Innovation in healthy communities can also mean taking advantage of a world where autonomous electric vehicles mean that thousands of petrol stations will be effectively redundant. The challenge here being, what is to be done with those locations? This was the question posed by Reebok to the global architects Gensler. The firm reimagined and repositioned these places as becoming hubs for physical and mental fitness, on an individual or community basis.

Communicating a health message

The communications industry has always had 'driving behavioural change' as a goal, and is an industry brimming with excitement at the major role it has to play. Hence the resulting products being promoted in the most creative manner via a comms sector in all its guises, ie across the worlds of advertising, PR, design and media, etc.

When it comes to communicating health issues, some incredibly creative routes to market have been used recently. And I believe that a great way to uncover a genuine 'human truth' on which to build a unifying insight for use by those tasked with creative campaigns, is to conduct ethnographic research in the context and 'real-life' social setting of the individual(s) concerned. Building an emotional link between brand and consumer is always a goal for companies, and as the World Federation of Advertisers points out 'emotional marketing is particularly potent in the health sector. Brands must help consumers to move beyond rational thinking, enabling audiences to re-evaluate their lives and achieve the long-term positive change they desire' (WARC, 2018).

For an example of best practice from the perspective of genuinely brilliant creative thinking that's inspired multi-generational, international action, then the award-winning 'Sea-Hero Quest' by Saatchi & Saatchi for their client Deutsche Telekom is one of my favourite campaigns. This multi-platform mobile game was the first mobile 'game for good' where players could assist scientists in their efforts to combat dementia, via helping to progress scientists' knowledge of spatial navigation.

It's well known that one of the first things that dementia sufferers experience is a loss of spatial awareness, ie the ability to find their way around places previously well known to them is lost. The idea behind the game, which brought this to life, was for the player to act as an explorer's son, travelling around the world finding places where the seafaring father had been, but who had now begun to lose the memory of his adventures. Therefore, essentially, 'finding his memories'. The data collected via the game has been given free to scientists on an international basis, along with University College London, a place renowned for its research into dementia. The concept was generated by the agency regarding 'the power of the Deutsche Telekom network and its 200 million users.'

The D-word

A staggering statistic that reflects incredible societal change is that today's 20-somethings have a 20 per cent chance of reaching their 100th birthday. On a demographic level, this #NewNormal will be one of the biggest social changes in history, and one that makes 'prevention rather than cure' an ever more pressing factor, eg as demonstrated in the 'productive healthy ageing' ethos espoused by the official organization, Public Health England, re better life-style behaviour.

While that is a cause for celebration in terms of a wide range of societal medical advances, it does of course come with serious implications, including who is to look after these Millennials when they reach old age, who is to pay for their care and how their healthcare is to be administered.

There are other implications of a range of healthcare issues including Alzheimer's (where stem cell therapy appears to hold out immense hopes) and diabetes, these being that while these people may have these diseases and illnesses that exist today, they'll have them for far longer.

Regarding these diseases, Leena Alanko of the think tank Demos says that 'they're already affecting today's society. It is not possible or even reasonable for society to provide care for everyone, which is why we need a new system. This should include transport, housing, town planning, and harness the power of technology to diagnose and monitor health as well as energize behaviour' (Buckland, 2018).

Meanwhile, and looking to the 'end of life' issue, The Future Laboratory note that 'dying well' is a point that's now featuring in trend presentations. They report that the 'death positive' movement means a 'better death' is becoming integral to the idea of a 'well life'. And of course, so it should.

An extraordinary array of corporates, start-ups and organizations continue to innovate in the area of dying and death.

An extraordinary array of corporates, start-ups and organizations continue to innovate in the area of dying and death, looking into areas ranging from the tech giants considering what happens to the digital memories held in the content we've placed online, and perhaps future messages we may wish to send loved ones after we've died, to ethical considerations around a 'polarization' of the 'death-sector' for the wealthy vs the poor.

In a series of articles commissioned by the Design Council, an article titled 'Reinventing death for the twenty-first century' noted how start-ups, corporations, venture capitalists and health providers are designing new, more meaningful ways of dying. The article noted how for both the dying and their carers involved in palliative care, all too often 'we don't get the death we want' and that 'the biggest challenge is in reframing death as part of life, not as the end of life.' After all, 'when well-designed technology can help improve our every living moment, why should it desert us in death?'

Of course, the various interests and involvements of those including religion, the law of the land, governmental policy, capitalism and free will may all combine and overlap in this most complex of issues. And as for the approach that those tasked with creating innovative products and services must take, 'they should tread carefully, with humility and with purpose'. And the key word they must consider is to take an approach to innovation that is 'incremental' rather than 'transformational' (Pallister, 2018).

Summary

This chapter has hopefully illustrated a range of innovation that's driving the health and wellness sector to a truly remarkable degree.

And a great deal of it is being driven by consumer desires relating to their treatment by brands in other sectors.

This sees a demand for convenience, along with low-cost quality products and services, completely altering their expectations for healthcare. This sees the opportunities for agile legacy brands and start-ups alike as being profound.

And I believe it's this 'cross-sector impact' above all others that is really driving genuinely revolutionary change in healthcare service provision and product development around the world.

Consumers today are already 'demanding and unreasonable' in their expectations, and this situation is one that is only set to continue at an increasing pace, eg regarding age being 'malleable'.

Our physical and mental well-being, of course, are also naturally intertwined with the well-being of the communities around us and the environmental condition of the planet. That each of these areas are being discussed on a holistic basis, as never before, is having profound consequences on individual, societal, business and political levels.

Meanwhile, and on a purely consumer basis, serious questions are therefore posed for those tasked with creating and delivering the results desired.

And that is why, when it comes to all the challenges and issues I've outlined in this chapter, disruptive and innovative thinking can provide a truly dynamic way forward.

CHAPTER SIX

Smart cities, the IoT and connected living

This chapter looks into a range of dynamic issues and trends affecting 'cities of today and tomorrow' and highlights some catalytic innovations impacting the people living, working and visiting them.

This is happening at a time when serious questions are being asked of those tasked with creating progressive answers to the problems facing citizens, businesses and governments. They seek insights for a world in which, according to the UN '55% of the world's population live in urban areas, a proportion expected to increase to 68% by 2050. Projections show that urbanization, combined with overall population growth, could add another 2.5 billion people to urban areas by 2050, with close to 90% of this increase being in Asia and Africa' (UN DESA, 2018).

Based on extensive research into the 'here and now' in addition to trend forecasting and scenario planning around cities, the approach I've chosen to take focuses on the 'chaotic realities' of urban life, alongside some extraordinarily innovative ways in which these realities are being addressed, regarding plans being developed and actions being taken.

The backdrop to any thinking in this area is formed by a clear realization that the city of the future will be faced with some fundamentally different challenges to those of the past. Innovations such as the impact of smart communication technology on citizen interaction are having, and will increasingly have in an IoT situation, such astonishing consequences for urbanites, that the old certainties of what city life actually means have to be reappraised.

There are many issues that any writer can take when looking into this subject, but I decided to concentrate on what I believe are the key overarching 'tension points' where innovation plays a vital role: population density and living spaces, action relating to social inequality and diversity, and environmental issues including carbon emissions and developments in mobility. (I shall cover, but won't look deeply into, issues around the future of work, specific health products and developments around car design in this chapter; those subject areas are covered in depth, in separate chapters.)

To add another caveat, I have also decided to focus on 'leading-edge' cities and innovative ideas impacting those cities, as opposed to either trying to cover 'all' cities or giving the possible inference that I assume all cities are the same. Which is, of course, far from the case.

During my research it was interesting to note how much uniformity there was around 'meta-narrative' issues, including chronic issues of water/energy/food, social issues such as inequality, and the ever-expanding role of disruptive tech: AI, biogas, renewables, robotics, etc. But what I found really fascinating were progressive viewpoints, widely shared, that when it comes to evaluating how and when actions taken are successful, the essential metric of success that we'll use will be 'citizen well-being'.

And a vital means of reaching that goal will be for all involved – the physical city and the inhabitants of it – to act together in collaboration. This is also why CX (customer experience) is an ever greater governmental obsession regarding the delivery of public services.

If this ethos is genuinely put into action as much as it is spoken of, then the reality of 'future city living' will be a positive one for all concerned.

The point I make about 'plans vs action' is deliberate, as cities are not programmable machines that strictly obey the urban planners' commands, but instead they portray the complexity and myriad outcomes that result from human, not robotic, populations, and therefore reflect their dreams, desires and demands, or the 'cultural layers and social interactions' of those inhabitants.

This means that, in cities as in the rest of life, the reality often turns out to be very different from the plan. And cities are adapting and changing all the time, of course. So while the London of today may essentially have the same layout (bar the occasional *Blade Runner*-esque building) as that seen by my great-great-grandparents, what goes on in that city from the perspective of homes, schools and workplaces, etc, has changed on a stratospheric level. Hence the 'form and function' buzzwords used by architects, when thinking about urban innovation, mean very different things in the modern age to those used by their forebears.

One of the key issues relates to population density and the impacts of this density on living spaces, the health of urban populations, and the opportunities available to them. Technological innovation is, to put it mildly, playing a vast role here, when hyper-connectivity, the speed of urbanization, and 'informed and demanding' citizens are driving innovation forward at an ever-increasing pace.

Acknowledging that many of those 'informed and demanding' citizens are also rejecting the city for either alternative life/work options, cost implications or as a result of innovative-mobility is also a subject area that's covered. I do so as it's naturally a highly significant element of the story, and indeed is alluded to by the World Economic Forum as 'given what we know of cities and digitization, this could herald deurbanization'. This all comes at a time when 150 metropolitan areas are already home to every seventh person, and cities are accountable for 80 per cent of global GDP. Noting this issue of collaboration, the World Economic Forum also reports that 'the next decades will see cities forging powerful international partnerships and taking the lead in solving global problems' (Puutio, 2018).

Noting the really big picture, that of answering the infrastructure challenges portrayed by the expected growth of world cities, in her book *Future Cities: All that Matters* sustainable development and regeneration expert Camilla Ween states that 'Never has the need to deliver so much been so urgent, and with dwindling resources. Tackling the challenges is complicated by pressure to develop sustainable solutions. Some advocate geo-engineering as the answer to tackling climate change. Others believe in behaviour adaptation.' But she believes the future is bright 'if you believe in our ability to innovate' (Ween, 2014).

So, for those interested in, or tasked with, innovation on behalf of the current and future urban citizen, in this chapter I've aimed to illuminate examples of dynamic concepts and action intended have a beneficial impact on their quality of life.

Meanwhile, the existing impact of the 'Four Great Modern Inventions' were highlighted by the *China Daily* newspaper as being 'high-speed railways, mobile phone-based electronic payments, e-commerce or online shopping, and bicycle-sharing apps' (Wei, Shijia and Nan, 2019).

Finally in this chapter, I also provide some 'headlight vision' on where we may be heading, but have aimed not to be diverted into forecasting something overly reminiscent of a cross between a J G Ballard novel, *Minority Report*, or Fritz Lang's *Metropolis*.

Urban tensions

Let's start by defining a city. A definitive quote came from the famous sociologist and expert on urban architecture Lewis Mumford over 80 years ago 'the essential physical means of its existence are the fixed site, durable shelter, permanent facilities for assembly, interchange, and storage; the essential social means are social division of labour, which serves not merely economic life but cultural process. The city in its complete sense, then, is a geographical plexus, an economic organization, an institutional process, a theatre of social action, and an aesthetic symbol of collective unity. The city fosters art and is art; the city creates the theatre and is the theatre' (Brown University, 2007).

Cities were first established about 10,000 years ago, but over the last few hundred of those, they followed a fairly similar plan, ie power and money at the nucleus, with everything flowing from that structure. But when it comes to forecasting what the future city looks like, the urban planning expert Professor Michael Batty reminds us that 'all this is changing. There's now a massive disconnect between what the city looks like and what goes on "under the hood". We can't assume that form follows function. The old certainties are disappearing. Cities are getting more complex at a faster rate and we're not able to keep up' (Batty, 2018).

Indeed, according to the internationally renowned architect Carlo Ratti 'the evolution of cities go through moments of radical change, turning points defining their very essence. We are in such a moment.' He also takes a fascinating approach (at MIT's Senseable City Lab) to thinking about the future. Not by stating a definitive viewpoint, but by employing 'futurecraft' scenario planning exercises, where he considers the future and then shares the resulting ideas for public consideration and feedback. Describing this, he says that 'futurecraft is not about fixing the present (an overwhelming task) or predicting the future (a disappointingly futile activity) but influencing it positively' (Ratti and Claudel, 2016). Ratti also references the 'speculative design' work done at the Royal College of Art in London.

Many of the problems that Lewis Mumford (mentioned earlier) saw around him, remain with us today of course. So how do those tasked with developing the successful 'cities of today and tomorrow' know what issues are important to urban citizens, businesses and organizations, and what actions are needed to satisfy their demands?

The development and delivery of innovation for these interlinked groups has to start with an empathetic ear to the challenges faced by citizens, businesses and services alike, and an observant eye for the cultural signals that act as early warning devices for existing tensions and emerging problems, alongside an appreciation of the societal make-up and economic realities that provide a clear picture of city life.

As a researcher, when it comes to understanding the 'tension points' that affect people on an everyday basis, there's nothing like sitting down with someone in their own living space and discussing the day-to-day realities of their lives, along with those of their families, friends and, when relevant, work colleagues.

This type of activity is being carried out around the world by a mass of people throughout the research industry on behalf of their clients, and the types of things that researchers like me hear consistently are the 'standard' issues that readers of this book will easily recognize. These range from the 'here and now' issues of cost of living, noisy neighbours, street crime and problems around commuting, to ones around a desire for faster and better communication, access to high-quality retailers, more engaging workspaces and the enablement of a healthier lifestyle. These issues, and many more, are what the research industry term 'signals' and those signals can be picked up across a wide range of sources.

And we need to get this right. Some of the most obvious signals, from a negative social and cultural perspective, seem to be omnipresent, such as intense traffic density, high levels of pollution and visible portrayals of societal division, where the 'social contract' between government and governed is under serious pressure.

The fundamental issue of affordability is, of course, one of the core 'tension points' impacting urban citizens.

That problem, familiar to us all and a contentious one over aeons of city-living, is a societal issue that has plagued city residents for centuries. In a report that Marx would recognize only too well, the *Financial Times* reported from demonstrations in Berlin, where rents have doubled in a decade, pointing the finger of accusation at Deutsche Wohnen, the biggest landlord in the city, which has over 100,000 apartments under its ownership. It also notes the blame attached to villainous developers and predatory investors.

The result being an ethos of bullying corporates against the bullied individual and what that article termed 'dramatic social cleaning. The cause being the growing financialization of the private rented sector'. In that article titled 'Residents' revenge' the *FT* quoted the think tank analyst Anthony Beach from the Centre for Cities as saying 'city planners and politicians should take this "anti-development politics" seriously'. He notes the reason why investors shouldn't dismiss the concerns and demands of citizens, and young people in particular, who are unable to enter the housing market due to inflated prices, is politicians can simply respond by 'taking away their social licence to operate' (Hammond, 2019).

And of course, some of the answers to these issues have turned out to bring their own problems with them, from a 'law of unintended consequences' angle. A current example, and a hot topic in 'urban innovation' circles, has seen the hipster movement, so lauded by urban mayors around the world as the answer to their dreams in terms of revitalizing run-down neighbourhoods, now being blamed for gentrification and 'cultural cleansing'.

Catalytic innovation provides a dynamic way forward, perhaps the only way forward regarding these areas, delivering the type of transformational impact that's demanded; whether it be of the citizen, community, business, service or political perspective. A key issue here, or possibly the key issue, is inclusion. All those hipsters may be, or certainly tell themselves that they are, bringing much-needed creativity and progressive change to these places, but often the existing community living and working in those areas have found themselves swiftly excluded from the newly 'repositioned' localities, viewed in a voyeuristic manner by 'underclass tourists' or simply priced out of their own homes.

Empathy and inclusion

Meanwhile, the reaction to unwanted urban developments has seen action taken in cities around the world and has involved high-profile action against some of the biggest corporates on the planet, with Amazon being a prime example. Their attempts to build a secondary headquarters campus named 'HQ2' in the Queens area of New York met with high-profile demonstrations, which involved the 'people's champion' and first-term congress-woman Alexandria Ocasio-Cortez, who CBS reported as saying 'it's incredible. I mean, it shows that everyday Americans still have the power to organize and fight for their communities and they can have more say in this country than the richest man in the world' (CBS News, 2019).

And the issue of 'localism' and indeed community activism, as shown by the local community reactions in New York, are key ones that were noted at the SXSW Festival, where an event focused on 'Reimagining power in a populist age' was intro-duced by the statement that 'power is shifting in the world: downward from national governments and states to cities and metropolitan communities... Where rising populism on the right and the left exploits the grievances of those left behind in the global economy, new localism has developed as a mechanism to address them head on' (SXSW, 2018).

A key answer then, and a way forward from the perspective of bringing 'wanted and welcome' innovation from the perspec-tive of urban development, is surely that investors must be seen as having an empathetic approach. This has to evidence a desire to add to the physical areas and the cultures and communities concerned via an inclusive approach, ie by creating jobs, vs a more brutal wish to simply grab more property or land, and price out both the existing residents and those that aspire to gain an initial and affordable foothold in the area.

Innovation is vital, and creativity is vital, but if we don't make urban areas inclusive, with opportunity and well-being at the core of the 'city offer', then we're really missing the point.

I saw a problem illustrating the issues of inclusion (or rather the lack of it) in the starkest terms when I was on a speaking tour of the US for my first book *The Post-Truth Business* during the mid-term elections, and noted how an explosion of highly paid jobs in Silicon Valley had meant that house prices and apartment rents in San Francisco had increased dramatically even in the two years since I'd last been in that city. This issue, that sees salaries paid to financial services or technology executives dwarfing those of people working in, for instance, public service roles, has dramatically increased levels of social inequality from the perspective of access to affordable housing.

Innovation and creativity are vital, but if we don't make urban areas inclusive, with opportunity and well-being at the core of the 'city offer', we're really missing the point.

The rise and rise of secondary cities

Hence a research report from PwC and ULI titled 'Emerging Trends in Real Estate 2019' noting the movement away, in the US for instance, from cities such as San Francisco, Miami, Washington, Los Angeles, Chicago and New York, in favour of 'secondary cities' including Atlanta, Dallas, Austin, Sacramento and Nashville.

The trade that people make when shifting to a secondary city is 'the trade from stress in return for a higher quality of life. Well-paid science, technology, engineering and math (STEM) jobs are flowing to some secondary locales, especially with start-ups that want to locate in affordable cities. One of the driving factors is a good relationship between universities and businesses' (Lerner, 2018).

And the demographics of this situation are fascinating, with numerous secondary cities noting their new population growth is coming as much via Millennials as from Baby Boomers, the generation who are now moving into retirement and hence are searching for a reduced cost of living.

That's something that links closely to the books *Rise of the Creative Class* and *Flight of the Creative Class* by the Harvard academic Richard Florida. His books have been enormously successful, and I enjoyed talking with him about his thesis when we both gave keynote speeches at a conference in Melbourne, Australia.

Florida's basic thesis is that, as Edward Glaeser put it, 'the economy is transforming. The urban lesson is cities that want to succeed must aim at attracting the creative types who are the future. They need to think about providing lifestyle, or consumption, advantages to their residents. Urban success comes from being an attractive "consumer city" for high skill people' (Glaeser, nd).

This all may sound positive, progressive and dare I say it, makes Richard Florida a genuine 'influencer and revolutionary'. However, several years after the book was published, and when 'no town was without its own arts and creativity strategy, innovation hub or pop-up poetry corner' the *Guardian* newspaper interviewed the man they termed the 'rockstar of regeneration, prophet of place-making, king of the downtown revival, patron saint of avocado toast', but who'd witnessed his 'blueprint for urban creativity' ('embrace the "Three T's" of technology, talent and tolerance') 'blamed for gentrification and inequality' (Wainwright, 2017).

Which takes us straight back to the point I made earlier about hipsters...

Indeed, Florida later wrote another excellent book *The New Urban Crisis* where his theory was that this crisis was about inequality and house prices. A review from CityLab noted 'winner-takes-all urbanism has deepened inequality, segregation and poverty. Urban revitalization, say the pessimists, is driven by rapacious capitalists who profit by rebuilding some neighbourhoods and running others down. Gentrification (which has escalated into 'plutocratization') and inequality are direct outgrowths of the recolonization of the city by the affluent and advantaged' (CityLab, 2017).

In the book, Richard Florida highlights five dimensions of the new urban crisis as being 'a growing economic gap between a small number of superstar cities. A crisis of success vexing these same cities. Growing inequality and segregation within virtually every city and metro area. The deepening suburban crisis regarding poverty, insecurity, and crime. Finally, the crisis of urbanization in the developing world' (Florida, 2017).

So how to put things right? The *Ohio City Observer* quoted his 'seven pillar solution' as being '1) Make clustering work for us and not against us. 2) Invest in the infrastructure for density and growth. 3) Build more affordable rental housing. 4) Turn low-wage service jobs into middle-class work. 5) Tackle poverty by investing in people and places. 6) Lead a global effort to build prosperous cities. 7) Empower cities and communities' (Grossman, 2017).

Security

But of course, before anything else can be considered, and taking into account the famous Maslow 'hierarchy of deficiency and growth needs' theory, something that's been getting an increasing amount of attention is innovation in the area of security, particularly with reference to policing. A country at the fore-front of utilizing technology with policing is China, where for instance, police are wearing augmented reality (AR) smart glasses, to catch criminals. As reported by the *South China Morning Post* 'when wearing the AR glasses, police can access real-time facial, ID card and vehicle plate information linked to the national database' (Yang, 2019).

The glasses were created by the AR company Xloong, which was set-up by a Huawei engineer called Shi Xiaogang, and which has also developed a smart helmet used by the Chinese army. Meanwhile, the company's AR glasses also include sports goggles that project digital maps for runners and cyclists, along with industrial glasses that can scan machines and share real-time video feeds with engineers, and they also make headsets used by those in sectors such as healthcare, tourism and real-estate. According to the *Nikkei Asian Review*, 'while surveillance tech-nology would generally trigger privacy concerns in western countries, Shi shrugged off such worries in China, as central government's emphasis on anti-terrorism and social stability, are important drivers for companies to thrive' (Chan, 2018).

The financial aspect of all of this high-tech innovation is phenomenal. As reported by the *Wall Street Journal*, 'China spends more on domestic security than it does on external defence. The country also has "176 million surveillance cameras operating in public and private areas"' (Chin and Lin, 2017).

Depending on your view of the current and potential uses of this type of technology including real-time data tracking, and its use in urban environments, the emerging and future city is one where residents may be reassured of ever greater safety, or an Orwellian one where 'surveillance capitalism' rules. Many argue that the destruction of privacy is increasingly becoming a disas-trous result of the involvement of corporates when they provide services to governmental institutions, often seeing the initially welcomed outputs of technological innovation being leveraged for unintended, and sinister, outcomes. I wrote about trust, privacy and surveillance capitalism in my previous book, referring to a 'reputational capital' issue for businesses being that of the immoral, unethical (and often illegal) leverage of our personal data.

Indeed, since I first wrote about surveillance capitalism, the UN passed its latest 'Right to Privacy in the Digital Age' resolution. This recognizes that 'more and more personal data is being collected, processed, and shared' and expresses concern about the sale or multiple resale of personal data, which often happens without the individual's free, explicit and informed consent. Since the first resolution, the UN has evolved its approach from being a mainly political response to mass surveillance to looking into more complex issues around data collection and the role of the private sector (United Nations, 2018).

An urgent problem today for many of those working in the marketing, media and tech industries, is that they're complicit in this key problem of our age. Brands have a fundamental role to play here when, for instance, the data that'll be transmitted about us by over 20 billion connected devices in the world by 2020 will be staggering. And, unless the safeguarding of that data is up to the task, an equally incredible, and tragic thing will be the final disappearance of our privacy.

With regard to citizens having their online lives 'watched, packaged and sold', an interesting and highly innovative player relating to this has been shown by the launch of 'Winston'. This service enables users to reclaim their privacy by anonymizing and encrypting their online data, and the company claim to offer the most advanced privacy solution in the world.

Indeed, Tim Cook, the CEO of Apple, called for a wide-ranging federal privacy law to protect individuals and society alike from the 'data-industrial complex' at a conference in Brussels titled 'Debating Ethics: Dignity and Respect in Data Driven Life'. It was just the latest clarion call to highlight this most vital of issues. He spoke of the four essential principles of privacy at the heart of privacy data and privacy rights as being:

'Companies should challenge themselves to de-identify customer data or not collect it in the first place. Users should always know what data is being collected from them and why. Companies should recognize that data belongs to users. Everyone has a right to the security of their data' (Cook, 2018).

Another key issue keeping urban mayors awake at night is the one of cyber-warfare and city resilience. At the suitably appropriate City of London University, an Institute for Cyber Security was established in 2019 to bring together world-class cybersecurity education, research and innovation. Their vision is to be a trusted hub for protecting the megacities from cyberattacks, and to tackle global challenges in privacy, trust and security. This will be done by implementing a comprehensive plan and by promoting an environment in which the general public, private industry and government can work together to address those cybersecurity issues specific to the megacity's digital infrastructures.

By their very nature, smart cities are unfortunately the perfect target for cyberattacks and those tasked with protecting urban populations, whether they be from next-generation start-ups, state cybersecurity teams, local councils or national government, need to reduce these cyber threats. This was demonstrated on a state level via the 'Web War One' cyber attack on Estonia.

Meanwhile, a real concern for the security services and governmental departments alike, is that increasingly connected infrastructures offer, from a criminal hacker or enemy perspective, potentially vital 'smart environment' weak spots. This is where 'cascade theory' comes into play, in terms of 'digital contagion' being truly dystopian.

It was interesting to note that, according to research from Gartner 'the number of IoT devices in existence already outnumbered the amount of people in the world...' (Knoll, 2018).

The reason I mention that, in terms of contagion theory, is directly linked to a point highlighted by *Wired* magazine: 'one benefit of cities being "smart" is their ability to use communications technology to integrate key industries and infrastructure in a way that generates growth and benefits everyone. However, this makes them attractive targets for large-scale malicious cyberattacks, as a single attack would have widespread implications' (Unal, 2019).

From both a business and city point of view, organizations are no longer asking, states the World Economic Forum 'if they can be attacked, but how they will be attacked, forcing increased organizational knowledge of cyberattacks and the adopting of new Tools, Tactics and Processes (TTPs) for defending their networks'. The WEF also highlight the persistency of often undetected 'Advanced Persistent Threats (APTs)' as being 'the most lethal vectors of attack today', known for their 'sophistication, bespoke software back doors and zero-day vulnerabilities' (Erez, 2018).

As for innovative ways of stopping them and maintaining or regaining 'network security', the WEF note organizations looking at automated attack simulation, and hiring security and defence personnel to conduct simulated attacks on their applications, data and networks, in order to judge the strength of their resilience.

Environmentalism: 'tell the truth, and act like it's real'

While on the subject of 'important issues' let's highlight one that, quite literally, could not be more urgent. It's a life or death issue, for all of us, and which is witnessing the emergence of 'permanent protest' in the current, and no doubt, future city.

Leading the way on this, is the 'Extinction Rebellion' (XR) socio-political movement, which uses non-violent resistance to protest against climate breakdown, biodiversity loss, and the risk of human extinction and ecological collapse.

The *Financial Times* highlighted the seriousness of the movement in the starkest terms, in an article about the incredible viral success of their bold action about climate change 'even as climatologists reveal the reality of the crisis, the environmental movement has shied away from graphic depictions of the dystopian future of harvest failure, starvation and anarchy that abrupt breakdown implies. The word "extinction" in the movement's title isn't just referring to plants, insects and animals. It means us' (Green, 2019).

As co-founder of this 'international apolitical network using non-violent direct action to persuade governments to act on the Climate and Ecological Emergency' Gail Bradbrook said at a speech to supporters who'd gathered in Bristol to plan for protest action 'if your government isn't protecting you and the future of your kids, you have a duty to rebel and a right to rebel. When you say "no" and do an act of civil disobedience, it changes your psychology, some of us need to turn the herd' (McLaughlin, 2019).

The network has three demands: 'Tell the Truth' (Government must tell the truth by declaring a climate and ecological emergence, working with other institutions to communicate the urgency for change); 'Act Now' (Government must act now to halt biodiversity loss and reduce greenhouse gas emissions to net zero by 2045); and 'Beyond Politics' (Government must create and be led by the decisions of a Citizens Assembly on climate and ecological justice) (Extinction Rebellion, 2019).

But an issue now being debated by policymakers around the world is how to police the peaceful but highly disruptive demonstrations that the 'XR' movement undertake. XR's point, of course, is that they need to force the fundamental change on a governmental level that their raison d'être entails; the implications of which affect all of society, and indeed all of our futures. For example, and in the context of this chapter, those living in Jakarta are unfortunately the inhabitants of the first megacity that looks set to be lost to climate change.

Megacities and smart cities

Talk of all things futuristic, and the idea of the megacity is never far away, despite the reality of this idea actually having been with us for years.

The world's first megacity was New York, but today it's been long surpassed by Tokyo, New Delhi, Shanghai, Mexico City and São Paulo. Following up are Cairo, Mumbai, Beijing and Dhaka. By 2030 it is anticipated that there'll be 43 megacities, ie those with more than 10 million inhabitants. The UN also report that while one in eight people live in 33 megacities worldwide, close to half of the world's urban dwellers reside in much smaller settlements with fewer than 500,000 inhabitants (UN DESA, 2018).

Is there one overarching reason that smart cities, and megacities in particular, are so dynamic? According to the World Economic Forum, it can indeed be summed up in one word: 'scale'. Their report references some famous research conducted by Luis Bettencourt who noted how 'cities take human and physical capital and scale them superlinearly. Defying traditional arithmetic, cities produce more units of output for each unit of input they use when it comes to issues such as GDP, wages, patents, and R&D expenditures. Cities also waste fewer resources per capita on infrastructure and services' (Bettencourt, 2007).

Meanwhile, according to the *Guardian* 'New research suggests that if Nigeria's population continues to grow and people move to cities at the same rate as now, Lagos could become the world's largest metropolis, home to 100 million people. By 2100, it is projected to stretch hundreds of miles, with enormous environmental effects' (Vidal, 2018).

From a positive business perspective, megacities are hugely important as they generate incredible opportunities for start-ups and legacy businesses alike, while generating vast amounts of income, and draw in wealth on a national and international basis, in a globalized environment. It's an environment in which disruption plays a pivotal role, from both a positive and negative viewpoint. And increasingly, those cities are 'smart'.

Smart cities are defined by IDC Government Insights as 'a city-state, county, city, town, or other non-national government organization that embraces technology and data-driven urban transformation to meet social, financial, and sustainability goals.' The role of technology here is central, but only to meet specific programmatic or city outcomes that are directly tied to meeting the needs of citizens' (IDC Government Insights, nd).

This, of course, comes at a time when the Fourth Industrial Revolution, which I write about in more detail in the chapter devoted to the future of work, is witnessing the combination of four truly dynamic and catalytic issues: augmented reality, cloud computing, automation and ambient intelligence.

An additional and existential issue is that of time itself, from the perspective of what this 'man made concept' actually means in an 'always-on environment'; how our shared understandings and interpretations of it may change in the future, and indeed the negative implications of this disruption for our physical and mental health.

I remember this being discussed by the visionary thinker Leon Kreitzman, in a speech about his book *The 24 Hour Society* when he spoke about the fact that the modern city never sleeps, and is thus always awake, and therefore 'a 24-hour society is the way forward' (Kreitzman, 1999).

A review by the Oxford University Press noted that 'this is more than simply all-night shopping and transit. It is about restructuring the temporal order. It leads to a different construction of daily activities, freeing people from the restraints imposed by rigid adherence to clock time. But there's a price to pay in terms of our natural circadian rhythms' (Kreitzman, 2016).

And as for which cities are genuinely leading by example and showing us a way forward, it seems that those including Tokyo, London, San Francisco, Singapore, Toronto, Paris and Sydney are prime examples of 'how to do it'.

These are some of the winning cities in the annual 'Innovation Cities Index' as noted by *Business Insider*, referencing research into urban innovation that's been taking place for over a decade. As they say 'cities are assessed based on 31 segments of their industries and economy, and 162 indicators of innovation.

Analysts compile each city's index score, out of 60, from three key factors: cultural assets, human infrastructure, and networked markets'. So why did Tokyo win? 'They showed clear direction by embracing smart technology changes to lead innovation' (Leskin, 2019).

Mobility 'connected, shared and self-driving'

Meanwhile, in gridlocked cities around the planet, the car (or 'mobility') industry is adapting to a brave new world that is completely reappraising the basic questions of 'what is a car, what is its function, and who is it for?' While engine manufacturers are, quite rightly, obsessing over electrically powered vehicles, the overarching innovative responses for future smart vehicles tend to focus around the sharing economy, AI-empowered autonomy and always-on, hyper-connectivity.

I spoke about this point with Carsten Beck, Direct of Futures Research at the Copenhagen Institute for Futures Studies, and Timothy Shoup from their explorative futures 'Smart City Team', whose catchy term for this is 'on-demand multi-modal transport options'. One of the major implications they spoke of was of autonomous vehicles giving people the ability to move further out from city centres, due to a key enabler being the far higher speed of safe commuting that these vehicles will offer. And, of course, the fact that these vehicles will be shared has benefits from both an environmental point of view and also an economic one from the perspective of the 'sharing economy'. Another 'sharing' example is the Gacha self-driving bus in Finland.

This issue is already witnessing a staggering rise in the amount of ride-sharing, app-based services, from America's Uber to China's Didi Chuxing. The numbers around this are equally staggering, with nearly 50 per cent of the global market taking place in China, and the research agency Statista GmbH forecasting an annual turnover of just under US $60 billion by 2020.

At the latest Auto Shanghai event, Zhao Guoqing, VP of the Chinese Great Wall Motor Co said 'we cannot just develop electric cars. They will have to be smart, interconnected and of course shared.' In an article reporting this, the *Taipei Times* noted that 'Didi unveiled an alliance of Chinese and foreign manufacturers including Renault, Toyota and Volkswagen, dedicated to exploring ways forward. Alibaba and Tencent joined hands with several manufacturers to develop a future platform for on-demand transport.' VW China stated that 'we can no longer be a conventional manufacturer, we must offer mobility solutions, connectivity' (Girault, 2019).

Meanwhile, the Science X site, reporting on the Shanghai Show, noted that 'Chinese authorities are encouraging service firms to build their own fleets, partly to spur the industry and push forward the futuristic transport concept. Some manufacturers are moving into ride-hailing, with Germany's BMW offering a high-end service in the southwestern Chinese city of Chengdu, and Volkswagen and Mercedes-Benz doing so in Shanghai'.

And with regard to those new and innovative technologies, China has given car manufacturers an ultimatum aimed at growing its electric vehicles market, and as reported by Bloomberg News 'from global giant Toyota and General Motors to domestic players BYD and BAIC Motor, all have to meet minimum requirements for producing new-energy vehicles, or NEVs (plug-in hybrids, pure-battery electrics, and fuel-cell autos). A complex government equation requires that a sizable portion of their production or imports must be green' (Bloomberg, 2018). A basic but vital issue here is the need for massive investment in EV charging points.

Summary

So, taking in just these few 'pressing issues' that I've selected to highlight, clarifies that the role of the innovator is key to our future success, in all the meanings of that word.

What happens to cities over the next few decades will determine our environment and the standard of living of what the UN calculate as a global population of over 11 billion people.

None of us can know with certainty or forecast precisely how the 'city of tomorrow' will develop. But you only have to look at those United Nations statistics to realize that just one issue, regarding the implications of a young and cumulatively urban populace, defines a deeply serious question that cannot be avoided, when 'humanity is expected to develop into an almost exclusively urban species with 80–90% of people living in cities. Whether those cities develop into sprawling, chaotic slums, with unbreathable air, uncontrolled emissions and impoverished populations starved of food and water, or become truly sustainable depends on how they respond' (UN DESA, 2017).

> What happens to cities over the next few decades will determine our environment and the standard of living of a global population of over 11 billion people.

Answering the definitive question, of how the 'future city' can develop into a sustainable, inclusive and welcoming location, as opposed to collapsing into a *Blade Runner*-esque dystopia with polluted air and a polarized society, is one where 'collaborative innovation' appears to me to provide the only coherent way forward.

The principal criteria that need to be considered were highlighted by *National Geographic*'s international challenge of designing the city of the future as being ecology, water, energy, waste, food, mobility, culture, liveability, infrastructure and economy. This is set against the statistic that by 2050 nearly 70 per cent of the world's population is projected to live in urban areas (Treat, 2019).

Thus, the need for the 'innovators of tomorrow' to step heroically into the breach and create answers to the seemingly nightmarish problems that confront us, is 'flashing red' urgent. If, throughout history, cities have been defined by people, then in the future it is ideas that will define their development. This means smart and sustainable concepts being retrofitted into existing locations that will need to flex around changing social dynamics, cultural needs, business functionality and political necessity.

That's quite a list of demands.

And while all of that activity is being implemented, we must not lose sight of the vital need for individual privacy in an IoT environment.

This being one where the brand ecosystems increasingly being offered by the likes of Apple, Google, Alibaba *et al*, means wearable tech interacting with our home-based smart speakers and smartphones, alongside a myriad number of products, services, structures and environments in smart urban locations. The project that Google-owned Sidewalk Labs have been conducting in Toronto is a prime example.

Elsewhere, ever more ubiquitous facial and gait recognition, eye-tracking and crowd-analysis systems are being added to by emotional-recognition technology.

What happens to and with the data collected, regarding the monitoring of, and interactions with the future citizen, is an issue of astonishingly profound importance.

So, it's time for the 'influential and revolutionary' thinkers of tomorrow to stand up and meet the challenge!

CHAPTER SEVEN

Intelligent and sustainable

A new era of tourism and mobility

In this chapter, I cover a range of trends and innovative activity taking place across the tourism and mobility sectors. I've joined these areas together from the perspective of similar cultural and social trends linking to product development and service provision, from both legacy brands and start-up operations.

The two issues that I find most compelling in these sectors (in all their guises) are environmentalism, from the perspective of 'conscious consumption' where sustainability (in all its forms) is a central concern, alongside ongoing digitization, particularly relating to artificial intelligence and the connectivity delivered by IoT smart technology.

To focus on the first of those issues, regarding the absolutely central issue of the environment – the 'golden thread' that runs through this book – I believe we'll see increasingly informed consumers making decisions that have environmentalism as a core concern. This consideration will also link to issues such as the human rights implications of local citizens in the destinations they'll be visiting, hence volunteering and purpose-based activity being very much part of the 'future traveller' ethos.

This notion of considering the well-being of local communities alongside one's own personal benefits, gives immediate rise to the notion of 'bad tourism' that is plaguing societies around the world. This is most visibly seen in 'bucket-list destinations' that are inundated with tourists to such an extent that the places in question are becoming unable to cope.

The environmental impact is immense, and as you'll read, I believe this genuinely existential issue is swiftly moving to become the central one that impacts this sector, as it does in so many others that are discussed in other chapters.

So, let's look at this in more detail, after which I'll move on to how innovation is being portrayed in other areas including – as the saying goes – planes, trains and automobiles.

Homogenized travel and 'social media similarity'

If you've been to any popular tourist destination recently, you'll probably have noticed one thing above all else.

There are too many tourists.

Simply put, everyone's going to the same locations, which are mentioned in the same 'Top Ten Places You Have to See' travel guides. Hence taking the same photos to put on their social media pages, which results in the content of so many social media platforms looking incredibly similar.

An example of this was given by Hongyadong in the Chinese city of Chongqing, which found itself suddenly transformed into one of the biggest attractions in the country due to being featured on Douyin, the social-media image-sharing platform. As pointed out by *The Economist* 'for some in China, the aim of travel is to create 15-second videos, where it's not about where you've been, but about where you're seen to have been' (*The Economist*, 2019c).

Now while there's nothing wrong with the frankly inconsequential subject of 'social media similarity' there certainly is a problem when one considers the real-life implications.

Popular tourist locations are inundated with outsiders who are essentially destroying what they've come to see. Complaints range from the personally irritating ('I can't get a table in my favourite restaurant because it's full of tourists'), to the effect on the community ('none of the local young people can find anywhere to live, as all the available apartments are now used for Airbnb'), to the effect on the local environment ('the traffic fumes from tourist coaches are out of control'), to the global environment ('does anyone seriously consider the overall carbon emissions of the travel industry and of the brands operating within it?').

The immediate problem in answering the above is that few of us tend to remotely consider that we, as individuals, might be part of the problem.

One answer to over-tourism (for those who still wish to travel) is the emerging move that sees people taking an 'anti bucket-list' approach, where they reject the idea of having an identical holiday experience to everyone else. Instead, they go 'off-grid' and, by meeting with local people who show travellers the authentic version of their neighbourhoods, this has the added benefit of giving something back to the genuine local economy.

To enable this to happen, we can follow our travel influencer of choice, who in putting up a list of suggestions online, means that in effect, a curated 'Spotify of travel' approach is being portrayed.

This approach also helps countries (such as those impacted by outdated images), which may benefit from some real-life advice from those who know them to be great places to visit. Hence, while places such as Lebanon and Colombia suffered from poor national brand images a decade or so ago, informed travellers now know them to be wonderful destinations.

In addition, from the perspective of destination-trends, an issue I also find absolutely fascinating is the impact of e-tourism. But as this also links to the gaming sector, from the perspective of spectacular disruption, it is within the 'entertainment' chapter that I'll address a trend that sees VR and AR as key elements of the immersive experiences desired by demanding consumers, be they travellers or otherwise.

Cruise ships and Tesla ships

Meanwhile, and for an example of a business that has both created and is now facing crisis-level problems, look no further than the cruise-ship sector, where innovation is framed as a 'do or die' option.

The numbers of passengers on these vessels reached nearly 30 million people back in 2018, with well over 100 new vessels currently being built, each of them able to take over 5,000 passengers.

When it comes to hugely negative media reports about the industry, and there are many to choose from, one of the most contentious areas being highlighted is that of cruises to the Arctic.

Trips to this environmentally critical region are partly a reaction to these ships being pushed away from locations like Venice (due to that city being both besieged by tourists and physically damaged by ever vaster cruise liners) and to passengers having requested more, dare I say it 'innovative' destinations, with places like Northern Canada and Greenland being favoured ones. The Arctic is thus a prime example of a last true frontier for those seeking an 'authentic experience'.

As for what this search for authentic experiences actually means, and in this case it surely means 'melting ice caps', this was noticed by the German explorer Arved Fuchs (the first person to reach both poles on foot) who said when interviewed:

'The number of cruise ships is rising, and they've no place in the Arctic. I've witnessed small Inuit villages inundated by day trippers. They do nothing more than gawp and give little back to the people who live there. The visitors are the only ones to profit, not the residents' (Connolly, 2019).

Two years ago, it was estimated that, in the waters around Europe alone, there were more than 60 kilotonnes of sulphur dioxide emissions from cruise liners, the effects of which are clearly related to cancer in humans, and acid rain.

Responses from the sector include the move towards using LNG ('low-pollutant liquefied natural gas'), which is claimed to reduce carbon emissions by approximately 25 per cent, while cutting nitrogen oxide by up to 85 per cent and the use of virtually 100 per cent less 'particulates' than fuels currently in use across the sector.

Regarding the attempts to reduce environmental damage, ships are also doing away with sea-bed damaging anchors, and increasing use of wind and solar power options. Meanwhile, the likes of MSC Cruises state that their journeys are now carbon-neutral.

A really innovative idea in river-shipping (from the perspective of cargo) is provided by so-called 'Tesla ships', these being battery-powered zero-emission barges, which operate from Antwerp, Rotterdam and Amsterdam, and are able to carry nearly 300 shipping containers each. A key environmental and social benefit of these 'future boats', and they were the first in the world to use carbon-neutral batteries, is their ability to take away nearly 25,000 lorries from the Dutch roads.

Elsewhere, there's a shipping industry-wide commitment to reduce the rate of carbon emissions by 40 per cent by 2030, as announced by the Cruise Liners International Association back in 2018. Indeed, the International Maritime Organization have a stated aim of the shipping industry as a whole being carbon free by the end of the century. To which many might answer 'that is a long time to wait'.

On board, the levels of innovation from the perspective of passenger experience, take the trends seen across the wider retail, sports and entertainment worlds to extreme levels, and specific trends in these areas are discussed further in those chapters.

As a final note on cruises, and from a hospitality viewpoint, the cruise-ship world is clearly one where 'less is definitely not more' and a 'Las Vegas meets Nemo' approach clearly seems to be in the minds of many architects and designers when it comes to this sector. Meanwhile, from a customer service technology point of view regarding personalization, artificial intelligence is increasingly being employed, including areas such as facial recognition, alongside app-based and wearable technology.

Hotels: cultural hubs, smart rooms and community integration

Moving on from the 'floating hotel' world of cruise ships to the land-based ones, a crucial foundation of their innovation activity is ongoing digital transformation. This, for example, means the benefits of AI will involve 'smart hotels' utilizing guest data to enable more efficient and personalized service automation; while facial recognition will improve security and enable simplified payments.

These innovations are absolutely intrinsic to helping the hotel sector be even better at what it has always prided itself on: guest service.

Voice search optimization is improving radically, as is speech recognition software (including easy-to-use language translation). Travellers are making increasing use of technology, ranging from guest-app-enabled pre-set customized room settings to informational chat bots, virtual assistants, and both virtual and augmented reality.

These innovations are absolutely intrinsic to helping the hotel sector to be even better at what it has always prided itself on: guest service. In this instance, smart technology can provide hotels with predictive information about guest desires, meaning that service can be more accurately, quickly and efficiently delivered on a truly personalized basis.

Looking to trends in the sector, according to Euromonitor, the hotel sector is witnessing 'the continuing rise of peer-to-peer sites, the ongoing increase in Chinese tourists, and Millennial travellers taking centre stage. Global hotel chains are aiming to benefit from technological innovations and the introduction of lifestyle, soft and boutique brands' (Euromonitor, 2019).

This viewpoint is reinforced at hospitality-sector travel conferences, where the talk is all about both qualitative and quantitative research insights telling of consumer trends. These include a desire for 'home from home' escapes (a particular favourite for those with young children, albeit a 'dream' home that is better ordered than the chaotic reality of their own), while other trends include a desire for more credible travel breaks where 'meeting the locals' is an option fulfilling the desire for 'cultural connectivity'.

The issues of locality and connectivity are also being evidenced by the way in which hotel lobbies have become such dynamic places. By day, the increased use of them as second-home or third-space locations for independent working zones is evidenced around the world; while their evening use as cultural hubs presenting local and visiting creative talent enables hotels to retain a sense of vitality and strengthen their community links.

Elsewhere, hotels are focusing ever more on providing 'surprise and delight' moments and treats for their guests, a very specific way in which they can deliver 'just for you' personalized service and demonstrate both generosity and creative thinking. In addition, the imaginative use of high- and low-brow design, and curated music and art are seeing hotels, and particularly independent ones, differentiate themselves by catering for discerning customers in a way that larger groups find incredibly difficult to match.

An absolutely key issue for hotels, or 'machines to make money' as they're known in the industry, is retail.

And when it comes to money, a fast-growing area is that of eco-luxury. According to The Future Laboratory 'as wealthy consumers become increasingly uneasy about their affluence and the privilege it provides, they are funnelling their spending into eco-conscious experiences, while not giving up their desire for quality'. An example of this that they give is the luxury-conscious 'QO Amsterdam' where the lessons to be learnt from this sustainable hotel is that 'guests staying in a beautiful place can feel less guilty if they're doing their bit for the environment' (Friend, 2019).

Business not as usual, and sci-fi futures

Meanwhile, it's also important to highlight the business travel market, which, according to the Global Business Travel Association, is worth $1.4 trillion.

The Times notes that the business travel sector 'while being fragmented and complex, remains largely undisrupted'. The possibilities for innovation are immense, particularly from start-ups operating at the edges of the sector, which like so many others is a difficult one to disrupt from the centre. The reasons for this are quite simple, 'Amazon, Google, Apple, Baidu and Alibaba have raised customer experience and expectations to an entirely new level. At the same time, most executives experience the exact opposite when they travel; business travel is a disjointed, stressful, disconnected mess' (Easen, 2019).

International travel also has the ever-present reality of geopolitics at its core, in an ongoing era that sees the basic security of international travellers as an always-on issue, alongside a basic reality that more people want to travel by air, more often.

The day-to-day impact for most of us is endless queues and irritating delays at transport hubs and border locations. The area of traveller security is also one that sees 'consumer-friendly' innovation as having a very strong level of consumer desire behind it, with increasing use of issues such as biometrics and (currently controversy-laden, regarding personal privacy) face-tracking technology being employed to smooth our way through transport hubs.

However, the issue of privacy is, as mentioned, of huge concern to civil rights campaigners and 'informed citizens' alike. The AI-enabled privacy debate, in this specific context, can be seen as 'personal security good' vs 'privacy infringement bad' and it's a complex one, growing ever more important in a societal context, that I discussed in my previous book *The Post-Truth Business*.

To return to the point about airports in particular, and a basic but very real irritant for stressed-out travellers, regarding lost or delayed cases, is being dealt with by the advent of luggage-tracking apps. This 'friction point' is finally, and at long last, being addressed for those keen to find where in the baggage hall – or perhaps where on the planet – their luggage is currently located.

Airlines, airships, air taxis and spacecraft

Regarding innovation in the airline sector, it's clear that fully electric and hybrid electric planes are absolutely key 'disruptive innovation' areas, albeit initially for local and regional travel.

Where is this all heading? Leading-edge reports tell us that 'better avionics point inexorably in one direction: pilotless aircraft. Airlines, passengers and regulators may take a while to come to terms with this so it is likely that pilots will sit in cockpits long after they're needed for anything other than the reassurance of the paying public' (Carr, 2019).

Meanwhile, advances in sustainable and alternative fuel developments are ongoing, with cryogenic hydrogen fuel cell systems being an area sponsored by NASA. According to the *Financial Times* 'electrical propulsion will be the biggest revolution for the industry since the 1940s (when it comes) and the industry is in the throes of the greatest revolution since the development of the jet engine. The catalyst for all this innovation is a global drive to clean up aviation pollution' (Pfeifer, 2019).

As part of that global clean-up drive, escalating media attention is reflecting the 'flight-shame' (or 'flygskam') movement, which portrays flying as a social taboo, and as a result, an increasing amount of people are opting for methods of travel that are less carbon-intensive.

Companies such as Rolls-Royce and Boeing reflect the obsessive environmental focus that's being taken by the airline industry in Asia, the US and Europe, due to governmental and societal pressure regarding carbon dioxide and nitrogen oxide emissions, along with complaints over aircraft noise pollution.

With regard to the point I make elsewhere in this book about innovators also 'looking backwards' for inspiration, then a fascinating example of this is airships. These may be finally about to see their moment, particularly where low-carbon and low-impact travel to inaccessible places, such as the North Pole or deserts, is concerned. Indeed, according to a luxury travel report 'the debate about sustainable aviation has completely the wrong focus. We're talking about the fuel, when we should be talking about the aircraft' (Mance, 2019).

Elsewhere, and when it comes to the look and feel of future aircraft, the traditional exterior and interior elements of aircraft design is changing along with the propulsion technology, with much talk in the industry of 'Flying V' shaped planes.

In addition, and just as seen in the chapters on retail, entertainment and future homes, the issue of immersive and dynamic consumer experiences being delivered via virtual reality are prime examples of digital innovation being delivered as part of the in-travel environment.

And while sci-fi fans have awaited flying cars for aeons, the much-heralded 'air taxi' or 'UAM' (urban air mobility) vehicle is a significant element of that focus via major legacy brands including Airbus, alongside start-ups such as the German company Lilium. With its VTOL (vertical take-off and landing) taxi jets, these effectively seek to take the military Osprey and reinterpret it in a smaller format.

To give an idea of just how much this market could be worth, Morgan Stanley estimate this as being a $1.5 trillion sector by 2040. However, the 'elephant in the room' in this area is the very real one of regulation with regard to issues such as noise (although air taxis will be quieter than helicopters, due to being electrically powered), and both physical and cybersecurity.

Whenever taxis are mentioned, Uber are naturally a part of the conversation, and their plans include offering flying taxi services in Melbourne, Los Angeles and Dallas by 2023. As part of this service, relevant take-off, landing and recharging places will have to be provided, hence serious funds being required for the building of so-called 'vertiports'.

Looking further upwards, and space is, to coin a famous phrase, 'the final frontier'. Innovation with relation to that most futurist area of travel is one with correspondingly high levels of media attention.

Over the next 50 years, according to *The Economist* 'falling costs, new technologies, Chinese and Indian ambitions, and a new generation of entrepreneurs promise a bold era of space development. It will almost certainly involve tourism for the rich and better communication for all: in the long run it might involve mineral exploitation and even mass transportation' (*The Economist*, 2019a).

This is evidenced by companies such as SpaceX, which was founded nearly 20 years ago to revolutionize space technology with the ultimate goal of sending people to live on other planets. It was, they point out, the first private company to return a spacecraft from low Earth orbit and was the first commercial spacecraft to deliver cargo to and from the International Space Station, alongside the launching of commercial satellites. They're currently working on the next generation of fully reusable launch vehicles, capable of carrying humans to Mars.

Back on Earth, and before we look at another sector impacted by phenomenal change for a wide variety of reasons (and where the leading one is its impact on the planet) I want to outline what I believe is a superb example of 'how to do tourism perfectly'.

CASE HISTORY

So, for an example of what beliefs about and trends in innovative ecotourism actually look like in a best-case scenario, I interviewed the highly experienced eco-pathfinder and revolutionary thinker Andy Middleton.

He's the 'Chief Exploration Officer' who co-founded the renowned outdoors company TYF Adventure in Wales.

As he told me when he was on dry land for a change, 'I often ask myself what might travel look like in a world that took its future seriously and where humanity's carbon budget and reliance on biodiversity was intelligently respected'.

So how, I asked him, would this change? 'One thing is for certain – it would be very, very different to today – there would be no carbon-powered cruise ships, far fewer flight-based holidays, and a reshaped relationship between the impact that our leisure choices have on others and the future'.

An easy accusation to make of any 'good company' is just how good are they, and how authentic is their ethical stance. It's an irritating line of enquiry, but I felt I had to ask Andy about this. He explained that 'when plotting our journey at TYF over the last 25 years, it was very clear that we had to earn the right to "walk the talk", so set out to learn what it meant to change for good. On that journey we became the first carbon neutral company in Wales, the first "1 per cent for the Planet" business, the first certified B Corporation, and so on. As pioneers we have to know what it was like to thrive on new ground, so we can help others do the same and importantly, prove that good practice is good business sense'.

As for the impact of all this, from a purely numbers perspective, he told me how this 'adventure business' had been set up 'with the aim of changing lives by teaching people how to play and we've had the privilege of giving over 200,000 customers memorable experiences in wild places. Our work is to help our customers fall in love with nature so deeply that it changes the way they live every day, and that has meant rethinking pretty much every element of the way that we engage them in a journey of adventurous, transformational change'.

When it comes to the overarching issue of the environment and climate change, Andy is adamant that 'the existing systems of quality management in most government and business relating to people or nature were rarely, if ever, designed to create conditions where life could thrive. Instead, they were designed, with good intent, to create "less bad" outcomes than whatever was already happening. When environmental and other legislators come to their senses, they'll start asking "how can we ensure that our rivers, air and oceans are clean to a standard that could have been written by nature itself?" When those questions start getting asked every day, we will know that the revolution has started'.

If that isn't an inspiring story, I'd like to know one that is!

Moving on from that 'adventure' aspect of the overall sector, let's move on and look to innovation in mobility, from the perspective of the car...

The life, death and rebirth of the automobile

About a decade ago, I was sat in a bar in Oslo having just given a trend speech at a Scandinavian advertising convention, when I got chatting to the editor of a soon to be launched magazine, called *Carl's Cars*. The magazine was the first to blend car culture with music, fashion, film and design, and the editor kindly suggested that I write a piece for it.

What I wrote was a piece not overly positive from his point of view, as I based it around that classic title *The Life of the Automobile*, written by Ilya Ehrenburg and originally published back in 1929.

Described as a 'masterpiece' by the press, this prescient book looked at the American consumer dream, and predicted the rise and fall of society's love affair with the car, despite the automobile being portrayed by advertising agencies, even back in the 1920s, as the ultimate 'freedom machine'.

The perspective that Ehrenburg provided would later have echoes in the writings of the author J G Ballard. In his book, Ehrenburg spoke of a Parisian visiting a cinema and being transfixed by a car racing across the screen. He longed to race down a highway in cinematic style and purchased a gleaming machine in order to do just that. But on his first drive, speeding as fast as it would go, he realized to his horror that the car had a mind of its own, and was out of his control. Indeed, it had gone insane. It went faster and faster, until the 'mad robotic vehicle' killed him in a crash.

That viewpoint seems rather prescient, nearly a hundred years later, doesn't it?

As it stands, nearly a century on, we've reached what many observers describe as a 'peak car' situation. An illustration of just one reason why this may be the case is delivered by numerous attitudinal surveys among Millennials, the results of which indicate that only a small percentage of that generation see cars as having the ability to genuinely reflect them as individuals.

Indeed, only about 30 per cent of them view cars as 'representing freedom', which is what had so motivated Ehrenburg's driver back in the previous century.

Their attitudes seem to combine both 'practical relevance and emotional motivation' and if you want to know why the car industry is facing such a crisis in consumer terms, when the next generation of cars buyers feels like that, then things are deeply serious for the industry.

This anti car-ownership attitude is a trend that began to be picked up years ago via consumer research and at events like the international Youth Marketing Summits, and it shows absolutely no sign of abating.

The lack of aspiration that cars represent to many young people, compared to that felt by the Boomers generation, has sent shockwaves through the car industry.

A key issue that has radically impacted those young people's viewpoint of cars, is, just as I described earlier and indeed throughout this book, the environmental impact of this sector.

It's estimated that over a quarter of greenhouse gases are, in the US for instance, released by the mobility sector, albeit in all its numerous forms.

It's estimated that over a quarter of greenhouse gases are, in the US, released by the mobility sector, in all its numerous forms.

Highlighting the emissions issues in the most dramatic way that one might think possible, was the infamous 'VW emissions cheating scandal'. For anyone not aware of the episode, the story goes like this: prosecutors charged the former CEO of VW of knowing the company had fitted illegal software (that understated their emissions) to over 10 million diesel cars and in doing so committed a breach of trust. According to *The Times* 'the scandal shattered faith in diesel technology and cost VW $19bn' (Crossland, 2019).

Which goes about as far as it's possible to go in undermining a 'consumer–brand relationship built on trust' that all brands desire. But the societal effects were far more important than the impact on VW's immediate finances and overall brand image.

And they weren't the only ones implicated, with VW's Audi and Porsche divisions, and BMW and Daimler, also potentially facing enormous fines. Another court case involving lorry makers MAN, Volvo/Renault, Daimler, Iveco and DAF ended with billions of euros in penalties being levied.

The *Guardian* reported that the EU's competition commission had charged the 'circle of five' carmakers with 'colluding to limit, delay or avoid the introduction of clean emissions technology. This includes SCR systems used to reduce toxic nitrogen dioxide emissions and "Otto" particle filters which are associated with tens of thousands of deaths a year' (Neslen, 2019).

Meanwhile, most cars actually spend the vast majority of their time static, which when added together as a physical mass, takes up a huge portion of our urban landscapes.

The response from an automobile industry under fire is to innovate, and innovate at a rate that they've never done before.

So, campaigners point out that the current societal issues relating to both static and mobile cars cannot continue into the future, as they are clearly unsustainable, in every sense of the word.

But, as well as being a hugely important environmental issue impacting each of us, it's also one where party politics is dragged into the equation. The reasons are obvious, given that a typical 'leftist' response may focus around the jobs impact on trade union members, while those on the right may point towards a 'statist and collectivist' approach, which takes power and choice away from individual citizens.

The response from an automobile industry under fire is to innovate, and innovate at a rate that they've never done before.

Autonomous vehicles, connected cars, electrification and shared mobility

An example is given by the Boston Consulting Group, who claim, for example, that 'the adoption of electric vehicles will reach a tipping point around 2025, alongside the commercial deployment of fully self-driving cars'. A decade later, BCG estimate that 'nearly 25% of new cars sold globally will be fully autonomous'.

Added to those changes, which are technologically based, will be a societal one (growing urbanization) and an ongoing behavioural one (the sharing economy), which shall both combine to increase the desire for shared mobility. Indeed, BCG forecast that by 2035, nearly 20 per cent of passenger trips will be those in 'electric vehicles shared on demand, and primarily autonomous' (Andersen *et al*, 2018).

So, facing huge demands for change, and in a bid to stay 'relevant and trustworthy' and indeed on the right side of history (in environmental terms) there are few sectors that are witnessing such extraordinary and game-changing innovation. Of course, elements of these trends are already visible around us today, if you're reading this book in a range of 'leading cities' in Asia, Europe and the US.

It's just one of the reasons we're seeing an increasing move from car companies around the planet to adapt their business approach to being one of selling 'soft services' rather than 'hard products'. It also sees a much-cited industry phrase coming to fruition, that 'currently the phone is a car accessory, but soon the car is going to be a phone accessory'.

And like any accessory, the cars of tomorrow will be lighter, safer and smaller than the ones around us today. Safety will also be enormously improved, quite simply by taking away the most dangerous element of the driving experience: human drivers.

Meanwhile, and showing that 'nothing happens in isolation', the move to autonomy also reflects how public transport is adapting to trends in urban planning. Described at trend conferences as 'multi-modality' this sees partnerships combining private and public ownership of vehicles (of all descriptions), providing an answer to consumer and societal demands for flexibility, personalization and on-demand access.

These resource-efficient provisions therefore mimic similar approaches taken to consumer desires across a range of other sectors, as described elsewhere in this book.

Vehicle passengers will benefit from the unseen utilization of always-on IoT data sharing links with smart roads; with those smart roads being deemed as such due to their traffic management and variable speed limiting technology. The cars will also transmit vehicle-condition information to central monitors for diagnostic feedback and management. Put like that, what's not to like?

Meanwhile, the technological benefits of HMI (human–machine interfaces) are also seeing huge innovative activity in 'conversational technology', alongside radical developments in the area of in-car entertainment, which is set to bring astounding changes. These 'fully connected ecosystems' by the way, are something about which advertisers are getting into something of a shark-like feeding-frenzy.

And while future passengers will no doubt be trying to avoid all that advertising, our digitally connected vehicles will seamlessly liaise with each other to improve car vs car and car vs pedestrian safety. What this also means is that vehicles will be able to travel in packs and travel (safely) at higher speeds.

One of the implications, as discussed in the chapter on 'smart cities' is that with commuting speeds going up, commuting distances may also increase, meaning the ability to commute further away may lead to the regeneration of 'fading areas'.

However, before we get too carried away, I must point out that attitudes and behaviour change fairly radically on both an Asian/European and urban/rural basis for a mixture of aspirational and practical criteria.

Meanwhile, what about the 'ultimate innovator' in recent years? It doesn't seem long since the arrival of Tesla caused shockwaves through the sector. Since then, ongoing international governmental decarbonization legislation has led to car companies rushing to develop lithium ion battery powered vehicles.

In innovation terms, this means that the opportunities for both start-ups and 'flexible and agile' legacy brands are staggering. But they're also complex and staggeringly costly.

The lithium ion battery was actually invented back in the 1970s at Oxford University, but Sony made the technology a commercial venture.

Tesla, of course, was the first brand to demonstrate that consumers would pay a high price for electric cars. But, as mentioned above, the sector finally woke up to its success, and the competitive set now includes Jaguar, BMW, Nissan, Kia, Chevrolet, Polestar, Aston Martin, Porsche and Hyundai.

Indeed, Elon Musk suddenly finds himself 'facing an all-out assault from Detroit and Frankfurt. The billionaire's at risk of being crowded out. One plan's for Tesla to become a $500bn giant via a plan to turn its global fleet into autonomous robo-taxis. When it comes to innovation, being first doesn't mean you win. Just ask Palm' (Fortson, 2019). But they're fighting back, ie with their Cybertruck, a new roadster, and by opening a 'giga-factory' in Germany.

And the competition isn't just coming from Detroit and Frankfurt. China has about 50 per cent of the world's electric cars, and according to an interview with the president of Aiways in *China Daily* 'we know how to produce a product that is high-quality, highly innovative, and our standards are high enough to meet the requirements of the European market' (McNeice, 2019).

From a specific Asian angle, exciting innovations in the electric car market are being shown by sector brands including the Arcfox 'ECF' and Aiways 'U5 Ion' SUVs in China. Meanwhile, the vehicle that I'm most looking forward to, as an ex-campervan owner, is a fully electric VW campervan. That is an innovation that surely has to happen sooner, rather than later.

I should also point to another area of transport innovation, and one that's already having an impact both on consumer behaviour and the infrastructure of cities. As noted by the *Financial Times* 'for sceptics of robo-taxis, something innovative that they can see right now are thousands of electric bikes and e-scooters appearing on streets across Europe, North America, Asia and Latin America' (Bradshaw, 2019).

But, unlike the safety benefits offered by autonomous cars, there are serious problems posed by e-scooters. As reported by *The Economist*, 'the day after e-scooters began to legally glide down

Sweden's streets, a rider was killed. The incident highlighted the riskiness of the vehicles which are notoriously unsafe and increasingly unwelcome'. For their fans however, PLEVs offer a dynamic alternative to public transport. A major obstacle is insurance, which the magazine describes as a 'complicated liability economy'. Indeed, and as they also point out 'it could get more complicated soon, with electric powered skateboards' (*The Economist*, 2019b). As the saying has it, what could possibly go wrong?

Sharing, insurance and the 'Third Transportation Revolution'

So, an absolutely key area amidst all this product innovation, is the crucial service of insurance. A typical context being the 'liability' question posed by those using a mixed range of vehicles for different purposes in different environments on a 'flexi-use' basis. The liability question is an essential one, much discussed in the media, of 'who's to blame when autonomous vehicles have accidents?'

These types of questions are dragging an insurance sector fast-forward into the future; a difficult task for many of the legacy businesses that have grown used to 'life as usual'. But it's providing fertile ground for a range of more agile players in the sector, alongside vibrant new start-ups who see a whole new world of possibilities opening up.

A crucial area of service innovation already sees consumers benefiting from ongoing developments seen in areas such as autonomous ride-sharing, being provided by an increasing range of brands such as Uber, Lyft, Grab, Go-Jek, Bolt, Ola, Kapten and Didi Chuxing. And alongside these will be ever more efficient delivery services care of those such as DoorDash and Postmates.

For the global management consultants McKinsey, the disruptions that the automotive industry faces can be summed up by the acronym 'ACES', ie autonomous vehicles, connected cars, electrification and shared mobility. As McKinsey point out 'by 2030 we'll see developments as profound as when the automobile was invented. We also see governments and cities playing a more active role in shaping the ACES ecosystem, by providing the crucial roadside infrastructure needed, and through investments in capturing and sharing data at scale' (Heineke *et al*, 2019).

That point about shared mobility is taken up, not surprisingly one might say, by Lyft, the US company that offers car rides, scooters and bicycle sharing. Its CEO claimed a couple of years ago that by 2025, 'private ownership will all but end in U.S. cities and autonomous vehicles will account for the majority of Lyft rides within five years. These two issues will see mobility become the ultimate subscription service'. He also addressed the staggering statistic that the average vehicle 'is used only 4% of the time' and went on to point out that as a result of the combination of these changes, the physical environment and structure of cities will be altered 'more than we've experienced in our lifetimes' (Zimmer, 2016).

A couple of years on from Zimmer's forecast, and where are we? An example was shown in the UK back in 2019, when the number of public places where electric cars could be charged overtook the number of petrol stations, and the government proposed that all new houses be built with charging points included.

It's clear that legacy automobile giants are repositioning and reinventing themselves for tomorrow's consumer to be 'lifestyle brands'. This is something seen across an array of sectors, where brands aim to elevate themselves above the 'mere' functional reality of their sector. Part of doing this will see them focus not on selling a specific vehicle type to a specific target consumer, but instead on offering the entire target market the option of a multitude of usage locations, via a product portfolio that may include every element of transport seen today in the private or public elements.

In practical terms this may see your 'premium or standard mobility package' including, or not including, and to rename a favourite film, 'flying taxis, hydrogen-powered trains and autonomous automobiles'.

The potential benefits of such a world are far reaching. These will impact an array of subject areas, which according to *NY Magazine*, will include 'urbanism (the end of parking!), work–life balance (the end of dead time!), the environment (the end of smog!), public health (the end of drunken driving!), manufacturing (the end of the car workforce as we know it!)'. But the magazine also highlighted the profound altered society that will result from a society affected by the changes brought by driverless cars, on an economic, political, cultural and experiential basis. The key issue they point to is a huge one in human behavioural terms: 'the American republic of drivers is poised to become a nation of passengers' (Moor, 2016).

As for that other 'ultimate innovator' in the sector (Uber) according to the *Financial Times*, its targets include the 'automobile industry, restaurants, haulage companies: all will have their worlds disrupted by an app that lets users summon a ride, order food or arrange road freight. They started out in ride-hailing but the scale of their ambitions are almost unbounded. They're bent on changing the sector as a whole' (Waters and Bond, 2019).

Trains and 'the fifth mode of transport'

A couple of years ago, while in the Middle East, I was on a speaker panel with the head of what was, at that time, the world's leading Hyperloop start-up, who enthused in suitably excited tones that this 'fifth mode of transport' technology really was the ultimate next big thing. The 'fifth mode' of course, relates to the one following on from boats, trains, cars and planes.

Just as we've seen in the areas devoted to the automobile, hotel and aircraft sectors, the issues of autonomy and green technology affect the rail industry in the same manner, with the desire for speed, safety and energy efficiency being key.

A pivotal foundation to this is the increasing global move towards urbanization, which I discuss in detail in the chapter relating to future cities. A key implication of this is the question around the ability of innovations in car technology to enable mobility solutions for all the new rail passengers that will also result.

Railways are uniquely set up to deal with this issue, from the obvious perspective of their ability to carry large numbers of people efficiently and swiftly.

Innovative responses include developments in Maglev (magnetic levitation), driverless and hydrogen-powered trains, with the first example being in Foshan, in China. The innovative results impact passengers on high-speed, metro and light-rail journeys as much as 'smart freight' and the implications for each are profound.

However, for mainstream passengers, the innovations in the rail industry are centred around increased efficiency and experience-based developments that have their foundations in the wider worlds of retail and hospitality. These are incredibly exciting, due to stations being increasingly viewed as combining best-case elements of both sectors. For examples, look no further than stations in Dubai and Tokyo, the Transbay Center in San Francisco or the Fulton Center in New York.

But the key issue in this context is that the 'green' rail sector is clearly being reappraised and revitalized.

Summary

In this chapter, what I believe all of the various trends and innovations I've highlighted indicate, is a future focused around key issues such as environmental protection, improved consumer choice and smart technology. Each being provided in product and service terms by relentlessly dynamic and 'positive' innovation.

Of all the current actions being taken by the overall travel sector, the ones I've found most compelling include the rise of ecotourism combining with a desire for authentic experiences.

The implications of the first may simply mean 'local or regional travel only'. The cost benefits of these also enable more frequent micro-trips, and these mini-breaks are clearly becoming a more popular option, with last-minute opportunities promoted to consumers well used to being offered on-demand options from brands in many other sectors.

Implications of the second point towards curated travel to places removed from the 'obvious Instagram' locations, visited by seemingly everyone else on the planet, which provide the traveller with a greater sense of absorbing 'genuine' local culture.

Elsewhere, a rejection of 'same old' offers from travel brands, is seeing innovative activity in skills-learning breaks, knowledge-based sabbaticals and mindfulness retreats from an ever more complex and anxiety-provoking world.

And, of course, the utilization of 'beneficial innovations' such as facial recognition, means that technology is enabling greater personalization alongside increased efficiency.

Meanwhile, and from the perspective of the mobility providers and transport manufacturers (in the range of formats I've discussed) I believe it's a combination of environmentally friendly products and technologically enabling services that shine a way forward. These will see a wide range of transport and mobility sectors being included, crucially doing so from the perspective of a combined 'people, planet, profit' ethos.

This, surely, is the future for business in general, and in the context of this chapter for innovation in particular, regarding a compassionate and 'brand positive' approach.

The transformation of entertainment by technology, experiences and personalization

In this chapter, I look into the entertainment industry, and a range of specific areas within it, including the games, sports, television, radio, film, video, music and festival sectors.

These areas all have two subjects in common from the perspective of innovation: the impact of ongoing developments in technology and a demand for ever greater levels of consumer experience.

In describing the implications of these, I cover a wide range of product offerings and service approaches, including those such as virtual reality, immersive entertainment, the impact of AR/VR, storytelling, community and individuality, streamed on-demand content, the home vs public space, massive growth in 'mobile-first' consumption, 'ear and voice' as the next big things, the rise of micropayments, short-form video apps, and the rollout of 5G in an IoT-connected world.

Most of the trends impacting the industry can be seen as having positive implications for the consumer. But when viewed through a negative lens, the issue of data privacy is one that, as seen in so many other areas covered in this book, poses significant ethical and legal questions for the overall entertainment industry, and particular areas within it.

While the range of areas covered in this chapter have natural overlap, they also need to be viewed separately. To avoid any risk of confusion, I've therefore discussed each area on an individual basis.

Among the most significant issues and trends covered in those separate areas are:

- **Gaming** – which is being impacted by a new generation of consoles and streaming tech. But, alongside the cloud-based 'gaming wars' between Google, Amazon, Sony and Microsoft, plus the growth of eSports, the issue of brand ethics is paramount.
- **Sport** – where augmented and virtual reality will offer fans a full-immersion 'live the game' experience. Meanwhile, female teams are revitalizing the global audience base. Elsewhere, I note the growth of links to cause-based campaigning.
- **Television** – where, despite a disrupted environment care of Netflix and Amazon, etc, and the ongoing rise of mobile-based viewing, broadcast TV is alive and well, via its dominance in consumer engagement, which will be deepened via Smart TV.
- **Radio** – where, due to its almost unique abilities in trusted community engagement and specific audience appeal, and where streamed video and social media are strengthening audience links, the sector has been refreshed, yet again.
- **Film and video** – where online viewing has transformed content consumption. And while box office records are regularly smashed by major studio successes, I note 'the advance of the disruptors' plus the implications of AI/VR/AR technology.
- **Music** – where live music, the key area that I look into, is continuing to transform the future of the industry. This sees,

just as with the sports sector, consumer experiences becoming ever more immersive, sustainable, engaging and rewarding.

- **Festivals** – where the number and variety of these that cater to niche audiences, who desire events providing tailor-made content, has proliferated amazingly. Meanwhile, organizers have been hugely empowered by technological innovation.

However, before looking into an array of exciting product and service developments, as the world of entertainment (in all its many guises) is linked by the notions of 'play, relaxation and happiness', and as play is at the centre of those issues, I shall start by illuminating the often overlooked, yet crucial, issue of 'why we play' regarding both the purpose and value of a pastime that is so often wrongly dismissed as being 'pointless'.

Play is a space where the past and future have no meaning

Over 2,000 years ago, Aristotle came to the conclusion that, as a central goal, people seek happiness. What's fascinating is that this primary goal sees all others, including our personal health, appearance, financial worth or notions of power, as being valued only because we believe that a sense of happiness will result from having them.

Meanwhile, ask those around you when they actually feel happiest, and common factors will be that they do so when they're with someone they love, doing what they find fulfilling, or engaged in an escapist activity that therefore removes them from the stresses of 'everyday life'.

Ask them to sum up that feeling, and as endless international social studies have reported in their analysis of responses, people will talk of 'playing' rather than 'working'.

But as Brian Sutton-Smith, who wrote numerous books including *The Ambiguity of Play* noted 'The opposite of play isn't work. It's depression'. And this is crucial. Because the concept of 'play' has been undermined as being essentially incidental and of having no genuine worth in an 'always-on, 24/7 society' where we are encouraged, indeed expected, to be productive and on call at all times.

Compare that with how you, yes you, feel when you're playing – in every interpretation of that word. You may well agree with the philosopher Jean-Paul Sartre, who said 'play is what you do when you feel at your most free, your most voluntary' (Kaufman, 1989).

Indeed, according to the excellent book *The Play Ethic*, which looked into how the trivialization of play was the work ethic's most lasting, and most regrettable achievement, from 'the Enlightenment to Eminem, Socrates to Chaos theory, Kierkegaard to Karaoke, play is fundamental on a societal and individual level. The dominant work ethic of the last few centuries isn't equipped to deal with our modern world. Without it, arts, business, politics, education, and our personal lives are fundamentally impoverished' (Kane, 2004).

So, let's look at the extraordinary number of ways in which the entertainment industry is innovating in order to (from its point of view) enable our lives to be enriched by playful products and services, rather than being impoverished by the absence of this crucial 'route to happiness'.

Their promotional departments would no doubt sidestep the question of basic social interaction being the simplest (and totally free of charge) route to potential happiness, but in order to understand the branded version, let's begin with the games sector.

Gaming: next-generation consoles, cloud-based gaming wars, eSports and ethics

The gaming sector has seen, from any perspective, phenomenal growth over the last few years, and the future appears set to be transformed by further developments.

It still amazes me that the sector is perceived by many people to be somehow a 'lesser' form of entertainment, possibly due to a lowbrow image, as opposed to its competitors in the music and film industries.

Those people should perhaps note that the gaming sector, purely from a bottom-line perspective, is worth more than both those markets combined.

What will surely change is a realization, for instance, of the enormous potential for brands to leverage in-game marketing. Indeed, this is already happening, as exhibited at the Cannes Lions event, where a campaign from Wendy's that was run in the hugely successful Fortnite game (played by over 250 million people) won a prestigious Grand Prix award in the Social & Influencer category, just beating the 'Dream Crazy' campaign from Nike. Others will surely follow.

And the numbers involved are dizzying. According to the *New York Times* 'revenue from PC games alone in 2019 are expected to rise to over $35 billion' (Bailey, 2019).

It's worth illuminating just how successful some of the key games have been, as pointed out to me by Geoff Glendenning, who's one of the industry's most renowned marketers and the brains behind probably the most impactful games campaign of all time: the original Sony PlayStation launch.

As he said when I interviewed him 'just think about GTA 5, which came out in 2013. They've sold over 90 million copies so far, and by 2018 had accumulated $6 billion in revenue, which is the biggest entertainment IP in the history of all entertainment. Fortnite was released in 2017 and made $4 billion in a year.

Much of that was on micro-transactions to personalize your game character, make you look cooler and, crazy as it sounds, provide dance moves: 'the Floss' was a global phenomenon in the 'real' world. Micro-transactions in the main, for a small amount of money, allow players to personalize their characters, but there are some games companies that have been complicit in the negative impact of their in-game micro-transactions. Fifa, for instance, makes a huge amount of money from their Gold and Premium Gold player packs, which allow you to gamble on getting a top player for your team, which will give you an advantage if you are playing online.

In addition, the issue of buying 'loot boxes' (virtual treasure chests that players pay for in order to uncover their mystery contents) has caused a huge amount of ongoing controversy. They're another ploy by the industry to essentially encourage players to buy an advantage over other participants, critics say, which not only effectively enables them to 'pay to win' but also reduces the impact of non-paying players, thus taking away the overall skill of the game.

They are, in many people's eyes, a gateway to gambling, and the industry is now under severe pressure to act on the issue, with governmental action already taking place in Europe and China.

I asked Geoff about this, and as he went on to explain, 'games, like anything incredibly enjoyable, are addictive. I've been a gaming "addict" since I first played on the Spectrum in the 80s. There's already a backlash growing because kids are, more than ever before, getting addicted to gaming... indeed it's a lot like gambling. Fortnite is so good that playing the game releases dopamine, endorphins and adrenaline. But, like a sugar rush there will be a guaranteed crash when that wears off'.

With regard to the corporate social responsibility of the industry, Geoff also says that there's a lot that could and should be done. 'There have been so many lost opportunities for companies to do some good. The games sector can truly make a difference, such as building amenities, supporting youth clubs, which would give safe havens for vulnerable kids, perhaps even helping to fight the rise of knife crime. They really need to identify their brand purpose, do something useful and make a difference.'

Meanwhile, any keen observer of the games industry takes inspiration from key events such as E3 in Los Angeles, the Consumer Electronics Show in Las Vegas (where the innovations on show link across a plethora of sectors) and Gamescom in Cologne.

At the E3 event, the overall mood this year was strange, with a lot of media coverage of the event pointing to this being a 'calm before the storm' atmosphere, as the industry awaits 5G, an explosion of subscription services, streamed games and next-gen consoles. And there was still something to do, with TikTok's short-form video app downloaded over 750 million times in 2019 alone.

As for the next game changer, most bets appear to be on Google, who presented their invention of, not a thing, but a place, at the Games Developer Conference. Or to be more precise, a virtual space: Stadia. This 'cloud stadium' enables players to play (via free or 'Pro' versions) anywhere on the planet where they have access to the internet.

This means goodbye to all that hardware, in the form of consoles or gaming computers, in favour of players purely required to be able to utilize the Chrome browser, and via it, streamed gaming care of any relevant device, from TV to mobile.

And just as I've outlined in the marketing chapter, where brands are hoping that 'weaponized consumers' will do their marketing for them via consumer-generated content, we'll no doubt see large numbers of game-obsessives showing off their skills and educating (in the promotional sense) vaster numbers of followers and viewers in the process, by their streaming of relevant content on YouTube.

Of course, other giants like Amazon (via Prime and Twitch) along with Microsoft (with 'xCloud') are in this fight, while Sony PlayStation is already part of the scene here care of its PlayStation Now offering. And, as expected, China's Tencent are also innovating in the area. Meanwhile, the impact of VR on the gaming sector has been notable by its lack of mainstream impact. Many think this is due to the sheer amount of computer power required, the impractical spatial needs, the fully immersive nature of player solitude, the faintly ridiculous headsets and the still frankly appalling controller environment.

Elsewhere, the rise and rise of eSports is remarkable, and shows no signs of slowing down, with over a billion people already making up the global audience. One of the points regularly pointed to for 'brand exploitation' is that, to state the obvious, football fans continue in their fandom once real-life matches have finished. This being demonstrated by their 'ecosystem' of support including the games sector, and with it, games such as the ubiquitous Fifa games. Hence innovative action is being taken by leading clubs, such as Tottenham Hotspur, who are acknowledging their eSports fans by providing specific gaming zones for them in their amazing stadium.

And just to clarify the size of the worldwide eSports audience for any doubters out there, this is currently ten times that of the Super Bowl and over twice that of Formula One.

Sport: AR and VR full immersion experiences and cause-based campaigning

I'll move on to sports in the 'real world' although I'll immediately state that there is such a blur between the two, that the distinction is becoming meaningless, eg the interactive sports (and music) live-streaming offered by game platform Twitch.

Meanwhile, the amount of innovation is astonishing, as seen at trade shows such as Sportec in Tokyo, where this year, innovations found by combining existing games such as football and table tennis (in 'Teqball') or in the creation of entirely new games such as Hado (in which players wear an AR headset) were shown.

As reported about Hado, 'this game sees individuals or teams destroying opponents by firing imaginary energy bolts across a real-life court, while diving to avoid oncoming salvos.' When it comes to the historic limitations of creating new games, the report notes, these have disappeared with Hado, where 'the swing factor is sensor technology and the algorithms empowering it'.

What does this all indicate for the future of sport? That report finishes by stating 'Bring on the laser frisbees. Futuresport is out of the movies and in the trade fairs' (Lewis, 2019).

Back to today, and one of the most fascinating, and obviously totally welcome, situations is that of the rise in women's sport, which is finally being properly acknowledged by brands. It's widely acknowledged that, around the world, sports fans find women's sport to offer a more progressive and inspiring vision than the sometimes staid reality of 'just another' match involving men. As shown throughout this book, issues such as inclusivity and diversity resonate hugely, and women's sport delivers this along with, of course, equality. This is effectively seeing sport combine with true social innovation.

We're seeing more and more sportspeople standing up for what they believe in, and rightfully gaining plaudits as a result. From the influential and indeed revolutionary 'Black Power' salutes at the 1968 Olympics, to Muhammad Ali refusing to fight in the Vietnam War, to Colin Kaepernick 'taking the knee' when the US national anthem played before American football matches; this behaviour is, like virtually all modern protest, given a turbo-boost by social media.

We're seeing more and more sportspeople standing up for what they believe in, and rightfully gaining plaudits as a result.

The protestor is (in the context of this chapter) seeking to combine the powerful social engagement of sport with that of politics. Kaepernick has, by the way, been awarded by Amnesty International, while also being the face of a massive advertising campaign called 'Believe in Something' by Nike.

Where this links directly with innovation, ie in the context of this book, is that sports sponsorship has been one of the most innovative areas of marketing and is incredibly lucrative, worth over $16 billion a year back in 2016 in the US alone, according to WPP. Something interesting is that, to date, many of the major brands involved in that sponsorship have effectively given their tacit approval to this type of activism (which I applaud) on the basis of it upholding freedom of expression.

That activism doesn't have to be of the political type of course. A really powerful area where athletes have also recently brought real benefit to society in general has been in their cause-marketing activity around raising awareness of, and dispelling negative attitudes around, mental health, which for so long has been a taboo subject. And, of course, this issue is regrettably still of taboo status in many parts of the world.

What all of this innovative use of their influence links to is how sports stars are encouraged by teams and sporting agents alike to promote their team, themselves, and with it, fan engagement, by generating their own media content.

In doing so, they're therefore both building fanbases and leveraging brand opportunities via platforms such as Instagram and Twitter, adding to the 'connection spaces' where fans can interact with their stars and team links can be deepened.

Television: the rise of the disruptors, mobile-based viewing and Smart TV

Let's move on to television, where any serious discussion about the future media landscape needs to clearly state that, far from being dead, broadcast TV is alive and kicking.

Yes, the media sector is incredibly turbulent, but no, TV isn't over. But what will be over soon are some of the major stand-alone names in the industry, as more studio consolidation continues.

Key trends have seen the impact of a generational shift from Millennials to Boomers, as the latter take over from the former in terms of binge-watching TV series, thereby adopting the viewing habits of their kids, as illustrated by streaming multiple episodes of their favourite series, be this *Stranger Things, Killing*

Eve, or any of the seemingly endless choices delivered by Netflix and Amazon.

This is why we're seeing the, as yet, unsatiated generations of older viewers being increasingly catered for by commissioning editors, who have wised up to the fact that Millennial audiences, in particular, are reaching burnout in terms of the astonishing amount of content they've already consumed.

In order to try to remain as a 'go-to' choice for those Millennials, and indeed, Gen Z and Gen X audiences, the broadcast television networks (and their disruptive rivals) are relying on tried and trusted consumer-brand strategies of conducting deep consumer research, in order to offer content that is relevant, motivating and entertaining, in an environment where the so-called 'attention economy' means that consumers are inundated with a constant barrage of alternative options.

So it's been fascinating to observe television schedules featuring programmes where the themes have evidently reflected the real-life disorientation of viewers; this is summed up by the famous academic and social theorist Francis Fukuyama as 'fear, uncertainty and doubt'.

Hence, endless series where the dystopian atmosphere was one of confusion and mistrust, Middle Eastern terrorists and environmental emergencies. And to guarantee that you couldn't sleep at night, perhaps combining those narratives.

Meanwhile, and in terms of the next big thing, 5G will, industry reports insist, change everything, along with emerging or next-generation technological developments in AR, MR, 3D and AI. A key element will see the viewer being put ever more at the centre of an immersive, ultra-high-quality experience, and with machine-reading curation delivering 'just for us' programming suggestions. This is where spatial computing is turbo-charging social TV.

Where we appear to be heading in the immediate future, if industry events like MIPTV are correct, will be forthcoming series featuring moves towards interactive programmes, episodic anthologies, more globally produced content, innovative shows featuring major stars in 'one-offs', along with content that is either surreal, or based around real-life drama, as in the fascinating yet horrifying 'Chernobyl'.

When it come to the first of those – interactive programming – an incredibly innovative example is *Black Mirror*. With immersive entertainment being such a theme across the entertainment world, television viewers demand this as much as any other audience, and in that internationally applauded series, they were given this in the most innovative manner.

The show's writer, Charlie Brooker, was interviewed by *The Times* about a famous episode called 'Bandersnatch', which featured multiple endings chosen either by the viewer, or automatically by Netflix. It was described in that article as being 'intriguingly clever and breathtakingly original' (Aitkenhead, 2018).

He explained that the idea came about when he and the show's producer Annabel Jones were discussing ideas for the series, one of which was about interactivity, 'the central conceit of which was that of somebody writing an adventure game in the past that we're then controlling in the future.' As if he thought the result was 'the future of television' he responded 'it's a future. But I don't think it supplants traditional storytelling. I think they're going to coexist'. Whether this will indeed be seen as 'the future' or merely a gimmick, will be fascinating to observe over the next few years, in media trend terms.

Which, I think, brings us neatly back to traditional broadcast television, with many of the programming traditions that have proved enduringly popular still helping it retain its place at the centre of the media environment, albeit with iterative innovations (including cross-media activity) ensuring that it retains an appeal that is fresh.

And for examples of just how involving broadcast television can be, look no further than the staggering genius of *Fleabag*, the power of *Blue Planet*, the escapism of *Game of Thrones*, the compelling inanity of *Love Island* or the community engagement delivered by watching a major sporting event.

The core issue about television, surely, is what one might term its 'cultural capital' and ability to influence the public conversation like no other form of entertainment.

Finally, there's the small matter of advertising, which obviously funds the whole sector. Television still sets the benchmark for creating emotive content, the type that connects consumers to brands. Until that changes, television retains its crown.

Radio: community engagement, audience appeal and social media

As for a medium not often associated with innovation, but which has quite extraordinary levels of emotional appeal and audience connection, nothing quite comes close to radio.

This part of the entertainment spectrum has, just like television, been written off many times, and yet always bounces back with renewed vigour, due to having a seemingly inbuilt method of reinvention.

Why? Because radio is both intimate and adaptable. By that I mean that while our favourite DJ may appear to be talking directly to us, the same medium serves as a perfect element of background noise which we're happy to seemingly ignore.

From the perspective of advertising, marketers are obviously obsessed with the idea (in a media planning context) of selecting a media route that'll connect with the relevant target market, and via an engaging promotional message, provide a solid return on their advertising budget invested in the process.

This is where a medium that delivers a personal relationship with its audience pays dividends to advertisers. It is also trusted, with a vitally important angle being its lack of association with fake news and disinformation. And advertisers are utterly preoccupied with their promotional messages being delivered in a trusted media environment.

Read any independent media industry report on the competitive media landscape, and you'll soon note from the radio element of this, that radio delivers in a multitude of ways, including its aura of authenticity, the immediacy of our interaction with it, its stress-reducing qualities, the way that it lends itself to 'music discovery', that we empathize with presenters and guests, its 'mood adaptability' in terms of relevance to different times of day and days of the week, and the levels of seriousness or frivolity with which messages and content are delivered.

At the end of the day, we are social beings, and radio delivers community like no other medium.

Brands love identifying and then advertising to specific groups of people, or 'communities of interest' to put it in an agency context.

At the end of the day, we are social beings, and radio delivers community like no other medium. By building communities of interest around genres, places, events, specific issues and DJ fanbases, it delivers precisely the types of audience targeting and engagement that brands desire.

As for current and emerging innovations, there's increased interest, for instance, around 'TV-radio' from the perspective of short-form programming where broadcast clips are live-streamed from the studio.

While I look into the implications of smart technology on the home in the chapter devoted to that subject, and on the issue of hyper-targeting advertising including personalized messages in the chapter on marketing, I also need to reflect the growth of 'ear and voice' technology in this chapter, and this section seems the appropriate place to do so. Audio-linked marketing for instance, is being enthusiastically noted by advertisers as being enabled by streamed content via brands such as SoundCloud and Spotify.

When it comes to the area of 'ear-based innovation' the growth of so-called audiotainment (ranging from music streaming and curated playlists, to podcasts, audiobooks, short-form storytelling and developments in radio-service engagement, to product innovation via earbuds and headphones) will also see, for instance, the much-awaited market introduction of translation devices worn on a semi-permanent basis for travel and/or business purposes.

Meanwhile, the rise of voice-activated technology has seen ongoing innovation (now well into its 'MkII' phase) from major players such as Google, Amazon and Apple via their Home, Echo and HomePod products. While the positive benefits delivered by these smart speakers are clear, in terms of easier shopping, there are also negative issues that are equally clear, ie the levels of trust associated with voice-activated software clearly need to be strengthened.

Before I move on to discuss the intertwined film and video sectors, I'd like to illuminate an issue that has been bugging me for years... that being a widely repeated statistic that has become an ever-present part of media industry trend reports.

This is the seemingly ubiquitous saying that 'by 2020, voice would make up over 50 per cent of all searches'. This quote is always attributed to Comscore and was understood to refer to the 'the world in general' and yet the remark was actually made by the chief scientist (great title) of the Chinese search engine Baidu. Yet he was not only referring to both image and speech search, but was also, crucially, doing so purely in the context of China.

However, the quote was repeated by Mary Meeker in her much admired Internet Trends Report, and then endlessly requoted by everyone else. The moral of that story is to always check one's references!

Film and video: how online viewing has transformed content consumption

Having discussed television earlier where, as I mentioned, the manner in which people are accessing content online has had a hugely destabilizing effect on a film industry that is also facing endless internal merger issues, let's now look at what the film industry is doing to fight back, and with it the specific issue of physical cinemas being undermined by streamed content.

If film could have been viewed in the past as more highbrow and elitist than television or video, then what we're now witnessing is television being viewed as way ahead in terms of scope and ambition; and video being viewed in a different context from the past, ie streamed content in the form of VoD (video on demand) where the likes of Amazon and Netflix (joined by Disney, Facebook and Apple) have totally upended the market.

Add to that the social media platforms like Instagram who are transforming themselves to deliver more video-based content than ever, and the entertainment world in which the film industry saw itself as having a 'fixed place' is clearly evaporating; major action needs to take place for it to realign and reposition itself in a consumer entertainment choice perspective.

And, just as we saw with the games and television sectors, the financial statistics related to the film sector are mind-boggling. To take Netflix as just one example, they're currently estimated to be budgeting over 20 billion dollars on original content.

Deep soul searching is now taking place in the sector, regarding how the 'legacy' film studios can fight back against this tidal wave of competition and financial power.

It also comes at a time when the latest home devices are technically superior to the vast majority of cinema screens. On the plus side for cinemas, be they of the art house or multiplex variety, it can confidently be said that they offer unique scale and a sense of communal watching, with streaming live theatre being a really exciting avenue. Which is indeed positive for advertisers and media planners seeking a particular audience environment.

But when it comes to the specific world of innovation, this is increasingly being seen as having to deliver on two distinct routes: a deeper level of audience experience and the utilization of next-generation technology. These are absolutely vital, if they're to avoid being utterly out-gunned by the streaming services and the allure of in-home or mobile viewing, as opposed to the 'inconvenience' required of urban cinema attendance.

When it comes to next-generation technology, and while a lot of the media-sector reports around this have focused around ongoing developments in virtual and augmented reality, which deliver more immersive and thus escapist viewer experiences, it's another AI-enabled technology that I find even more fascinating from the perspective of 'viewer involvement' actually being facilitated. That is: the 'viewer as star'.

An example of this was given by the Chinese app Zao that utilized deepfake digital manipulation technology to transpose the viewer's face into film content, it thereby enabling us to be the star in our film of choice. The implications for advertising are obvious, while the implications for politics are, frankly, terrifying. (And those were covered in my last book *The Post-Truth Business*, regarding the search for authenticity in a mistrustful world.)

Music: the transformation of immersive, engaging and rewarding experiences

Let's move on to another industry that has been massively disrupted over recent years, but which is now, just as we've seen with film and radio, pushing back and looking to innovative business models as a route to re-engaging with fans.

After enduring a torrid decade, the industry woke up to the realization that, more than ever, music fans demanded more memorable and intense live experiences, just as they do with regard to other areas of the entertainment sector.

So, in particular, I'd like to focus on the live music experience, as this is becoming richer, with deeper immersion and interactivity alongside 'consumer convenience' being fuelled by technology such as augmented and virtual reality, wearable devices, advanced mobile apps, blockchain and a myriad of other emerging tech products and services.

What does this mean in reality, from the viewpoint of innovative actions? One example relates to a long-held wish of fans: for traditional gig experiences to be enriched, and that includes the desire for meaningful interaction with their band or artist of choice. This also, for instance, means things like that interaction being shared via social media content and curated playlists being provided by bands on SoundCloud.

Once fans are at or inside a venue, AR and VR technology are adding to the existing lighting and sound already being produced, to deliver even deeper concert involvement. Although we're currently making use of what are, essentially, 'Version 1' types of virtual- and augmented-reality technology, innovations in these areas via platforms like Snapchat or Instagram are clearly set to deliver ever more immersive experiences for fans.

And these may also connect to next-generation apps, including content-creation ones that help fans produce their own content (sometimes with a variety of elements given to them via the artist or music label) for them to then share and discuss on platforms like YouTube, in a similar manner to the industry's close cousin, the games sector.

But with so much of the above activity producing ever greater amounts of personalized consumer data, the issue of privacy once again rears its head. Elsewhere in this book, I look into the implications of personal data from the perspective of areas such as retail, health and fintech, and of the gathering, storing and use (or abuse) of our personal data. So while the ease of financial payments across the entertainment world may be welcomed by fans, the safety of the data gathered is a vital issue, particularly when fans may not be as 'clear-headed' at a music venue as they are when in a typical retail environment.

As for one other issue so closely aligned to the music industry – influencers – then it's to China that we can look for an illustration of where influencer marketing may be taking us.

There, key opinion leaders (or KOLs) and bloggers include the ubiquitous influencer Becky Li, who has phenomenal social reach among her obsessive Millennial followers. The key issue to note is just how much more powerful the impact of these people is, due to the most obvious issue (the size of population) and other closely aligned factors such as a more deeply integrated digital ecosystem relating to social media and shopping, via players such as WeChat, Taobao, Red and Weibo. (And influencers are not always 'real' of course, as demonstrated by the virtual influencer Lil Miquela.)

And when KOLs have their own content studios, then from the perspective of fan connections, artist liaison and marketing production, some of the innovative 'retailtainment' activity set to hit US and European markets is self evident.

Festivals: the rise and rise of tech powered niche audience events

Finally, let's look at an area very closely associated with the music sector, the world of festivals.

And I really mean a 'world' as the festival sector, which just like radio, was being written off not so long ago, in many cases due to a perceived lack of choice or 'customer empathy', has dramatically increased in terms of scope and variety, by taking an innovative and intuitive approach to meeting consumer needs.

We're now seeing festivals designed around more unique interests, hobbies and passions. These range from dance music to artisan foods, political discussion to 'meet the maker' and from highly targeted youth events to multigenerational ones, spa and glamping, and work- and religion-based events.

What links these to the trends we've seen throughout this chapter, is festival organizers delivering more personalized choices than ever, and on-site technology massively improving the attendee experience, and indeed in the reimagining of other sectors in a festival environment, via lo-tech and high-tech interpretations. In effect 'bringing the city to the field'. However, the environmental impact of festivals needs to be addressed further.

Add these types of trends together, and it's clear why growth in the festivals sector is set to continue, as they reflect the desire for more customized events regarding ticket choices offering different food, accommodation and travel options, to special-interest ones focused around everything from cat videos to military hardware to psychics; and where innovative use of digital technology such as RFID wristbands and prepaid smartcards can be utilized on-site, rather than cash, along with festival-specific programme apps to enhance and simplify the overall consumer experience.

I wrote about the Burning Man festival in my last book from the perspective of cultural marketing activity and authenticity; I'll give two very different examples of leading-edge festivals here.

The Byline Festival was set up a couple of years ago with a very specific aim: to enable debate about, and promote the concept of, independent journalism and free speech; with a tagline of 'dance, discuss, laugh and change the world'. Something I think the festival does incredibly well is to utilize a 'hybridization' approach that sees it put together an eclectic yet complementary array of speakers, bands and activities. This concept of what is essentially an 'ideas festival' links to a wide range of others centralized around debate and discussion (and plenty of socializing) such as the TED events or the superb Do Lectures.

The second I'll highlight is the South by Southwest (SXSW) range of interactive media, film and music festivals in America. It also runs an educational innovation event and has done similar ones focused on innovative start-ups and the environment. In turn, the event had links to earlier ones in Portland (NXNW), NXNE in Toronto and the renowned 'SXSL' (South by South

Lawn) event that was run in conjunction with President Obama at the White House and the US Film Institute.

Among all the performances, speeches, panels and breakout sessions at SXSW, for me one of the most innovative, engaging and staggeringly worthwhile things to come out of the festival saw them team up with the American Red Cross. The vision was to help completely alter the image of a vital service that had unfortunately suffered previously from a distinct lack of engagement with a Millennial generation on which it must now, or soon, heavily rely.

The story goes that, in a moment of genius, the agency Giant Spoon created the concept of combining the act of giving blood with the enormously popular series *Game of Thrones*. To do so, they came up with the concept of 'bleeding for the throne' in order to portray the act of giving blood as an entertaining ritual.

According to a report on the event by JWT Intelligence, the theatrical environment for the activation included 'actors and musicians dressed in *Game of Thrones* costumes recreated a Westeros world. The authentic Iron Throne was there, surrounded by a robed choir and stony-faced soldiers guarding the grand prize. Visitors who "bent the knee" in deference to the Throne were rewarded with a Hand of the Throne pin' (Chiu, 2019).

In doing so, they linked the 'leading-edge meets mainstream' popularity of the show with an experiential scenario that also brought to life a deeply important social cause. The 'blood drive' was also enacted in cities across the US and was enormously successful in terms of units donated, donator data gathered and the 'brand image' of blood donations reframed for a younger generation. Now that, in my mind, is about as innovative a way to approach a vital issue as one could hope for, in this instance by using the entertainment industry in a very specific way as a 'force for good'.

Summary

In looking through the wide array of trends and innovations that I've explained in this chapter, I think it's clear that taking an approach that sees the combining of methods such as hyper-targeting and experiential products and services, leveraged by leading-edge technology, is enabling the entertainment industry, in all its many forms, to reconnect with consumers and provide them with more satisfying results.

From the future of gaming consoles and streamed content, to the deeply immersive offerings of AR and VR, to mobile consumer engagement, community enrichment, individual empowerment and cause-related activity, the entertainment world finds itself absolutely centre stage in the innovations being provided by highly creative thinking and technological developments.

For the last quote, and with reference to my earlier overview of the reasons behind and the benefits offered by play, I refer to the United States Declaration of Independence, and within it, those inspiring words about 'unalienable rights'. The last of which I believe connect directly with the entertainment industry: 'Life, Liberty and the pursuit of Happiness'!

CHAPTER NINE

The future of work

Goodbye to certainty and stability.
Hello to Industry 4.0

This chapter outlines how a range of trends are impacting the future of work from a range of perspectives including future workforce desires, the catalytic impact of technology, the enablement of autonomy and the broadening remit of creativity. I'll also illuminate why the future workplace will become a more emotional, diverse, inclusive and responsive 'exchange space' and why issues ranging from sustainability to wellness, flexibility and virtuality are becoming ever more key considerations.

I'll look into specific areas such as 'conscious coworking', multi-generational teams, life-long learning, the search for meaning and value creation, and how we're witnessing a move from 'talent owning' to 'talent attraction' in the era of the gig economy and pro-working environments. All of these issues are framed by the 'conscience' of business: ethics.

Closely aligned to this is, of course, an ever more informed consumer empowered by an always-on media spotlight that shines an unremitting light on dubious business behaviour. This means that how organizations treat their workers is an important element of the 'Brand A vs Brand B' competitive set consideration when it comes to brand adoption or rejection.

Furthermore, I'll explain how we need to fundamentally reappraise work by taking a fresh look at this most vital of economic and political issues, and the corresponding impact of social and cultural trends regarding the 'who, how, why and where'. The future workforce will look very different to the work we've traditionally come to accept, from the aspect of progressive trends linked to age, gender, diversity and education. These will, in turn, be affected by a range of issues including fluid, alternative, flexible and adaptable employment. Thus a reformulation of the very concept of work, and both how and where this takes place is required.

Playing catch-up to these dynamic changes are governments and institutions who are having to adapt to a world that is fast leaving them behind but is of course still one where vital matters such as social benefits, pensions, childcare and healthcare provision need to reflect the new reality of work in the emerging economy and modern society.

So, when it comes to work, be under no illusion that we're living in revolutionary times, where bland organizations led by conventional leaders look more dated and unappealing by the day.

Defining the issue...

If you're looking for a subject with no singular definition, then the future of work is a great place to start. That's an unusual situation for an area witnessing a staggering amount of creative thinking, with catalytic activity influencing expectations regarding next-generation workforces and workplaces on a global basis.

An essential foundation of the 'Fourth Industrial Revolution' or 'Industry 4.0' is a continuing reappraisal of the notion and role of work. Because how and where we work, who with, why and to what ends are issues radically impacting us all, and the societies around us.

What's clear is that it's becoming more inclusive, motivating and adaptable, and therefore more fit for purpose at a time when work has become more horizontal in nature, ie peer to peer and less hierarchical.

The 'Influencers and Revolutionaries' in this area innovate around the blending of emotional, physical, digital and machine. And to achieve the elixir of a truly engaged, motivated and more productive workforce, agility, flexibility and empathy are key requirements from business leaders and managers.

When even major companies like Spotify are renowned for using 'agile scaling methods' via placing their workforce into 'squads, tribes, chapters and guilds' then it's obvious that the catalytic approaches of these innovators, with autonomy and motivation at the core of their thinking, present incredible challenges and opportunities to individuals and employers alike. Indeed, they require us to reappraise the nature of 'what is a workforce?' and 'what is a workplace?'

According to *Business Insider* 'previous generations of workers wanted security and stability from their employers. Today's workers don't necessarily expect that – instead, they want a sense of personal fulfilment, whether that comes from one job, two jobs, or a job and a side hustle' (Lebowitz, 2018).

Hence, descriptions such as 'digital nomads' being used to describe workers are no longer met with derision but recognition of a self-evident reality, when workers are no longer judged on 'presenteeism and timings' but effectiveness and production. For people like these, achieving the required end results means a combination of every trend researcher's favourite buzzwords: 'collaboration and connectivity'.

Both are issues where 'constant evolution' is a new reality in our #NeverNormal world, and both have immense implications for businesses that wish to, and indeed have to, appear competitive against other organizations also seeking the most skilled workers.

Pulling these various strands into key themes defining the next generation of working life, what is clear is that more and more people seek 'meaning' from their work.

From an employer perspective, this means an increasing desire, particularly noted by HR departments, as being expressed by Millennial candidates in terms of a search for organizations whose 'purpose and vision' are based on authentic values such as creating 'social value'.

In due course, businesses made up of teams who share similar values will benefit from increased levels of commitment.

That's why the results of seemingly endless research reports into the subject talk of a search for purpose, fulfilment, friendship, collaboration and mutual encouragement. They also talk a great deal about 'adaptability', which has gone through a 180-degree shift where it is organizations that are now adapting to workers, and not the other way round.

There's been a fundamental change in the overall context of the contemporary environment vs the days when work was primarily a manual one. This is because when manual work was essentially all that was available, whether a worker felt emotionally happy or not was, unfortunately, far less relevant than now, when the majority of us essentially work via our minds, not our bodies.

We're now in an age when the atmosphere of the workplace, team interaction and modern leadership attitudes have an ever more direct impact on productivity and company profits are directly related to workers' feelings.

Reflecting the seismic changes brought to us via ongoing transformations in technology, sites like Upwork permit organizations to outsource tasks to freelancers, while they can rely on digital comms tools like Zoom to make multi time zone team liaison easy. Meanwhile, software products like Zendesk enable the smooth start-up of a new company.

What these all show us is that flexibility and speed are vital enablers for individuals or coworking teams who operate on a short-term, in-house or external basis. That all goes to make next-generation workspaces an essential commodity that can only become more useful and sought after.

Meanwhile: artificial intelligence, language interfaces and augmented reality

Endless discussions in human resource departments focus around social and emotional intelligence, alongside creative thinking, as being the most reliable means of safeguarding ourselves in a hyper-competitive 'future-worker' context, where technology will increasingly be a greater competitor for jobs than human competition. But this means huge opportunities for those with appropriate skills.

A report into economic forecasting from the Creative Industries Federation, conducted in liaison with Nesta, discussed a future economy shaped around 'creativity and technology. With artificial intelligence taking over routine tasks, there will be immense opportunities for people who combine creative, technical and social skills – those that are resilient to future automation. Hence, interpersonal, cognitive and systems skills are likely to be in particularly high demand' (Easton and Bakhshi, 2018).

Future-proofing ourselves against the ongoing jobs disruption is something that we all need to do, by embracing change and adapting accordingly.

Future-proofing ourselves against the ongoing jobs disruption is something that we all need to do, by embracing change and adapting ourselves accordingly. Because while we've all grown used to apocalyptic stories relating to the destruction of job roles, far less attention is given to the myriad benefits that change is bringing.

Deloitte describe the advent of AI as making it possible to 'reconceptualize work as a collaborative problem-solving effort where humans define problems, machines help find solutions, and humans verify the acceptability of those solutions. Therefore we anticipate a movement towards a "STEMpathetic" workforce. One that co-mingles technical knowledge and cognitive social skills, such as connecting with other people and communicating effectively' (Schwartz, Stockton and Monahan, 2017).

Other major areas of technology becoming key drivers of workplace transformation are natural language interfaces, alongside augmented reality, which will be of particular use for those working in separate locations, but who would like a simulated physical interaction.

So which specific roles and skillsets are considered to have a positive future? In his book *The Globotics Upheaval*, author Richard Baldwin talks about the positive and negative impacts of globalization and robotics; he states that these jobs relate to 'managing and developing people, applying expertise, interfacing with stakeholders, unpredictable physical tasks, plus sports and recreation'.

Another absolutely vital issue of 'job displacement' due to automation is a corresponding problem that will see only certain megacities and urban hubs generating the majority of future (human) jobs, leaving other areas behind.

The nucleus of this problem is that, in the context of this chapter, so many societies have become essentially static, as opposed to earlier generations who dealt with displacement of their jobs (via the innovation of the era) by then moving to where the next work locations appeared.

That 'mobility deficiency' reflects social dynamics (for instance in the US) around matters such as ageing populations and rates of home ownership. The answers will come via empathetic and innovative political policies, but these appear notable by their absence at present.

Diversity, inclusion and cognitive diversity

Alongside the growing use of AI in the workplace, another key trend is the re-evaluation of the roles of individuals, companies and communities. Of an ageing, diverse and educated workforce, which is going to present organizations of all types with a whole new raft of challenges and benefits.

This also has a generational twist to it, as attitudes and behaviour around diversity have clearly changed over recent years. For instance, Millennial views towards diversity appear to be different to previous generational cohorts.

According to *Forbes* 'Millennials encourage diversity because they're living it. As opposed to older generations that were overwhelmingly white, today's Millennial workforce is divided across a number of races and backgrounds. They see it as something much deeper than skin colour. It's a blending of different backgrounds, perspectives, and experiences: "cognitive diversity"' (Johansson, 2017).

And this is of course a vital issue from an external perspective as much as an internal one. For issues ranging from liaising with globalized supply chains to interacting with local customers in an age of increased migration amidst ongoing social and cultural change, an appreciation of diversity is a key attitudinal skillset required for the modern worker.

Illuminating the point about cognitive diversity, *Psychology Today* notes a crucial point relating to effectiveness as it relates to successful innovation. 'Companies produce the best results and are better able to innovate when team members don't all think, process information or see the world in the same way. Leaders who innovate and make an impact seek out those who don't share their opinions and resist the tendency to over-rely on their experience and what's worked in the past' (Canaday, 2017).

This issue of cognitive diversity is also focused on by the *Harvard Business Review*, who illuminate the subject with an additional viewpoint. As they point out 'we discovered the kinds of diversity we most commonly think of – gender, race, age – has no correlation to results. What does make a difference is different perspectives and styles of processing knowledge' (Reynolds and Lewis, 2017).

The impact of this issue is illustrated in the starkest terms by the crisis in digital skills in the private sector. It's obvious to any onlooker that the technology sector – in all its many forms – is in dire need of a more diverse workforce. This means the opposite of the 'tech-bro' photos we probably all associate with the sector.

But a crucial issue is that this doesn't mean firing existing workforces – they just need to be retrained, or 'upskilled', and then redeployed accordingly.

And that diversity also means a diverse range of workforce ages to effectively generate innovation. That's because, according to *Adweek*, organizations need those with 'diverse opinions and backgrounds willing to challenge the status quo. Ensure you have enough women, people of different ethnicity and that you don't kick out everyone over fifty. We tend to think of Millennials as being the big innovators, but that's not necessarily true' (Tynan, 2019).

The practicalities for leadership in this area are that it needs to be transparent, communicative and engaging.

Rateocracy: from 'owning' to 'attraction'

When it comes to flexibility enabling companies to attract the best talent, then a closely linked area is the reversal of employers demonstrating outdated beliefs that they 'own' their workforce, akin to an 18th-century factory boss. Instead, what's now witnessed at forward-looking organizations is a disposition that sees 'talent attraction' vs an 'ownership' ethos as offering a far more attractive proposition for gaining the best people available.

Something that would horrify those 18th-century factory bosses is our 'rateocracy' culture that, in a work context, sees people rating their employers, workplaces and the tasks set before them as much as employers rate their staff.

In this context, something that I believe we'll be increasingly seeing more of is 'workplace activism'. By this I mean the desire of workers to work for 'good companies' being clearly and consistently reflected by positive environmental and social actions sanctioned by the leaders of those organizations. And if leaders are not prepared to implement this type of activity, then workforces (along with investors) will agitate for their replacement.

The modern office needs that element of humanity and gentleness that you or I feel in our home.

The modern office needs that element of humanity and gentleness that you or I feel in our home. This explains why design values are so vital and why harshness and sterility are so outmoded.

Finally, it seems, it's understood that having access to sunlight, plants, water, natural materials and fresh air have enormous benefits for our psychological and physiological well-being. They enhance our moods, reduce stress, improve our cognitive abilities and help make us more creative.

One example of this sees architects taking a lead from the hospitality world, which has led to office reception areas mimicking the feeling of a hotel lobby space, ie they're as inclusive and welcoming as possible. Hence 'biophilic design' being such an important part of successful offices, indeed in any 'built environments' where we might work.

Generational issues: challenges and opportunities

Meanwhile, in a world grown used to watching increasing numbers of Boomers depart the workforce and Gen Z workers streaming in, something becoming ever clearer is that this is only one version of the next-generation work story.

Because, just as social trends relating to demographic changes around age and gender have altered radically over recent years, the attitudes and behaviour of the workforce has also undergone equally seismic change.

Something that is focusing more and more attention in HR circles is that we're now starting to witness something that has long been anticipated: the rise of the multi-generation work-force, one that may include up to five generations working together. (This multi-generation approach will also increasingly be reflected by living arrangements, a situation that is covered in the chapter on the future home.)

This trend sees a wide range of workers carrying with them their own, often extremely different, life experiences, skillsets, communication approaches and collaborative practices.

While Millennials may be more associated with being completely familiar with issues ranging from mixed reality to mindfulness, Boomers, for instance, bring their own inbuilt bene-fits such as a more collegiate and less hyper-competitive approach. While the obvious attractions of good pay and a good corporate reputation are key to attracting them, what will actually help them to stay are diversity and inclusion. Ensuring that these types of policies are put into place has the direct knock-on effect of making the overall workplace one that is engaging and satisfying.

Looking at Gen Z, a crucial generational issue is that they are actively thinking about not taking the traditional college educa-tion that their elder siblings may have taken. By utilizing alternatives such as UnCollege they're not getting into the levels perhaps associated with their older siblings, but are simply going straight to work.

They also have a very different attitude to themselves, which some describe as being 'micro-entrepreneurs'. The BBC reported on this, and how 'if you've grown up managing your personal brand on Instagram, you're much better wired to think of yourself as an individual brand instead of a cog in an organizational machine. "Micro-entrepreneurial" ventures have replaced traditional career paths. "Entrepreneurial" is the critical differentiator. Gen Z is more likely to be practical and risk-averse' (Lufkin, 2018).

As for Gen X, while they may be heading for retirement age, the 'most-connected' generation that grew up playing video games are also associated with being highly entrepreneurial and self-reliant. Both are key skills for 'next generation' roles.

Education and lifelong learning

For a stark illustration of just how much the 'world of work' is changing, the World Economic Forum states that '93% of college-educated freelancers say their skill training is more useful in the work they are doing now than their college training, whilst 65% of children entering primary school will end up in jobs that don't yet exist' (WEF, 2018).

Elsewhere, some of the findings of a major project conducted by Edelman highlighted that the future of work is becoming all about job skills, not degrees, which has huge implications for traditional educational establishments and institutional frameworks.

This means that a whole new range of options have to be provided in the educational sphere. As their report states 'In many industries and countries, the most in-demand occupations or specialties didn't exist five years ago, and the pace of change is accelerating. This points to something much larger. Rapid technological change, combined with rising education costs, have made our traditional higher-education system an increasingly anachronistic and risky path' (Bloxam, 2019).

This means that employers have got to provide learning resources if they want to attract and retain Millennials.

And this is naturally where a host of catalytic companies have made in-roads, particularly with regard to educating students (of any age) about the skills required for sectors that are renowned for their high employment ratios. General Assembly was an early mover, with what they describe as 'outcome focused coding bootcamps offering new career opportunities in code or data science.'

A typical example is the Flatiron School based in New York. Elsewhere the education platform 2U linked up with WeWork, enabling online students to use WeWork's offices on an international basis. Although, following the chaos of WeWork's IPO and their ongoing PR debacle, 'watch this space' appears to be a relevant phrase.

Gender-specific

Another aspect to the demographic story is the specific issue of gender.

Something that's caused a huge amount of debate regarding future work trends is that of gender-specific (usually female-only) workspaces. This has really grown out of the original coworking boom, yet that world is evolving, with the latest trend being for women-only coworking.

An example of this is All Bright, which was established 'to celebrate female talent and support women to thrive in their careers, with a mission to help smart women gain the skills, confidence and network to achieve their career ambitions. Featuring a wellness studio, beauty salon, café, flexible lounge areas for events, exhibitions, meetings and co-working and cocktail bar'. What's not to like?

Developing this female-only idea are GTG, or Girl Tribe Gang to give them their full name – an award-winning collective for women who describe their offering as 'an eco-system of support of like-minded women who work for themselves, are spinning a side hustle or who are aspiring to quit the 9–5. As well as reducing loneliness, confidence upping, knowledge gains and new friendships formed, members collaborate via events, inspiration & motivation'.

Meanwhile, and aligned to this, early movers around the world in the 'workspaces with childcare' sector (aimed at entrepreneurial parents who need flexible childcare) include Trehaus in Singapore, CoworkCreche in Paris, Collab&Play in Los Angeles, EasyBusy in Berlin and Second Home in London.

Emotional and empowering – the future workspace

The most obvious example of the biggest trend to have hit work over recent years is that if you drop into virtually any city on the planet, you'll soon be able to set yourself up in a coworking space. That trend has had a radical impact on how and where we work, and who we work alongside.

And coworking spaces can be scaled as much as you like of course. A personal favourite is the world's largest start-up campus, the truly incredible 'Station F' in Paris. It's a location where they've gathered a whole start-up ecosystem under one roof, in a space for over 3,000 desks (yes, you read that correctly) divided into specific areas titled 'Share, Create and Chill'. There's a tech laboratory, which is dedicated to prototyping, and in a really influential move that is being replicated elsewhere, they've also launched a 'co-living hub', which has space for 500 people, for exhausted Station F entrepreneurs to relax after a hard day at this staggeringly dynamic place.

Another dynamic example is Makerversity, which has bases in Amsterdam and the beautiful Somerset House in London. Aimed at 'Makers with a Mission' they provide cutting-edge making and prototyping facilities for designers, inventors, technologists, craftspeople or engineers: all the physical kit they need for their business. Each being aimed at those entrepreneurs who intend to 'kickstart the Fourth Industrial Revolution'. Elsewhere, the School of Machines, Making and Make-Believe in Berlin operates at the intersection of art, technology, design and human connection.

A personal favourite is Brooklyn Boulders, which is a highly innovative space that grew out of an exercise/bouldering location. When the owners noticed people checking their phones and working in between 'working out' an idea to create a coworking space that also made you physically fitter was born. 'The long commute between your workplace and gym is a thing of the past', as they state. It's been interesting to note similar ideas and services put forward by the likes of Endeavour in South Carolina and Re:Creative in Belgium.

> *The blurring of our personal/social and private/public personas is clearly being understood and creatively reproduced by trend-forward architects and designers.*

The blurring of our personal/social and private/public personas is clearly being understood and creatively reproduced by trend-forward architects and designers.

Meanwhile 'four recurring themes reveal why creative working environments and virtual collaboration tools are facilitating the next generation of idea exchange', according to *Forbes*. They state that these themes are 'meaningful connections happening easier; barriers to cooperation being reduced; honesty and openness leading to better outcomes; and success coming from a generous exchange of information'. They go on to question what creative collaboration will come to look like during the next couple of decades: 'unplanned like the neighbourhoods of Montmartre and Greenwich Village, or coworking environments and social tools?' (Wolff, 2018).

What is increasingly being leveraged in this area, is the move from major corporates who wish their staff to benefit from rubbing shoulders with independent workers and start-ups.

The collaborative nature of all this is summed up by the tech workspace accelerator Huckletree. Their Dublin and London based organization brings together a community of start-ups, scale-ups, innovation teams and global brands powered by a belief that collaboration is the key to a successful business.

And on that most obvious of issues of a collegiate approach, as pointed out in *The Times* 'ultimately, we are social animals and we like to work collaboratively with other people. You are more productive and creative when you are with people with similar objectives in the same space for at least some of the time' (Frary, 2018a).

Silicon Valley has, of course, got its attention firmly fixed on this area, hence things like the Google Startup Campus, which provides tailored mentorship and workspace for growth-stage start-ups. TechHub, the international community for tech entre-preneurs, counted Google as their original sponsor in Shoreditch and now has a global partnership with them.

With Silicon Valley companies and work practices often being accused of mimicking a 'culture of cool' while being as hard-headed as any investment bank, it's interesting to look at one of the first big brands that grew directly out of youth culture, specifically club culture, to see how it's reacted and adapted to the workplace revolution. Hence, The Ministry, which is a work-space that caters specifically for creatives, set up by that famous club, the Ministry of Sound. (I remember the launch night, although not very well, if you know what I mean.)

And I have to point out that charities are another fascinating type of organization in this sector, an example being Launch 22, which linked with charity Catch 22 in Liverpool to help those facing the greatest challenges to entrepreneurship. The charity has a highly unusual story with regard to virtually any other organization in techland, in that it can trace back its history over 200 years to the formation of the Philanthropic Society in 1788. Beat that, Silicon Valley!

Forget coworking, think proworking

The highly innovative outfit Fora have as their raison d'être 'reimagining the entire work experience'. They state that they are 'leading the workspace revolution providing the most inspiring, comfortable & productive work environments one can find.'

They name this reimagined experience 'proworking' by embracing the best aspects of hotel hospitality and providing beautiful professional work spaces. As they say 'Trailblazing businesses need revolutionary environments, completely molded to their needs.' Just the sort of thing one might hear a hotel guest in an upmarket and stylish hotel say.

And of course, hotels are entirely aware of this trend, and are fighting hard to ensure their business offerings are as 'on point' as possible, hence having lobbies full of hipsters hard at work on their laptops. Those at the leading edge of this include the uber-cool CitizenM, Hoxton and Ace hotels.

An ever-expanding trend in office design sees them becoming more like 'soft sanctuaries' than 'hard factories'. An integral element of this is biophilia, hence hydroponic plants, along with an ever greater awareness of mindfulness and the promotion of mental health.

And this is the exact tack taken by all those members' clubs that are now a staple part of seemingly every city on the planet. These are created 'for people that want dedicated workspace and also appreciate design, functionality, friendly service and attention to detail' says the Creative Director of Soho House (Treggiden and Tucker, 2019).

Soho House set the standard one might say, with an offering including meeting rooms, screening rooms, phone booths, an all-day café and bar, members' kitchen and roof terrace, alongside offerings like a photo studio, craft workshop, 3D printer, library, reading room, concierge service, etc.

Meanwhile, the home/office hybrid is represented by the likes of The Collective, whose ten-storey building may look like a hotel, but on launch was thought to be the world's biggest large-scale house-share, offering modest rooms and upscale services for hundreds of young adults.

Cultural planning and social action

A different issue, in fact one of the biggest problems facing many start-ups, is naturally that when they're starting up, they have minimal funds. Helping local start-ups to actually 'get started' is therefore a combination of structural political policy meets social impact via community empowerment.

An example of how to do this well is provided by the Impact Hub Network, which describes itself as 'part innovation lab, part business incubator, and part community centre' and has been lauded for its practical approach to solving the problem of delivering social-impact coworking spaces. Others have clever offers like free coworking space for the first six months for creative sector start-ups, or quick-hit schemes for entrepreneurs, gig economy workers and independent operators. Elsewhere, the superbly named Bathtub to Boardroom activates a belief that this type of dynamic thinking should be formally built into the education process, via assisting students with advice and practical assistance.

A problem relating to existing, and indeed future, organizations is the age-old one of 'first-movers' being priced out of the initially 'unknown' areas where they're based (from a mainstream business perspective) which have perhaps become gentrified, or just less edgy than they were when they moved in, meaning new start-ups can't afford the workspaces and nor can their workforces afford the living expenses.

An 'Artists' Workspace Study' for the Mayor of London highlights the ways of tackling the issue of losing these potential creative populations via the experiences of other cultural capitals, including New York, Berlin and Montreal. The report states that 'tactical interventions including planning protection, direct investment in under-occupied buildings and creative uses of city-owned properties. The creative sector's huge contribution to economy and the positioning of our "national brand" means we simply cannot afford to lose them' (Mirza, 2014).

A great example of those taking action in this specific area are Eat Work Art, who reclaim and unlock abandoned buildings and transform them into spaces for independent creative businesses to grow. The venture has grown organically and now provides studio spaces for over 600 creative practitioners. As their site says 'collaboration is what keeps the hubs alive, the ethos is to always seek innovative ways to bring together all those with a desire to create and share, including residents and the wider community via industry talks, galleries, theatre productions, workshops, gigs, sample sales, street food, cafés and live music'.

Cultural clustering and the battle for authenticity

However, all this reclaiming and reinterpreting of old buildings comes with a downside. That downside is illustrated by a cultural battle being under way – one of authenticity.

As Vishaan Chakrabarti, the author of *A Country of Cities: A Manifesto for an Urban America* puts it 'people are looking for a sense of grit and authenticity, but we're now entering a world where what's defined as attractive has changed. Has the sleek, futuristic newness of many of the new workspaces gone too far, particularly when they've rendered the old and original unrecognizable or indeed ironic?'

That's because many of those old warehouses and factories have been taken over by creative workers, who also tend to cluster together in what urban planners term 'collocationing'. This all seems fine at the beginning, but what can easily follow, and in fact usually does, is the evaporation of the sense of authenticity that was such an allure to the original movers if 'outsiders' then move in, when the location gains the aura of coolness that others desire.

This is of course a standard accusation levelled at, for instance, retail sites and hoteliers that have gentrified run-down areas, but which may have lost a sense of authentic humanity in the process.

A classic example of this is Coal Drops Yard in Kings Cross, London, which, as the *Observer* newspaper put it 'touches a desire for the artisanal, a nostalgia for the authentic and work-aday. Those very things squeezed out of city life by the same economic forces that enable a £1000m shopping complex to come into being in what was an industrial and then an ex-industrial badland. A frankly posh place' (Moore, 2018).

Vogue magazine also wrote about this extraordinary (and extraordinarily expensive) redevelopment, but in their piece they described Coal Drops Yard as 'progressive' which was a some-what bizarre misappropriation of a term more often linked, as the *Observer* noted, to political idealism.

Global brands have also run aground in this area, Apple, for instance, some of whose new locations are described as blurring the boundaries between public and private spaces.

Brand purpose and a new social consciousness

Meanwhile, organizations that develop the idea of community move the future workspace story neatly, and one might say 'authentically', into the overall one of brand purpose.

A classic example of this, in the context of the 'future of work' area, is WeWork, widely acknowledged as being in on day one of the coworking sector. While their troubles have been a media obsession, I still feel their story is worth telling.

Led by the discredited ex-chief exec Adam Neumann and by co-founder Miguel McKelvey, the company rebranded itself into separate businesses. These included the original WeWork alongside temporary co-living via WeLive and nursery schools to look after its members' kids via WeGrow.

The company, like so many of the giant new brands of our age, claim that they're actually tech companies – data gatherers and analysers – who are definitely not merely constricted by whatever sector they happen to be famous for operating in. They may still have aspirations to build towns via WeBuild, alongside fitness sites WeGym and a broader education offering, WeLearn.

Developing this point, there was even talk of an entry into the financial sector. All part of a master plan that, according to the *New York Times* article about their vast coworking space Dock 72 in Brooklyn, illustrated just how big their intentions were by also including 'a luxury spa, a juice bar, real bar, gym, restaurants, dry cleaning services and barbershop. It will be the kind of place you never have to leave until you need to sleep, and if Mr. Neumann has his way, you'll sleep at one of the apartments they have nearby' (Gelles, 2018).

After their 2019 rebrand, the *New York Business Journal* noted that WeWork had approximately '400k members at 425 locations in 100 cities across 27 countries. Their technology platform provides a complete solution for space needs, has disrupted a multi-trillion-dollar industry, and their valuation is now US$47 billion' (Noto, 2019). This was before their dramatic fall...

As mentioned earlier, a fascinating element of the 'coworking space revolution' has been the coming together of major corporates with start-ups. In this instance, according to the same *New York Business Journal* article that reported on their financing deal with the SoftBank Corporation 'in late 2018 approx 30% of the Global Fortune 500 were with WeWork' (Noto, 2019).

According to an interview in *Property Week* magazine 'the prospect of a "WeWorld" is a real one. Neumann was convinced the business could change the world and achieve its corporate goal of creating a "new social consciousness"'. At which point, you either took his point very seriously, or just laughed out loud.

It's been fascinating to see how brands in sectors apparently entirely unconnected with the workspace, ie the motor industry and in this instance the BMW-owned Mini, have been getting in on the coworking act. Their A/D/O creative space in Greenpoint, Brooklyn is based in, of course, a converted warehouse. The reason, as reported by *The Drum,* was two-fold 'to prove its worth as a lifestyle brand – not just an automotive dealer, and to future-proof itself against the tide of ride-sharing and autonomous cars. The large-scale experiential space houses a workshop for designers, and "Urban-X" an accelerator program. They're now working on "MiniLiving", which has been referred to as "their take on WeWork's accommodation brand WeLive"' (Deighton, 2018).

The notion of social consciousness includes a very strong desire, and indeed requirement, for sustainable workplaces and sustainable workforces.

That notion of social consciousness includes, of course, a very strong desire, and indeed requirement, for sustainable workplaces and sustainable workforces.

At the Amsterdam office, or 'smart building' named 'The Edge', which was built for the global advisory firm Deloitte, the building acts 'as a catalyst for Deloitte's transition into the digital age. Everyone is connected to the building via a smartphone app; a radically new working environment has been created that is enabled by sustainable technologies'. Nearly 30,000 sensors track motion, temperature, and humidity, also adapt to the number of people actually in the building. This is, according to their publicity 'an inspirational and healthy environment that attracts talent, leads to higher satisfaction and higher productivity'.

The issue of a sustainable economy, and of future jobs being massively impacted by actions identified in the 'Green New Deal', which is endorsed by numerous progressive politicians, is another key one to note in the content of this chapter, and with it, the vital area of employment protection. As pointed out by the admirable Naomi Klein (who, I remember, was kind enough to give me her insights for an article I wrote for *The Face* magazine way back in the 1990s) 'what is needed is an industrial transformation similar in scale to that undertaken by Roosevelt as a reaction to the Great Depression. This is emphatically not a "jobs vs the environment" policy, which is a false dichotomy, but a practical means of approaching the existential emergency of our time' (Klein, 2019).

The future work manifesto: 'empowerment, flexibility, collaboration, empathy and autonomy'

While I've highlighted some of the revolutionary activity taking place in the emerging and future workspace and for the future workforce, this doesn't mean complete destruction of the old order, in fact far from it. Lots of what has existed over the ages naturally remains useful and entirely relevant.

To state the obvious, that's because... it works. But this doesn't mean that innovation shouldn't be an ever-present consideration.

As reported by *Raconteur* 'Almost every market is fragmenting, becoming more niche, and being disrupted more frequently. In that world, as a leader, do you really think being inflexible is a competitive advantage?' (Frary, 2018b).

For instance, in terms of many office layouts around the world, while workers appear to want privacy, the open-plan office has been in existence for the best part of a century. The *Financial Times*, noting the latest workplace trends from Silicon Valley, points out that for company bosses 'an obvious incentive to seating workers together is cost. The downside is lack of focus, when endless disruptions are par for the course. But unless remote working via video or hologram replaces communal offices, open-plan layouts are not going anywhere. The next big Silicon Valley perk could be workplace privacy' (Bird, 2019).

Where a lot of the new transformations offer real impact is in the way that they enable workers to be both happier and more productive. A combination of autonomy, comfort, 'collegiate efficiency' and flexibility is something that needs to be communicated over and over again to companies of all descriptions, in locations far away from the original 'future workspace' havens of Williamsburg, Shoreditch, Kreuzberg and Shimokitazawa.

So what are the future workplace rules? According to the global architecture and design firm Callison RTKL it's all about wellness, experience, an ongoing technology revolution, internal/external workforce connections, personalization, and safety being paramount. The specific details that they cover in these areas include 'real-time integrated wellness measurements and preventative health interfaces, the workplace becoming one of collaboration, choice and control becoming dominant issues, IoE (Internet of Everything) meaning more elements being connected for data collection, and as more and more data is captured and transmitted electronically, cybersecurity will become complicated and even more important'.

And what about the workers concerned about those ubiquitous media reports describing a future where robots will steal our jobs? In an excellent report compiled by Accenture titled 'Principles for an Inclusive Future of Work' they advise that the answer is all about 'Shifting the Conversation' where employers start courageous conversations with workers about AI and equip them for successful transitions... 'Reimagining Work' where employers pivot the workforce by redesigning roles to support continuous learning... and 'Recognizing Inherent Value' where organizations build workers' confidence and resilience, developing new talent pools by prioritizing potential over pedigree.

Unfortunately, all of this incredible change is happening at a time when the need for leadership has never been more needed;

and even more unfortunately, leadership is evidently in short supply in these uncertain times.

On that subject, a while ago I spoke at a 'corporate trust' event alongside Robert Phillips, the ex-CEO of Edelman. He later wrote a message to the business and political elites attending Davos, just prior to the annual World Economic Forum meeting. In it, he drew attention to what he called 'Employee Liberation Movements' where, as he said 'Employee Liberation recognizes the importance of fair and equal representation and voice. It speaks to the real diversity agenda and control shift. Movement captures the power and momentum of networks and that trustworthiness flows horizontally. Trust cannot be imposed from above or by centralized machines, if it ever really could' (Phillips, 2019).

Summary

To finish, when it comes to discussions around people's desires toward the type of work that they want, the most consistent things I've heard are the need to feel connected, to have a purpose and to have a sense of community. The understanding that a collaborative approach is the best way forward, being part of an environment that promotes diversity and seeking work with a genuine sense of meaning, are issues that you'll hear from Tokyo to Los Angeles to Melbourne to Helsinki.

It's therefore no surprise that these types of desires are noted by successful organizations who take action at every level. Thus, demonstrating that the business in question clearly has an understanding of, and empathy with, their workforce, complementing and mirroring their attitudes and behaviour, and genuinely empowering those viewpoints.

The workforce and workplace trends I've described reflect in many cases not an idealized future of 'what ifs' but instead are rapidly becoming the status quo, the types of things that organizations are having to realize are not 'nice to have benefits' that future workers may request, but are instead straightforward expectations that future talent will demand.

Business has, and will continue to, go through radical changes, and those organizations that either ignore these issues or attempt to deny their existence will soon find that their future is growing darker by the day.

Meanwhile, for those that heed the 'influencers and revolutionaries' illuminating the path ahead in our brave new world, the future is bright.

CHAPTER TEN

Fintech and insurtech, and the battle of choice vs privacy

This chapter looks into the dynamic areas of the banking and insurance markets, where the level of disruptive innovation, particularly in Western markets, is at long last catching up with those in the East.

The supercharging of the financial services industry (in all its guises) by Big Tech provides them with a dynamic challenge, or a 'perfect storm' problem depending on your point of view. The latest and ongoing moves from Silicon Valley that I'll describe are a clear indication of the enormity of the disruption set to transform this area. From a consumer perspective, there are at least two positive end results to all this: services are set to become both cheaper and less complex.

I deal with the banking sector first in this chapter, which until recently (particularly in the US for instance, as opposed to China) has been a byword for being both inefficient and outdated. The legacy players are also viewed with often great suspicion due to the cataclysmic role played by numerous high-profile individuals and organizations in the financial crisis.

The repercussions of that disastrous episode led to additional levels of government regulation supplementing those already in place. (A great deal of it being absolutely vital, of course.) But seen through the prism of this chapter, from a US and European angle this had the added and unforeseen result of stalling innovation in the wider sector. Prime examples being illustrated via the hurdles faced by early movers involved with the 'libertarian' concept of bitcoin and ongoing concerns over biometric services.

The resulting barriers for the Western tech players have been political, ie regulatory, and social, in terms of trust (or rather the lack of it) due to a decade of seemingly endless data breaches and privacy encroachment.

A list of those could fill a book by themselves, but the impact included companies such as Marriott (where 500 million customers had their data stolen), eBay (145 million) and Equifax (150 million), along with those across a wide spectrum of sectors, ranging from Uber to JP Morgan to Sony PlayStation. And, of course, and as mentioned elsewhere in this book, the No 1 position in that dubious list goes to Yahoo!, where the biggest data breach in history saw its entire database of 3 billion users compromised.

In short, the sector has been ripe for a serious overhaul, where a desire for fresh products and services (from a consumer viewpoint) and an intent to boost competition (from a governmental policy perspective) mean that the need for 'genuine innovation' is immense, while ensuring that customer security is paramount.

A personal favourite innovation of mine saw the Swedish fintech start-up Doconomy launch the world's first credit card 'Do Black' featuring a carbon footprint limit. The card not only helps consumers track and measure CO_2 emissions associated with their purchases, but also puts a limit on the climate impact of their spending. Another example of brands enabling ethical consumption via digitization is the 'Almond' app, which also estimates the carbon footprint of users' purchasing behaviour, but in addition, provides monetary rewards for responsible purchasing.

As shown by these inspiring examples, opportunities will present themselves to those organizations in both the banking and insurance sectors that welcome change and open themselves to imaginative ways of thinking and operating.

The opposite will be the case in a brutal 'survival of the fittest' environment, where the winners will win big and the losers will find themselves facing the harsh reality of being left behind by fundamentally altered market conditions and unforgiving consumers.

And yet, and just as we've seen from numerous other industries highlighted in this book, despite being faced with this market turbulence, an apparent unwillingness to change and a failure of leadership (that could have enabled companies to be agile and adaptable) has left many companies around the world in a perilous position.

However, and this is critical, unlike many other sectors where the public have traditionally been quite happy to see new players come to market, while existing ones disappear, banks also have a 'social stability' role to play. They act (or at least should act) as symbols of trust, dependability and resilience, amidst volatile political and economic conditions that often seem increasingly dystopian. As the saying goes, when they catch a cold, we all sneeze.

So the implications of ever-increasing technological progress, the impact of stricter regulations and the effect of increasingly demanding consumers, set against a broader backdrop of changing social expectations, mean that both these sectors are set for a turbulent ride over the next few years. Common denominators include innovation based around increased consumer choice, and a key part of gaining competitive advantage will be to answer increasing demands for the safeguarding of consumer privacy.

Meanwhile, exciting sector developments include a myriad number of product and service innovations, where open banking, crypto-trading bots and AI-enabled auto-credit risk modelling are typical examples. And as we've seen, much of this originates far away from New York, Berlin or London. And while the legacy players have stood still, the 'influential and revolutionary' rise of catalytic fintech and insurtech companies are answering the call for a new, or at least experimental, approach. Of which more later.

Capitalism under attack, and the need for greater accountability

To illustrate these issues and to indicate a way forward, in this chapter I outline a range of brands and personalities across these sectors, who are demonstrating a best-case approach to business.

And while much of the energy is held by 'insurgents and start-ups' this isn't always the case, due to the absolutely vital issue of trust that I highlighted earlier. It's important to observe, particularly when issues such as 'identity management' are so critical, that the levels of trust held by certain (and it's only a fortunate few) sector legacy brands, are key differentiating assets.

This will be an increasingly critical issue as we see dynamic product and service developments appear from new but untested, and thus unproven, next-generation players.

That relates to what I termed the 'reputation capital' of a brand in my previous book *The Post-Truth Business*. This is summed up by three key foundational points, where the brand in question has to give a convincing and coherent illumination of their behaviour around the questions of whether they are 'competent, reliable and trustworthy'.

Because if a brand fails to evidence their credibility across these crucial areas, then I believe that, when choice is available, they will be rejected in favour of a brand that can provide proof of their corporate integrity regarding those vital issues.

On one hand, the evidence of this is usually shown more in a reduction of market share than instantaneous rejection, while on the other, rival businesses benefit from consumer trial and 'sector promiscuity'. If they then match up to the customers' wishes, brand loyalty to them is strengthened while the 'untrusted' brand is further weakened.

Examples range across a myriad number of sectors and go right to the top of the business charts. Hence they include 'Ratner moments' (where a brand is effectively destroyed overnight) to 'Boeing or VW episodes' where the reputation capital of a brand is deeply damaged, and the impact of this involves a long recovery and immense financial damage.

What's crucial is that issue of choice that I just mentioned, ie if given the chance, how many people would stay with Facebook if, as in any other sector, 'mirror image' competitors were available?

To give added context to this, the famous Edelman 'Trust Barometer' states that less than 50 per cent of consumers trust business at all, while Accenture estimate that a lack of trust 'costs global brands US $2.5 trillion a year. Yet for most companies, trust has been viewed as a "soft" factor, its value to a company being unclear. But today, to be truly competitive, companies must look at it as a critical component of their business strategy' (Long, Roark and Theofilou, 2018).

As the great Steve Jobs once said 'a brand is simply trust'.

Another relevant and crucial point is that not all innovation is beneficial when viewed in hindsight, in fact far from it.

For instance, any college debating society student could easily present a case that the 'law of unintended consequences' has played a central role in the knock-on effect of the consumer debt explosion that resulted from the introduction of credit cards into societies around the world. That's in addition to issues such as the housing loans that, encouraged by the US Government for 'progressive' ethical reasons, were offered with such ease and did so much to eventually spark the sub-prime crisis with disastrous results.

It's also important to point out the broader, indeed existential, context here, very much linked to the above: that the concept of capitalism itself is under attack. We're in an era when young people in particular are viewing alternative political systems like socialism from a fresh and positive perspective, in the context of individual vs societal well-being, and seemingly endless media exposés of corporate malpractice and senior management greed acting as a backdrop to the public's viewpoint.

The famous 'perspective fail' of the usually brilliant academic Francis Fukuyama, was that we had reached 'the end of history' due to the rise of liberal democracy and the collapse of the Soviet Union after the Western victory in the Cold War. That statement was tragically incorrect (depending on your political leanings) and indeed today we're witnessing democratic capitalism under assault in a manner not seen since the Cold War, and with it, Fukuyama's prediction.

Yet no serious commentator would argue against the perspectives of those like the sadly departed Hans Rosling that, for the vast majority of humanity, there has never been a better time to be alive, and that a great deal of the credit for this can be put down to the 'disruptively liberating' powers of innovation and free markets.

But what's missing from that statement about the economic benefits of capitalism is a moral one. Indeed, as the (pro-market) think tank the Centre for Policy Studies acknowledges 'There has to be more to it than the numbers. Of course, there is plenty of moral worth in a system that lifts billions out of extreme poverty. Yet there is a deeper point about markets that goes beyond living standards and to the heart of human nature' (Wiseman, 2019).

A capitalist system only really works efficiently when it is seen, or at least understood, to act with transparency.

Without getting too earnest, a capitalist system only really works efficiently when it is seen, or at least understood, to act with transparency. But currently it's increasingly viewed as being a system that's controlled and rigged in favour of a minority. When issues ranging from personal inheritance to corporate tax to executive compensation appear wildly unfair to the vast majority, and it appears to have inequality built into its DNA, then it's clear that the system requires a serious amount of innovative and structural reform. For if the foundations of meritocracy, opportunity and fairness aren't in place, then the whole structure is in a perilous state.

Indeed, to quote the *Financial Times* 'the superiority of private enterprise and free markets in creating wealth is no longer seriously challenged. But plainly, there is disenchantment... the financial crisis dented faith in the economic system and political and business elites... Western Governments must ensure that multinational corporations are taxed fairly and curb excessive executive pay' (*Financial Times*, 2019c).

Furthermore, and in what until only recently would have been considered a shocking statement from one of the ultimate 'pro-capitalism' media titles, the *FT* announced on their front page 'Capitalism: time for a reset. Businesses must make a profit, but should serve a purpose too' (*Financial Times*, 2019b). And of course, throughout all areas of life, power must be held accountable.

The sun rises in the East...

On the other side of the world, it's in the Asian markets where the most exciting innovation has taken place, ie via companies that also feature elsewhere in this book including those Chinese behemoths Tencent (who own WeChat and thus WeChat Pay) and Alibaba whose affiliate Ant Financial includes its payment app Alipay, consumer credit arm MYbank and wealth management division Yu'e Bao.

For instance, Ant has links with online payment companies in countries from Mexico to Thailand, as a result of a digital 'belt and road' initiative (that is to say, in addition to the physical one), which enables its customers to utilize Alipay while travelling or working internationally.

Other examples of dynamic Asian brands in this space include the massively successful South Korean chat app Kakao, financial app Toss and the Indonesian Go-Jek (and its mobile app Go-Pay), which moved into financial transactions and other financial services a few years ago and has since expanded into Thailand, Vietnam and Singapore.

On the global stage, this type of innovation is vital according to the World Bank, whose president Jim Yong Kim, when talking of Go-Jek, said 'this is good news for Indonesians, and their country's economy. The World Bank views access to financial services as a "critical step" toward reducing poverty and inequality. Financial inclusion allows people to save for family needs, borrow to support a business or build a cushion against an emergency' (Maulia, 2018).

It was thus interesting to see moves from Facebook-owned WhatsApp Pay, mimicking the existing array of financial services offered by messaging app WeChat and Alibaba-owned Paytm, as they began trialling their payments offer in India, back in 2018. This could be prime territory for the brand, as there are over a billion mobile users in the country. (South America, and particularly Brazil where WhatsApp is hugely successful, appear to be next on the list.)

Hypertargeting meets privacy... and Libra

Meanwhile, those like Apple who've achieved high levels of public trust, due in part to their commitments to individual privacy (which is a recurrent theme in this chapter) are in a prime position to make substantial inroads into the financial services space, in all its numerous variations.

The most overt instance saw Apple launch their own credit card in conjunction with Goldman Sachs, utilizing Mastercard's network. This being the self-titled 'Apple Card', which linked to a whole raft of financial services and products such as their

Apple Pay and Wallet app, and links with Apple Maps to show where payments have been conducted.

One might say this is typical of 'late to market' Western brands that are desperately attempting to draw level with those like China's WeChat, with its array of easy-to-use financial services. In addition, the US card system itself is also playing a seriously delayed game of catch up, regarding the staggeringly slow roll-out of contactless payments across the US.

What all of this also points to, of course, is that Apple are aiming themselves squarely at the existing sector giants, ie Mastercard and Visa. Key differentiators include being more 'now', as reflected by being both stylishly designed and made of titanium.

The privacy angle that I alluded to earlier is another incredibly powerful differentiator here, with Apple stressing that all financial data will remain purely on the iPhone and Goldman Sachs agreeing not to share or sell the data to advertisers. They certainly needed to do something dynamic in this space, as the mainstream and mass adoption of Apple Pay had been anything but 'mainstream and genuinely mass' prior to the launch of Apple Card. It also reflected moves from the brand to make more revenue from services as opposed to products, as sales from items like the iPhone slowed.

Other moves from key players have seen Amazon launch their person-to-person unified payments interface (or Pay UPI) service for Android users, meaning they can pay bills, send money to friends and family, and pay for things such as the inevitable Amazon delivery services. In doing so, they are clearly aiming to compete with, for example, Google Pay.

The resulting amount of added behavioural analytical data, in this instance 'how people are actually spending their money' is of immense use to the tech giants and therefore their advertising clients, from the perspective of targeting and messaging efficiency.

And when advertising rears its head, Facebook are a seemingly omnipresent element of the conversation. However, one place that they haven't really been until recently was inside our wallets.

That all changed with the announcement of their own crypto-currency 'Libra', which was built on their own blockchain technology. As the *Observer* newspaper stated 'First it had your friends, then it had your pictures, then it had your diary. Now, in the latest effort to entwine its systems still further into the everyday lives of its users, Facebook wants to get into your wallet' (Hickey, 2019).

The purpose of Libra is, according to their official announcement, 'to foster more access to better, cheaper, and open financial services'. The proposal being seamlessly transferring money on a peer to peer, or buyer to seller, basis 'as easy as sending a text'.

But the omnipresent issue of privacy was one of the main reasons given by the chair of the US House Financial Services Committee, Congresswoman Maxine Waters when she said about Facebook that it 'already has data on billions of people and has repeatedly shown a disregard for the protection and careful use of this data. With the announcement that it plans to create a cryptocurrency, Facebook is continuing its unchecked expansion and extending its reach into the lives of its users' (Paul, 2019).

Meanwhile, an influential report outlined two key points about the company, noting first that it's an 'unlikely guardian of other people's money, given its habit of privacy abuses and evasion'. But it went on to say that 'like or loathe them, its new scheme has legs. If Facebook's 2.4bn users adopt Libra to shop and transfer money, it could become one of the world's biggest financial entities. That would herald a consumer revolution' (*The Economist*, 2019).

So it will be fascinating to observe how successful (or not) Facebook's cryptocurrency Libra will be, regarding what one might charitably call its 'issues' with trust, after their previous failure to provide financial services. Anyone remember 'Facebook Credits'?

It was no surprise that they arranged for their 'low volatility' digital currency to be overseen by a third-party Libra Association, based in Geneva. Initially made up of 28 different backers including Visa, Coinbase, Uber, Stripe, PayPal, Mercy Corps, Spotify, eBay, Anchorage and Mastercard, this number is set to change, dependent on factors such as increasing regulatory scrutiny. Indeed, just before their first association meeting, that initial figure dropped to 21, as numerous 'partner' companies dropped out, causing considerable embarrassment to Mark Zuckerberg.

Indeed, already the media have reported that, from that list alone, the likes of 'PayPal, eBay, Visa, Mastercard and Stripe have jumped ship' (Feiner, 2019). Meanwhile, Reuters note that governments including those of Germany and France have currently agreed to clock the cryptocurrency, reporting that 'in a joint statement, the two governments affirmed that "no private entity can claim monetary power, which is inherent to the sovereignty of nations"' (Frost, 2019).

A clear target is the millions of people (with estimates putting this at over a billion) who, while having a mobile phone, don't have a bank account. For them, this 'instant mass-availability' concept could be an enticing proposition, despite, or perhaps because of, it being so revolutionary.

Gambling and open banking

However, a deep concern is the very real one of encouraging debt. The launch of credit cards led to a boom in consumer debt, as mentioned earlier, with a key reason for this being 'saliency'. Simply put, this means that (according to behavioural economists) our psychological relationship with cards is essentially 'removed' from the very personal relationship we have with physical money.

Unfortunately, the links to similar consumer usage of digital wallets, perceived as having 'mental-distance' from real cash in your hand, mean that the warning lights are flashing (or not, depending on your stance) over this issue.

As a slight aside, it was no surprise that the noir masterpiece *Mr Robot* series was such a hit, as its central theme of 'the people's champions', ie a group of rebel hacktivists who managed to cancel all debt records, clearly struck a highly sensitive public nerve.

Meanwhile, my previous book shone a spotlight on the so-called 'G-Mafia' of Silicon Valley and impact of the behaviour and failings of, for instance, Facebook, that were described by the *Financial Times* as having 'between data breaches, hate speech and smear campaigns, set a standard of sorts in Silicon Valley scandals' (*Financial Times*, 2019a).

That they've now turned their attention, once again, to the fintech world means that many are rightly concerned about the impacts of issues such as yet more data breaches and the leverage of private financial data by third parties.

Meanwhile in Europe, as the impact of the 'PSD2' (revised payment service directive) becomes ever more apparent, the inroads made by existing competitors alongside new ones means that the levels of disruption have been increased even more.

The whole point of this legislation is to encourage 'secure innovation', in this instance meaning that banks are legally obliged to enable authorized competitors to have access to customers' account information, with the customers' permission of course, via application programme interfaces, or APIs for short.

The benefits are 'a world in which, with a few swipes of a smartphone, you could find a better mortgage, compare household bills, cancel unwanted subscriptions, control direct debits, and track payments across your accounts. It's not a fantasy: it's called open banking, the idea of which was to drive competition and innovation' (Warwick-Ching, 2019).

Bitcoin, smart contracts, neobanks and... Extinction Rebellion

As I mentioned earlier in this chapter, underpinning all of this activity, of course, is trust.

Or rather, a worrying lack of it.

This is just one of the reasons why many believe that block-chain, a technology that's been written about and commented on seemingly endlessly in recent times (for instance with regard to clarifying the world of 'immutable contracts') will shape the future of banking.

It will put power back into individuals' hands and drive a radical shift in power from big financial institutions back to the consumer, allowing people to have total control and vision of their finances, from their credit score and financial data to their overall banking footprint.

Blockchain technology-enabled bitcoin, of course, was credited with being the first mover here, with huge associated interest around smart contracts and 'programmable money'.

But there are downsides, eg as bitcoin fails to live up to many of its promises, alternatives like altcoin offer additional benefits as emerging technology ushers in a new era of more consumer-friendly transactions.

Key issues for the sector are that, while bitcoin promises transparency, it also opens up the users' entire payment history to the public and is therefore unable to match the privacy given by cash. An answer to this problem is offered by Zcash, which uses zero-knowledge cryptography (authentication in which no passwords are exchanged) to promise secure transactions.

Elsewhere, and in light of growing concern from consumers around climate change, the staggering usage of computing power and electricity by bitcoin mining and functioning underlines the need for a vastly more sustainable alternative. A fact that those like Extinction Rebellion point out is that, in one month alone, the bitcoin network consumed more energy than the Republic of Ireland.

The fintech sector isn't strictly new of course, as operators in this area have been making great efforts to disrupt the sector for over a decade, with the winners taking advantage of an incredibly slow-moving market. According to McKinsey, the reasons are clear: 'many began as start-ups, functioning with a much lower cost burden than traditional banks, free of the burden of banking operations, branch networks, and legacy IT systems. By developing innovative products and delivering them digitally and swiftly, they made inroads into business lines traditionally dominated by incumbents' (Catlin and Lorenz, 2017).

Another legacy issue is the frustration that consumers have with traditional banks, who use SWIFT payments to transfer money. With these bank-to-bank transfers typically taking a couple of days, alternatives include Ripple, who use pre-mined coins to offer faster bank transfers in a matter of seconds. This all comes at a time when, as already explained, a huge challenge for the banking sector is from the tech giants of Facebook, Google and Amazon offering financial services, at both lower costs, on a cross-border basis, at lightning speed.

Elsewhere, smartphone-based 'neobanks' such as Starling, Simple, Empower, Chime, Moven and Germany's N26 (named after the elements of a Rubik's Cube) have come to market with a combination of dynamic consumer offerings and equally dynamic business models.

The neobank concept has been centre stage at many of the trend events that flag up interesting activity in the market, but it's the Asian markets that have really proved to be 'first-movers' (in innovation terms) in this area.

According to *Business Insider* 'driven by innovation-friendly regulatory reforms, these companies have gained traction in Europe. The US neobank ecosystem has lagged behind largely because of an onerous regulatory regime that has made it hard to get a banking licence. However, developments suggest US start-ups are finally poised for the spotlight' (Tesfaye, 2019). One could argue that PayPal effectively kick-started this area, although legally speaking they were in a different legal situation as they operated without backing from the Federal Deposit Insurance Corporation.

As for that 'lagging behind', it's worth reiterating that what's being discussed here is one of the biggest business sectors in the

US, which also just happens to be one of those least affected, so far, by genuine disruption. In addition, and to put it mildly, very few people have any sense of emotional attachment to brands in this enormous industry.

It's therefore no surprise that innovators are getting so excited at the potential prospects.

Meanwhile, those like Monzo, Varo or Revolut, what one might call 'challenger banks', also offer far greater, or certainly far more immediate, levels of transparency that young people in particular wish to see, as part of their 'open-banking protocols', which combine multi-source yet secure data, enabling easy and 'smart consumption' decision making by account holders.

Big brands fight back, and criminal networks see an opportunity

Of course, it didn't take long for those major legacy players to take note and join in this vibrant area, hence those like Chase Bank setting up their Finn online bank, while the Goldman Sachs brand Marcus is set to be developed further, into a full-service online bank.

The move may have seemed somewhat at odds with consumers' views of the Goldman Sachs brands ('sceptical' might be a generous term) and indeed the *New York Times* described their actions as being 'somewhat unexpected, like Maserati making a push into the motorized bicycle market, given it's long been known as the most upscale firm on Wall Street. But if successful, it could provide a valuable public perception payoff by softening the firm's image as a remote bastion of power and wealth' (Popper, 2018).

But among those using technology to promote their businesses, criminal networks are always at the forefront of tech innovation. As shown by dark web drug dealers turning to popular apps to peddle their products, often using street graffiti to advertise their accounts to customers.

According to the *Independent* 'they then utilize automated bots to communicate with them, together with the introduction of encryption into apps that allows users to remain anonymous i.e. via messaging apps like Telegram, WhatsApp and Facebook Messenger, with semi-anonymous cryptocurrencies facilitating the payments' (Cuthbertson, 2019). Telegram gained notoriety after it became the comms choice for terrorist groups, for example.

So, encryption apps that started out with good intentions, such as helping to protect private communications from government spying, have unfortunately seen this functionality abused.

Elsewhere, when it comes to how cyber-criminals attempt to steal from, or defraud us, ie from the perspective of e-commerce where this is prevalent, then it's hoped that the implementation of 'strong customer authentication' (more easily referred to by the acronym SCA) will have a transformative effect on the world of online payments.

Unlike many new financial innovations, this one is simple to explain: by utilizing multi-faced authentication care of secure hardware or via tech developments, including personal biometrics such as facial recognition or fingerprints, it replaces those old rigid passwords on which we used to rely.

The biggest hurdle to this becoming a 'mass-use' system remains the basic conundrum of speed vs security, where the actual behaviour of consumers vs their professed attitudes shows that the former usually outweighs the latter, particularly when it comes to small purchases or those done under time pressure.

Which for most people, of course, means all the time.

Insurtech and 'Policy 2.0'

The insurance sector has been disrupted as much as any other by a combination of political, economic and technological developments.

And, just as in the world of fintech, their 'insurtech' start-up associates in the insurance world have proved to be far more agile, adaptable and closer to consumer-need states than the dinosaur-like legacy brands whose inertia has prevented them from taking advantage of a changing market environment.

So for those running legacy insurance companies, the issue of these catalytic new players driving the insurtech agenda has to be at the top of their agenda from a business strategy and brand development perspective.

The insurance sector has been disrupted as much as any other by a combination of political, economic and technological developments.

Hence a similar pattern is developing in the insurance sector to the banking one care of dynamic insurtech companies leveraging new technologies to offer consumers more relevant and attractive coverage, with these offerings reflecting the portfolio approach and digital platforms usage of their banking equivalents.

The sectors have often taken a very segmented approach to consumer product and service innovation from a generational perspective, ie as they see the Boomers retiring and the Gen-Xers take over followed by the Millennials. These 'always-on' digital natives desire personal service at a low price, and what they demand is speed, delivered via efficient online (preferably mobile) platforms.

What the traditional brands really lacked were the key factors now catalysing the industry: hyper-personalization and cost reduction. Both are key elements of the brand offerings of dynamic new players such as Thing Co, Nimbla, Dinghy, Canopy and Pluto.

But an added, and absolutely vital, issue is that of privacy, just as we've seen in banking, indeed across virtually every other sector. According to *The Sunday Times* 'the explosion of health apps and devices, from the heart monitor in your watch to sleep apps and gene testing kits has created a treasure trove of sensitive medical data. The problem is that this deluge of digital data is being bought, sold and passed around unbeknown to users' (Fortson, 2019).

The accuracy of that data is what brands are after. This is keenly felt in the advertising world, where it's long been realized that traditional categories of age, gender, location, ethnicity, etc are, while being far from meaningless, also far from reflecting the 'real person' via those crude demographic indicators. So what's the answer?

According to KPMG 'the industry must target digital customers. Interaction with clients has been isolated to policy anniversaries and renewal periods and fails to build on existing relationships. This makes it easy for the insurer to be cut out of the loop if another carrier offers the same, or more appealing, products and experience than them. Customers are expected to be increasingly segmented upon their behaviour, as this is the data that insurers are beginning to capture' (KPMG, 2019).

Elsewhere, a commonly held complaint about insurance company contractual small print is that it enables them to wriggle out of paying for consumer claims. However, according to McKinsey 'because of data and AI advancements, insurers can do so much more for their customers, regarding predicting, monitoring and reducing risk.' This could mean 'a personal assistant app alerting you when you're about to engage in activity that could increase your insurance premiums, as the industry shifts from a 'repair and replace' model to a 'predict and prevent' approach' (Jefferies, 2019).

Meanwhile, ethical considerations may not be an immediate link for many people when considering the business model of insurers, which is why the B Corporation certified Burnham Benefits Insurance Co attract customers interested in social causes and environmental issues. This is due, for instance, to the company's involvement in local community and charitable activities.

The 'cheaper, faster' app-based brand Celo offers personalized motor, health, travel and electronics insurance for those doing business on web-based platforms like Amazon. It uses AI-powered telematics (the merger of telecommunication and infomatics) and behavioural analytics to promote 'good behaviour' by offering rewards such as gift cards, free coffee and discounted premiums.

Or if you just want your headphones, laptop or smartphone insured, then the on-demand platform Trov, who describe themselves as 'reinventing insurance for the mobile generation' offer to do it for you on an instant and 'on–off' basis.

Sharing, collaborating, pricing and not-for-profit

And as a really sector-shaking trend, the ever-expanding trend for sharing means that the so-called 'collaborative economy' has led to a fundamental reappraisal of what insurance is actually for, in an environment where 'ownership' is increasingly done on a temporary basis.

The growth of the sharing economy has been extraordinary, with its global impact being felt in virtually any sector one could imagine. According to a report released by the World Economic Forum 'access over ownership' is a shift that has taken root, as digital and mobile technologies make it ever easier to access goods and services on demand. No longer just a Millennial preference, it's part of modern society. The focus has shifted towards convenience, price and transactional efficiency: 'community as commodity' (Rinne, 2019).

So the issue, for instance, of collaborative platforms where 'what's mine is yours, for a fee' will continue to pose a deeply serious challenge to the insurance market for many years to come, with extraordinary opportunities for organizations that are agile, efficient and attractive in terms of their products and services, and who manage to position and promote themselves in an impactful, engaging and motivating way.

The implications are clear for those legacy players that remain bonded to outmoded business models, inflexible service behaviour (that fails to cater for 'real-time' insurance needs) and unemotional communication activity, ie they need to 'adapt or die' as the industry saying has it.

And absolutely crucial to all of this, of course, are the equally 'agile and attractive' pricing models that are put in place.

While the denizens of advertising creative departments have traditionally found the subject of pricing to be unexciting, the opposite is the case for real people (or 'consumers') who view price as being of the upmost interest. In many cases, either to the exclusion of all other considerations or as the absolute primary consideration.

The Boston Consulting Group note that consumers will always be interested in a better price, stating in a high-profile report that 'companies that don't tackle pricing in a strategic and concerted manner are likely to face a number of predators. The long-term trend in global trade is toward more open markets and fewer barriers to cross-border commerce. And digital technology opens up whole new avenues for buyers and sellers to connect' (Schürmann *et al*, 2015). This is, of course, as relevant for the insurance sector as it is for a vast array of others.

A prime example is Lemonade, who were part of the new wave of digital insurance brands that shook up the US sector by leveraging the abilities of leading-edge technology, powered by their own imaginative approach to business, before then developing the company via international expansion.

Their business plan mirrors the attitudes held by many Millennials (and Gen-Xers) towards the financial services market, from the perspective of demanding a more transparent, ethical and empathetic approach.

The 'fresh appeal' of the brand was noted by the *Financial Times*, which pointed out that young people 'use Airbnb for travel and Spotify for music, so why not Lemonade for insurance?' (Ralph, 2019). This sees the company's fees paid by their customers being utilized on a not-for-profit model, with an end result being that 'good causes' benefit from being given the proceeds of unused premiums, ie those that were not absorbed by customer claims.

A key element of their appeal is that they do away with the type of indecipherable legalese with which anyone who's attempted to 'read the small print' of a contract will be only too familiar. Instead, they massively reduce the amount of confusing legal information with which consumers have to contend under what they term a 'Policy 2.0' approach.

Summary

When it comes to consumer demands and innovation in the fintech and insurtech sectors, the future is bright for those companies who heed the types of trends that I focused on in this chapter, and indeed in many other parts of this book. These organizations are both enabled by, but also held accountable via, appropriately innovative regulations. This means the respecting of personal privacy, delivering consumer control and evidencing guarantees that, for instance, customer data will be erased after 'task-specific' usage.

As for the future, *The Economist* notes a tectonic shift in financial services for slow-moving banking institutions and their 'digitally inducted nightmares. In hindsight, the pivotal year was 2007, when the credit crunch started, and the iPhone was launched. The consequences of the crunch have preoccupied bankers everywhere for more than a decade. The smartphone it is becoming clear, will matter at least as much for their future' (Joyce, 2019).

An almost continual note of reinvention is required in order to align with, and answer, the demands of increasingly 'unreasonable' consumers. Today's consumers have grown used to a world in which those demands are met swiftly and efficiently. And if yesterday's financial services companies were often defined as being slow and inefficient, then it's in the past where they will remain.

An almost continual note of reinvention is required in order to align with, and answer, the demands of increasingly 'unreasonable' consumers.

And as for what's coming over the horizon at speed, a good place to look is Switzerland, where their stock exchange operates on a leading-edge basis from the perspective of next-generation technology.

I'd make one final point about the moves from Silicon Valley. In my previous book I covered, in great detail, how the misuse of the products and services provided by 'tech titans' (and their own almost criminal ineptitude) had such a negative impact on societal cohesion, across deeply foundational areas including politics and culture.

The destabilizing impacts of those 'early years' of social media from the perspectives of distortion, disinformation and destabilization will simply not be allowed to disrupt the global financial markets in an equally negative manner.

Indeed, as Chris Hughes, a co-founder of Facebook said about Libra's potential control of monetary policy 'it could hand over much of this from central banks to private companies. Inevitably, these will put their private interests – profits and influence – ahead of public ones. "Move fast and break things" was an appropriate slogan for a college social network. It's not appropriate for the global monetary system' (Hughes, 2019).

So when it comes to banking in particular, let us all hope that consumers and society benefit from the incredibly positive outcomes potentially offered by the tech innovators.

It's starkly obvious, for instance, that cryptocurrencies are set to become a far more mainstream offering in the future; so it's vital to ensure that society benefits from 'positive innovation' while potentially negative outcomes are constricted by strong oversight and powerful regulation. For in the banking and insurance sectors, the societal costs of market failure have been shown, time and again, to be too onerous for us to accept.

When it comes to 'positive innovation vs negative outcomes' then the world of cryptocurrencies offers a classic example of where the oversight and regulation that I mentioned are, obviously, utterly vital. A recent example of this requirement was shown by the BBC investigation into Ruja Ignatova, the self-named 'Cryptoqueen' and inventor of OneCoin. This supposed 'Bitcoin Killer' turned out to be, as the BBC noted, 'a familiar scam with a digital twist – a new and hugely successful take on the old pyramid scheme, which represented the dark side of rapid technological change' (BBC, 2019).

And of course, companies must be ever vigilant with regard to understanding the potential actions of both shareholder activism and environmental campaigners. This is all set in the context of an era when considerations over environmental, social and governance (ESG) issues have at long last become part of mainstream activity, and the 'green bond' markets have proved wildly popular with investors and entrepreneurs alike.

What this all goes to show is that, just as I mention elsewhere in this book, a mantra for those wishing for long-term success in the banking and insurance sectors is 'be trustworthy, reliable and competent'.

Summary

The Influencers and Revolutionaries
Innovation Manifesto

As I've illustrated throughout this book, businesses in all sectors are challenged by the environmental crisis, disruptive technology, unforeseen competitors, unpredictable customers and swiftly changing trends.

Around the world, people are looking for alternatives and demanding a better way of doing things; with desires including more sustainable, inclusive, ethical, flexible, personal, collaborative or radical options, with those 'radical options' possibly being of the nostalgic or futuristic variety.

A vital issue is that we're increasingly seeing emerging issues becoming mainstream trends, at speed, due to the fragmentation of markets and the sheer size of 'mass-niche' consumer groups. Those groups are frequently attracted by issues such as the authenticity offered by more 'personable' brands with strong customer engagement, and of course, the excitement offered by challenger brands with edgy, innovative offerings.

Yet too many businesses seem to ignore this new landscape and aren't adapting quickly enough in order to innovate and generate growth. They need to stay ahead of the competition and understand dynamic cultural, economic and social trends, and innovate around emerging ways of living and consuming that are dictating new methods of doing business. Hence, a 'design thinking' ethos being so important.

The response must be a transformation of the way in which businesses are led, strategies are developed, concepts are generated, products are created, customers are served, and of the overall approaches to be taken in a circular economy.

And, of course, they must act in a trustworthy manner and note their moral obligations with regard to the outputs of their activity. For example, the tension between innovation and ethics, regarding AI and predictive algorithms, is of immense significance.

It's fascinating to observe how modern management theory has shifted away from the one apparently set in stone by the economist Milton Friedman, for whom the responsibility of business was purely to increase its profits. This means that a deeply meaningful realignment of the 'Overton Window' has taken place in corporate terms.

We now see leading businesses having a very different overall 'accountable capitalism' stance, with the 'purpose of business' being viewed as one that has improving society as a central aim. This also links to a global 'Contract for the Web'.

That is a hugely important shift, and these modernized principles reflect a very different business world than that inhabited by Mr Friedman. For instance, they must make ever stronger efforts to achieve the sustainable development goals set before them.

Throughout this book, I've aimed to illuminate an extensive range of exciting ideas and actions taken by influential and/or revolutionary thinkers and doers, regarding the delivery of dynamic solutions to problems and tension points affecting people around the world, from the perspective of a wide variety of industries and sectors.

Of course, some of the changes that I've described, and the implications of them (in terms of governmental, organizational, business and brand innovation) will happen at slower or indeed faster rates than forecast, in different places, across different sectors, for different audiences. A prime example being the global scope and personal impact of the Internet of Things.

It'll be fascinating to observe and, when relevant, experience the products and services produced, and the choices made available as a result of altered consumer behaviour and new business models. A key trend driving systemic change is that scarcity, not abundance, will be a defining element of our futures.

But innovators must also beware of creating change when none is required, and authenticity, in terms of nostalgia and a dependable past, is what's desired instead. They need to take heed of the search for escape from the 'simulacra world' that Jean Baudrillard so abhorred, and that Guy Debord's *Society of the Spectacle* and his Situationist followers highlighted as 'the beach beneath the street'. Those influencers, or perhaps revolutionaries, pointed to the 'real' and not 'manufactured' world as the one we should evoke, hence their critique of homogenized modernity, and the empty promises of the consumer dream.

Their ideas have gone from the margins of the 1960s counterculture to the centre stage of the 2020s zeitgeist and have clear links to those who also point with alarm to, for instance, the innovations that Silicon Valley has brought us. Those innovations have delivered highly welcome positive outcomes, alongside increasingly rejected negative ones, to societies around the world. Hence, we should be mindful of 'the law of unintended consequences' which is one that is regularly mentioned with regard to, for instance, developments in artificial intelligence.

The aims of those anti-establishment thinkers and activists had obvious links to the anti-capitalist protestors of the 1990s and 2000s. Those events sent shockwaves through government departments and corporate boardrooms, and the protestors attending them directly connect to current activist movements. Which brings us neatly back to today's environmentalist groups who relentlessly identify a sustainable future for all as a central goal. Hence an obsession with the crucial COP26 summit.

The existential issue of the climate and biodiversity emergency matters to all of us, and it needs to be endlessly stressed in a business book as much as any other type of title. Indeed, according to the Governor of the Bank of England (not someone normally given to extreme statements) 'firms ignoring the climate crisis will go bankrupt'. But he also noted that 'there will be industries, sectors and firms that'll do very well, because they will be part of the solution' (Carrington, 2019). I'll use just one more quote to illuminate the issue, from one of the most pro-business international media sources available.

According to the *Financial Times* 'everything is dying out. Half of all wild animals have been lost since 1970. The Amazon is burning, as is the Arctic. Carbon dioxide in the atmosphere has reduced the plants' nutrient value by 30 per cent since the 1950s. Regarding this catastrophe looming over our heads, it's with us for good' (Ings, 2019). Tragically, the science is crystal clear.

The business community need to get on 'the right side of history' with reference to this vast challenge. In the specific context of this book, innovators within organizations must make their voices heard and their leaders need to act upon their recommendations, with a growth mindset and a 'brand positive' approach. Hence increasing numbers of 'regenerative' businesses.

Many have called for not just a fundamental rethink of how we approach solving business problems (and as I said at the beginning of this book, innovators are those who 'seek problems to solve') but that we look at innovation as a whole, and its place in the world we live in, as a point to be endlessly deliberated from the perspective of making life better for the largest possible number of people, for instance via biohacking.

This is ever more important in a chaotic political setting that sees companies (and, of course, religious groups) moving into vital areas where a 'policy vacuum' exists, in order to generate solutions to complex issues impacting society. These are framed by debate about issues such as a 'Green New Deal' that links climate action with the idea of greater social justice, in addition to whether we've worryingly reached 'peak democracy'.

Meanwhile, in a trend-saturated world that sees us inundated with the rise of 'endless possibilities' I've tried to highlight both anomalies within sectors, and the connected trends that link across them, from a pattern recognition perspective.

Why? Because by looking for signals and being aware of emerging trends, organizations can prepare themselves for the disruptive impacts on their own particular situations, from strategic planning and tactical action perspectives.

To summarize my thoughts, I believe we need a more humanistic approach to innovation. One that promotes environmentalism, diversity, social progression and individual well-being as a foundation of the concepts, products, services and experiences that organizations and businesses create. One that, frankly, delivers hope.

Finally, and in order to have an easily referenced innovation checklist, I've produced a guide – or manifesto to give it a more grandiose title – and this is it:

The Influencers and Revolutionaries Innovation Manifesto

Question and confront

Be sceptical, and challenge established thinking. So... think like René Descartes.

- For example: clarify if you're to take an iterative or inventive approach. Iterative versions are where brands improve on past offerings, with major examples including Amazon and Deliveroo. The original social media brands, meanwhile, effectively invented a whole new category, and with it, changed the world. Remember that most sectors have 'set-in' beliefs about business success, many of which are, quite simply, no longer fit for purpose. Meanwhile, many believe, for instance, that Silicon Valley has created nothing genuinely innovative in a decade.

Look and listen

Be aware of cultural signals and market dynamics. So... think like William Gibson.

- For example: take an empathetic approach and aim to understand the areas in society or business where a brand can make a relevant and welcome offering. In a world where sustainability is a central concern, and when many consider that society has passed being at 'peak-stuff', innovators need to think of the genuine benefits that they can bring us, while being ever mindful of the circular economy.

Research and develop

Conduct consumer research re needs, desires and tension points, then test innovative concepts. So... think like Peter Drucker.

- For example: in a world of ultra-personalization across an expanse of industry sectors, focus relentlessly on the customer, asking yourself if they will say 'this is ideal for me'. Consumers have grown so used to being targeted and offered increasingly fine-tuned products and services, that most generalized offerings are perceived to be, correspondingly, ever weaker. Quantum computing may also play a vitally innovative role here, ie regarding personalized medicine.

Collaborate and utilize

Leverage a range of team abilities and organizational assets. So... think like Don Tapscott. (Or indeed, Mariana Mazzucato.)

- For example: companies are increasingly looking to 'weaponize' their consumers by encouraging them to promote the brand in question themselves. Meanwhile, corporations are seeking many of their innovative ideas on an external, rather than internal basis. Collaboration is good, because we're social beings and are more creative and productive when we liaise with others, who share the same goal, in an empathetic manner.

Be a good corporate citizen

Take note of, and try to help fix, social and environmental problems. So… think like Tom Siebel.

• For example: companies need to be a 'positive force for good' and this impacts product and service innovation alongside social and environmental innovation, eg regarding the way we eat, dress, travel and work. Organizations, particularly purpose-driven ones, should demonstrate their part in confronting climate change and social problems. Ethics has also moved from being a 'nice to consider' issue to a key 'must have' factor for those desiring good reputations and long-term success. Ethics is also an absolutely central point when it comes to issues such as AI, privacy, IoT, cybernetics and robotics.

What this all points to, I believe, and as stated at the very beginning of my book, is that the core buzzwords for successful innovation are hyper-relevance, ultra-personalization, collaboration, ethics and sustainability.

I finish with a final point: only a few years ago, when asked to identify an extraordinary figure who was an 'Influencer and Revolutionary' many people would have thought of an individual like Elon Musk, who created a radical new range of consumer products, and in doing so, made better things.

But in today's world, I'd like to highlight someone who, quite simply, is the most important 'influencer and revolutionary' of our era. Crucially, instead of 'just' being interested in making better things, she takes a more profound approach, and wants to make things better for humanity. I'm talking, of course, about Greta Thunberg.

I believe we must take note of both those remarkable individuals, and of others in my book, blend innovation with ethics and, in a paradigm shift, ensure that 'good business is good business'.

References and further reading

Introduction

Ford, H (nd) [online] https://www.thehenryford.org/collections-and-research/digital-resources/popular-topics/henry-ford-quotes/ (archived at https://perma.cc/8ZWT-J25K)

Chapter 1

Adair, J (2015) *Effective Innovation*, Macmillan

Creative Education Foundation (2016) Creative Problem Solving Tools & Techniques Resource Guide [online] https://www.creativeeducation foundation.org/wp-content/uploads/2015/06/ToolsTechniques-Guide-FINAL-web-watermark.pdf (archived at https://perma.cc/M5S9-C3ZT)

Denning, S (2015) How to create an innovative culture, *Forbes*, 30 November [online] https://www.forbes.com/sites/stevedenning/2015/11/30/how-to-create-an-innovative-culture-the-extraordinary-case-of-sri/#2ba7fe7f6ad3 (archived at https://perma.cc/5UM5-S6BD)

Drucker, P (2002) The discipline of innovation, *Harvard Business Review*, August [online] https://hbr.org/2002/08/the-discipline-of-innovation (archived at https://perma.cc/FN98-HCKB)

Gibson, W (2003) *Pattern Recognition*, Penguin

Kotler, P (2003) *Marketing Insights from A to Z*, John Wiley & Sons

Levitt, T (2002) Creativity is not enough, *Harvard Business Review*, August [online] https://hbr.org/2002/08/creativity-is-not-enough (archived at https://perma.cc/6Q44-KYYT)

McKinsey Quarterly (2014) Tom Peters on leading the 21st-century organization [online] https://www.mckinsey.com/~/media/McKinsey/Business%20Functions/Organization/Our%20Insights/Tom%20Peters%20on%20leading%20the%2021st%20century%20organization/Tom_Peters_on_leading_the_21st_century_organization.ashx (archived at https://perma.cc/3EVS-Q2Q2)

MindTools (nd) TRIZ – a powerful methodology for creative problem solving [online] https://www.mindtools.com/pages/article/newCT_92.htm (archived at https://perma.cc/W9AW-6VB8)

Royer, I (2003) Why bad projects are so hard to kill, *Harvard Business Review*, February [online] https://hbr.org/2003/02/why-bad-projects-are-so-hard-to-kill (archived at https://perma.cc/WWH8-XPAR)

Schwartz, P (2004) *Inevitable Surprises*, The Free Press

Sternberg, R (2001) *Perspectives on Thinking, Learning, and Cognitive Styles*, Routledge

Tapscott, D (2018) The spirit of collaboration is touching all of our lives, *The Globe and Mail*, 9 May [online] https://www.theglobeandmail.com/opinion/the-spirit-of-collaboration-is-touching-all-of-our-lives/article12409331/ (archived at https://perma.cc/9Z8R-9KAK)

Wharton College (2001) How Siebel Systems found its groove, 19 December [online] https://knowledge.wharton.upenn.edu/article/how-siebel-systems-found-its-groove/ (archived at https://perma.cc/YH3V-N33Q)

Yu, H (2018) *Leap*, PublicAffairs

Chapter 2

Arrigo, Y (2019) Extinction Rebellion disrupts Cannes Lions, *Campaign*, 19 June [online] https://www.campaignlive.co.uk/article/extinction-rebellion-disrupts-cannes-lions/1588146?bulletin=campaign_agencies_bulletin&utm_medium=EMAIL&utm_campaign=eNews%20Bulletin&utm_source=20190622&utm_content=Campaign%20Agencies%20(331)::&email_hash= (archived at https://perma.cc/HYK6-9Q2P)

Bregman, R (2018) *Utopia for Realists: And how we can get there*, Bloomsbury Press

Dams, T (2019) Cannes Lions takes place in a time of change for ad world, *Variety*, 17 June [online] https://variety.com/2019/biz/festivals/cannes-lions-happens-as-ad-world-adjusts-to-shifting-landscapes-1203238623/ (archived at https://perma.cc/Q794-SRLP)

Davis, E (2019) Sixth sense analysts: the marketing roles of the future, *Campaign*, 29 July [online] https://www.campaignlive.co.uk/article/

sixth-sense-analysts-marketing-roles-future/1591051?bulletin=
campaign_brands_bulletin&utm_medium=EMAIL&utm_campaign
=eNews%20Bulletin&utm_source=20190729&utm_content=
Campaign%20Brands%20(351)::&email_hash= (archived at https://
perma.cc/TAA4-WD84)

Elmhirst, S (2019) It's genuine, you know?: why the influencer industry is
going 'authentic', *Guardian*, 5 April [online] https://www.theguardian.
com/media/2019/apr/05/its-genuine-you-know-why-the-online-
influencer-industry-is-going-authentic (archived at https://perma.cc/
LA24-VE6K)

Extinction Rebellion (2019) Our Demands [online] https://rebellion.earth/
the-truth/demands/ (archived at https://perma.cc/Y935-RNUN)

Horton, A (2019) Fighting Fyre with Fyre: the story of two warring
festival documentaries, *Guardian*, 16 January [online] https://www.
theguardian.com/film/2019/jan/16/fyre-festival-documentaries-hulu-
netflix (archived at https://perma.cc/XS6Q-8MU2)

Kelly, J (2019) Netflix's Fyre Festival documentary is a cautionary tale of
bad leadership, *Forbes*, 29 January [online] https://www.forbes.com/
sites/jackkelly/2019/01/29/netflixs-fyre-festival-documentary-is-a-
cautionary-tale-of-bad-leadership/#533ee1eeea28 (archived at https://
perma.cc/9Y99-U3NW)

Kemp, N (2019) Should the advertising industry be doing more to tackle
climate change? *Bite/Creative Brief*, 22 July [online] https://www.
creativebrief.com/bite/should-advertising-industry-be-doing-more-
tackle-climate-change (archived at https://perma.cc/J45C-BWE4)

Murphy, H (2019) Advertising industry closes in on a new target:
influencers, *Financial Times*, 13 July [online] https://www.ft.com/
content/3510eaf0-a3af-11e9-974c-ad1c6ab5efd1 (archived at
https://perma.cc/EGN3-7TP7)

Rogers, B (2019) Accenture Interactive disrupts ad agency industry by
engineering better customer experiences, *Forbes*, 19 July [online]
https://www.forbes.com/sites/brucerogers/2019/07/19/accenture-
interactive-disrupts-ad-agency-industry-by-engineering-better-
customer-experiences-qa-with-ceo-brian-whipple/#2bf4ef9a536f
(archived at https://perma.cc/GG49-FAL5)

Trott, D (2019) Bad influence, *Campaign*, 11 July [online] https://www.
campaignlive.co.uk/article/bad-influence/1590398 (archived at
https://perma.cc/S93U-PUUW)

Vallance, C (2019) Isn't it ironic? *Campaign*, 29 July [online] https://www.campaignlive.com/article/isnt-ironic/1592124 (archived at https://perma.cc/YJ28-5PZR)

Vizard, S (2019) Keith Weed: great advertising is the best way to build trust, *Marketing Week*, 5 March [online] https://www.marketingweek.com/keith-weed-great-advertising-build-trust/ (archived at https://perma.cc/3T8S-USL2)

Chapter 3

Bradshaw, T (2019) Hey, Siri: from virtual assistant to BFF? *Financial Times*, 20 April [online] https://www.ft.com/content/f9a13062-5fd7-11e9-b285-3acd5d43599e (archived at https://perma.cc/842X-BWE2)

Bramley, E V (2019) Extinction Rebellion: 'Fashion week should be a declaration of emergency', *Guardian*, 26 July [online] https://www.theguardian.com/fashion/2019/jul/26/extinction-rebellion-fashion-week-should-be-a-declaration-of-emergency (archived at https://perma.cc/2PZV-72WG)

Deloitte (2019) Redefine Work, *Deloitte Insights* [online] https://www2.deloitte.com/content/dam/insights/us/articles/4779_Redefine-work/DI_Redefine-work.pdf (archived at https://perma.cc/8A4J-4NUL)

Fenner, J (2019) Prada's newest travel bags are made from 100% recycled ocean trash, *Robb Report*, 1 July [online] https://robbreport-com.cdn.ampproject.org/c/s/robbreport.com/style/fashion/pradas-sustainable-re-nylon-bags-are-made-from-recycled-ocean-waste-2856553/amp/ (archived at https://perma.cc/XYQ7-ER5V)

Ricker, T (2018) What is the Home of the Future anyway? *The Verge*, 6 August [online] https://www.theverge.com/2018/8/6/17636538/home-future-grant-imahara-solar-energy-5g-smart-gadget (archived at https://perma.cc/C4F9-B5NZ)

Schumpeter (2019) Sleepless in Silicon Valley, *The Economist*, 16 May [online] https://www.economist.com/business/2019/05/16/sleepless-in-silicon-valley (archived at https://perma.cc/QF9A-FNEJ)

Siegle, L (2019) Scrap the catwalk: Extinction Rebellion is right – London fashion week is unsustainable, *Guardian*, 9 August [online] https://www.theguardian.com/fashion/2019/aug/09/scrap-the-catwalk-extinction-rebellion-is-right-london-fashion-week-is-unsustainable#img-1 (archived at https://perma.cc/RCA8-KUVZ)

Tett, G (2019) Why Japan isn't afraid of robots, *Financial Times*, 15 June [online] https://www.ft.com/content/87ac09b0-8c9a-11e9-a24d-b42f641eca37 (archived at https://perma.cc/8NJS-XAP8)

Wood, Z (2019) Unilever warns it will sell off brands that hurt the planet or society, *Guardian*, 25 July [online] https://www.theguardian.com/business/2019/jul/25/unilever-warns-it-will-sell-off-brands-that-hurt-the-planet-or-society (archived at https://perma.cc/L2AA-34P2)

Chapter 4

Angus, A (2018) Clean Lifers: a top consumer trend for 2018, *Euromonitor International*, 2 May [online] https://blog.euromonitor.com/clean-lifers-top-consumer-trend-2018/ (archived at https://perma.cc/ET55-NJBH)

Doward, J (2019) Virtual fences, robot workers, stacked crops: farming in 2040, *Guardian*, 17 February [online] https://www.theguardian.com/environment/2019/feb/17/robots-future-farming?CMP=Share_iOSApp_Other (archived at https://perma.cc/B9VR-BRE3)

Impossible Foods (nd) Mission [online] https://impossiblefoods.com/mission/ (archived at https://perma.cc/Q5KD-4UUZ)

JWT Intelligence (2018) The Future 100: 2019, November [online] https://www.jwtintelligence.com/trend-reports/the-future-100-2019/ (archived at https://perma.cc/M9QX-C8XZ)

Lempert, P (2017) 10 food trends that will shape 2018, *Forbes*, 13 December [online] https://www.forbes.com/sites/phillempert/2017/12/13/10-food-trends-that-will-shape-2018/#67a9bac84104 (archived at https://perma.cc/C89S-KPVG)

Mintel (nd) Global food and drink trends 2019 [online] https://www.mintel.com/global-food-and-drink-trends/ (archived at https://perma.cc/8Q8W-KG9M)

Nicolaou, A (2018) Coca-Cola joins push to cut plastic waste, *Financial Times*, 20 January [online] https://www.ft.com/content/9059c2dc-fd30-11e7-9b32-d7d59aace167 (archived at https://perma.cc/VFV6-K7VD)

Qureshi, W (2019) P&G to launch reusable and refillable packaging after joining LOOP initiative, *Packaging News*, 24 January [online] https://www.packagingnews.co.uk/top-story/pg-launch-reusable-refillable-packaging-joining-loop-initiative-24-01-2019 (archived at https://perma.cc/FG85-W56C)

Sax, D (2018) End the innovation obsession, *New York Times*, 7 December [online] https://www.nytimes.com/2018/12/07/opinion/sunday/end-the-innovation-obsession.html (archived at https://perma.cc/ETW8-G56P)

Splitter, J (2018) What can blockchain really do for the food industry? *Forbes*, 30 September [online] https://www.forbes.com/sites/jennysplitter/2018/09/30/what-can-blockchain-really-do-for-the-food-industry/#3d38bb9488ef (archived at https://perma.cc/EF8N-KESC)

Wilson-Powell, G (2017) 'In Nature there is no waste'. Behind Silo, the UK's first zero waste restaurant, *Farmdrop*, 30 August [online] https://www.farmdrop.com/blog/silo-brighton-zero-waste-restaurant/ (archived at https://perma.cc/6P55-88WD)

Chapter 5

Armstrong, N (2018) Brave new world, *The Spectator*, 25 November [online] https://www.spectator.co.uk/author/neilarmstrong/ (archived at https://perma.cc/P2ED-3TRN)

Avery, B (2018) Drinks for thought: nootropic beverages offer brain benefits, Bevnet, 14 November [online] https://www.bevnet.com/news/2018/drinks-for-thought-nootropic-beverages-offer-brain-benefits (archived at https://perma.cc/ZBH3-SJ8Y)

Barlyn, S (2018) Strap on the Fitbit: John Hancock to sell only interactive life insurance, Reuters, 19 September [online] https://www.reuters.com/article/us-manulife-financi-john-hancock-lifeins/strap-on-the-fitbit-john-hancock-to-sell-only-interactive-life-insurance-idUSKCN1LZ1WL (archived at https://perma.cc/2HMK-AZZL)

BBC (2018) Diabetes: Smart patch micro needles 'to revolutionise' care, *BBC News*, 15 July [online] https://www.bbc.co.uk/news/uk-wales-44546252 (archived at https://perma.cc/C2PD-S6VS)

Bell, L (2019) The best health tech and fitness innovations at CES, *Forbes*, 11 January [online] https://www.forbes.com/sites/leebelltech/2019/01/11/the-best-health-tech-and- fitness-innovations-of-ces-2019/#49d3243a74c8 (archived at https://perma.cc/RE5T-HP4E)

Buckland, D (2018) Preventative healthcare and tackling challenges of an ageing population, *Raconteur*, 28 March [online] https://www.raconteur.net/healthcare/preventative-healthcare-tackling-challenges-ageing-population (archived at https://perma.cc/L5XK-FBDT)

Cannes Lions (2017) [online] https://www.canneslions.com/ (archived at https://perma.cc/2ZPC-JPD2)

Dans, E (2018) Insurance, wearables and the future of healthcare, *Forbes*, 21 September [online] https://www.forbes.com/sites/enriquedans/2018/09/21/insurance-wearables-and-the-future-of-healthcare/#26de7791782f (archived at https://perma.cc/4GWH-2LW6)

Davis J (2018) Hackers breach 1.5 million Singapore patient records, including the prime minister's, *Healthcare IT News*, 20 July [online] https://www.healthcareitnews.com/news/hackers-breach-15-million-singapore-patient-records-including-prime-ministers (archived at https://perma.cc/3ACN-YVU4)

Global Wellness Institute (2017) New research on the booming wellness lifestyle real estate and communities market, Global Wellness Institute, 10 October [online] https://globalwellnessinstitute.org/press-room/press-releases/new-research-on-the-booming-wellness-lifestyle-real-estate-and-communities-market/ (archived at https://perma.cc/SU9Y-RQJC)

Gottlieb, S (2018) FDA budget matters: advancing innovation in digital health, US Food & Drug Administration, 26 September [online] https://www.fda.gov/news-events/fda-voices-perspectives-fda-leadership-and-experts/fda-budget-matters-advancing-innovation-digital-health (archived at https://perma.cc/XN2K-SWAT)

Government of South Australia (nd) Healthy communities [online] https://www.sahealth.sa.gov.au/wps/wcm/connect/public+content/sa+health+internet/healthy+living/healthy+communities (archived at https://perma.cc/VH39-HSZE)

JWT Intelligence (2018) The Future 100: 2019, JWT Intelligence, November [online] https://www.jwtintelligence.com/trend-reports/ the-future-100-2019/ (archived at https://perma.cc/M9QX-C8XZ)

Moy, J (2018) Want to know yourself better? Blockchain can help, *Forbes*, 1 March 2018 [online] https://www.forbes.com/sites/ jamiemoy/2018/03/01/want-to-know-yourself-better-blockchain-can-help/#172b67972d69 (archived at https://perma.cc/L2AF-6AH5)

NHGRI (nd) Genomics and medicine, National Human Genome Research Institute [online] https://www.genome.gov/27552451/ what-is-genomic-medicine/ (archived at https://perma.cc/T6J2-5T8S)

National Institute for Play (nd) [online] http://www.nifplay.org/ (archived at https://perma.cc/4NSE-6EE8)

Pallister, J (2018) Reinventing death for the twenty-first century, Design Council [online] https://www.designcouncil.org.uk/news-opinion/ reinventing-death-twenty-first-century-0 (archived at https://perma. cc/8HUA-K28Z)

Proteus Digital Health (nd) Transforming care with digital medicine, Proteus Digital Health [online] https://www.proteus.com/evidence/ (archived at https://perma.cc/R23F-N3XR)

Pursel, B (2018) Smart tattoos for improving health, Penn State University, 2 September [online] https://sites.psu.edu/ ist110pursel/2018/09/02/smart-tattos-for-improving-health/ (archived at https://perma.cc/UZ9Q-WCYS)

Reuters Editorial (2018) Digital health market size, share, report, analysis, trends & forecast to 2026, Reuters, 18 April [online] https://www. reuters.com/brandfeatures/venture-capital/article?id=33613 (archived at https://perma.cc/7CWT-7NJC)

The Economist (2018) A revolution in health care is coming: Welcome to Doctor You, *The Economist*, 1 February [online] https://www. economist.com/leaders/2018/02/01/a-revolution-in-health-care-is-coming (archived at https://perma.cc/9WE7-UYDJ)

WARC (2018) Brands must adapt to the wellness trend, WARC, 7 December [online] https://www.warc.com/newsandopinion/news/ brands_must_adapt_to_the_wellness_trend/41429 (archived at https://perma.cc/ATL4-4DEN)

WHO (2014) Mental health: a state of wellbeing, World Health Organization, August [online] https://www.who.int/features/factfiles/mental_health/en/ (archived at https://perma.cc/752S-4ENW)

Wired (2019) The future of healthcare is collaborative, *Wired*, 14 March [online] https://www.wired.co.uk/article/nhs-future-collaborative-healthcare (archived at https://perma.cc/68MK-3PXK)

Chapter 6

Batty, M (2018) *Inventing Future Cities*, MIT Press.

Bettencourt, L (2007) Growth, innovation, scaling, and the pace of life in cities, *PNAS*, 6 March [online] https://www.pnas.org/content/pnas/104/17/7301.full.pdf (archived at https://perma.cc/EL7X-F6LU)

Bloomberg (2018) China is leading the world to an electric car future, *Bloomberg Businessweek*, 15 November [online] https://www.bloomberg.com/news/articles/2018-11-14/china-is-leading-the-world-to-an-electric-car-future (archived at https://perma.cc/NJA4-QTZE)

Brown University (2007) Urbanism in the archaeological record: what is a city?, 11 September [online] https://www.brown.edu/Departments/Joukowsky_Institute/courses/urbanism/3981.html (archived at https://perma.cc/XYX4-MBEG)

CBS News (2019) Alexandria Ocasio-Cortez celebrates Amazon move to scrap New York headquarters, *CBS News*, 14 February [online] https://www.cbsnews.com/news/amazon-cancels-new-hq-alexandria-ocasio-cortez-celebrates-amazon-move-to-scrap-new-york-headquarters-today-2019-02-14/ (archived at https://perma.cc/8GAC-GMZL)

Chan, M (2018) Chinese startup makes facial recognition glasses for police, *Nikkei Asian Review*, 21 August [online] https://asia.nikkei.com/Business/Companies/Chinese-startup-makes-facial-recognition-glasses-for-police (archived at https://perma.cc/4CSM-L4XQ)

Chin, J and Lin, L (2017) China's all-seeing surveillance state is reading its citizens' faces, *Wall Street Journal*, 26 June [online] https://www.wsj.com/articles/the-all-seeing-surveillance-state-feared-in-the-west-is-a-reality-in-china-1498493020 (archived at https://perma.cc/9MQK-9CVQ)

CityLab (2017) Confronting the New Urban Crisis, *CityLab*, 11 April [online] https://www.citylab.com/equity/2017/04/confronting-the-new-urban-crisis/521031/ (archived at https://perma.cc/67JJ-SUSR)

Cook, T (2018) Debating Ethics, 24 October [online] https://www.privacyconference2018.org/en/press-media/press-releases.html (archived at https://perma.cc/KJ8F-GZVT)

Erez, N (2018) Cyber attacks are shutting down countries, cities and companies. Here's how to stop them, World Economic Forum, 22 June [online] https://www.weforum.org/agenda/2018/06/how-organizations-should-prepare-for-cyber-attacks-noam-erez/ (archived at https://perma.cc/SU2P-8ECL)

Extinction Rebellion (2019) Our demands [online] https://rebellion.earth/the-truth/demands/ (archived at https://perma.cc/Y935-RNUN)

Florida, R (2017) *The New Urban Crisis*, Basic Books

Girault, J (2019) Coming soon to China: the car of the future, *Taipei Times*, 21 April [online] http://www.taipeitimes.com/News/biz/archives/2019/04/21/2003713759 (archived at https://perma.cc/Z5FA-75G9)

Glaeser, E (nd) Review of Richard Florida's *The Rise of the Creative Class*, OpenScholar @Harvard [online] https://scholar.harvard.edu/files/glaeser/files/book_review_of_richard_floridas_the_rise_of_the_creative_class.pdf (archived at https://perma.cc/2E9L-XBXZ)

Green, M (2019) Extinction Rebellion: inside the new climate resistance, *FT Magazine*, 11 April [online] https://www.ft.com/content/9bcb1bf8-5b20-11e9-9dde-7aedca0a081a (archived at https://perma.cc/Q4BN-C3PP)

Grossman, B (2017) The Seven Pillar Solution, *Ohio City Observer*, 16 July [online] http://ohiocityobserver.com/read/2017/07/16/the-seven-pillar-solution-conclusions-from-richard-floridas-new-book (archived at https://perma.cc/689A-HT48)

Hammond G (2019) Residents' revenge: how citizens are taking on city developers, *Financial Times*, 13 April [online] https://www.ft.com/content/2c869db2-5abc-11e9-939a-341f5ada9d40 (archived at https://perma.cc/GDU5-958Y)

IDC Government Insights (nd) Worldwide smart cities and communities strategies, IDC [online] https://www.idc.com/getdoc.jsp?containerId=IDC_P23432 (archived at https://perma.cc/VCS6-6VC8)

Knoll, L (2018) Developing the connected world of 2018 and beyond, *Forbes*, 16 March [online] https://www.forbes.com/sites/forbestech-council/2018/03/16/developing-the-connected-world-of-2018-and-beyond/ (archived at https://perma.cc/S84K-54KB)

Kreitzman, L (1999) *The 24-Hour Society*, Profile Books

Kreitzman, L (2016) How the 24-hour society is stealing time from the night, *Aeon*/Oxford University Press, 22 November [online] https://aeon.co/ideas/how-the-24-hour-society-is-stealing-time-from-the-night (archived at https://perma.cc/6DZ4-8MUW)

Lerner, M (2018) The new boomtowns: why more people are relocating to 'secondary' cities, *Washington Post*, 8 November [online] https://www.washingtonpost.com/realestate/the-new-boomtowns-why-more-people-are-relocating-to-secondary-cities/2018/11/07/f55f96f4-d618-11e8-aeb7-ddcad4a0a54e_story.html?utm_term=.b9e97b685b7f (archived at https://perma.cc/E5NB-H5SY)

Leskin P (2019) The 50 most high-tech cities in the world, *Business Insider*, 2 April [online] https://www.businessinsider.com/most-innovative-cities-in-the-world-in-2018-2018-11?r=US&IR=T (archived at https://perma.cc/AVH4-6A5N)

McLaughlin, M (2019) Climate Change: where Extinction Rebellion is going wrong, *The Scotsman*, 17 April [online] https://www.scotsman.com/news/opinion/climate-change-where-extinction-rebellion-is-going-wrong-martyn-mclaughlin-1-4908627 (archived at https://perma.cc/HC2Y-DQ7E)

Puutio, T (2018) Here are 5 predictions for the future of our cities, World Economic Forum, 15 February [online] https://www.weforum.org/agenda/2018/02/here-are-5-predictions-for-the-cities-of-the-future/ (archived at https://perma.cc/6CR7-A34G)

Ratti, C and Claudel, M (2016) *The City of Tomorrow: Sensors, networks, hackers and the future of urban life*, Yale University Press

SXSW (2018) New localism: reimagining power in a populist age, SXSW, 12 March [online] https://schedule.sxsw.com/2018/events/PP98705 (archived at https://perma.cc/LV55-RGWT)

Treat, J (2019) Cities of the Future, *National Geographic*, April [online] https://www.nationalgeographic.com/magazine/2019/04/see-sustainable-future-city-designed-for-people-and-nature/ (archived at https://perma.cc/7ACR-4QB3)

Unal, B (2019) Smart cities are an absolute dream from infrastructure cyberattacks, *Wired*, 14 January [online] https://www.wired.co.uk/article/cyber-attacks-smart-cities (archived at https://perma.cc/3G39-97DY)

UN DESA (2017) World Population Prospects 2017, UN Dept of Economic and Social Affairs [online] https://esa.un.org/unpd/wpp/Publications/Files/WPP2017_KeyFindings.pdf (archived at https://perma.cc/6ZKH-5BEV)

UN DESA (2018) 68% of the world population projected to live in urban areas by 2050, says UN, UN Dept of Economic and Social Affairs [online] https://www.un.org/development/desa/en/news/population/2018-revision-of-world-urbanization-prospects.html (archived at https://perma.cc/9GL5-G3L5)

United Nations (2018) The right to privacy in the digital age, United Nations [online] https://www.ohchr.org/EN/Issues/DigitalAge/Pages/DigitalAgeIndex.aspx (archived at https://perma.cc/2JUE-UUXY)

Vidal, J (2018) The 100 million city: is 21st century urbanisation out of control? *Guardian*, 19 March [online] https://www.theguardian.com/cities/2018/mar/19/urban-explosion-kinshasa-el-alto-growth-mexico-city-bangalore-lagos (archived at https://perma.cc/TJ42-89MR)

Wainwright, O (2017) Everything is gentrification now: but Richard Florida isn't sorry, *Guardian*, 26 October [online] https://www.theguardian.com/cities/2017/oct/26/gentrification-richard-florida-interview-creative-class-new-urban-crisis (archived at https://perma.cc/VY6A-FRAK)

Ween, C (2014) *Future Cities: All that matters*, Hodder & Stoughton

Wei, H, Shijia, O and Nan, Z (2019) Innovation pays rich dividends, *China Daily*, 11 March [online] http://www.chinadaily.com.cn/a/201903/11/WS5c85b68da3106c65c34edd2b_2.html (archived at https://perma.cc/MFA7-KRJH)

Yang, Y (2019) Chinese AR start-up develops smart glasses to help police catch suspects, *South China Morning Post*, 6 May [online] https://www.scmp.com/tech/start-ups/article/3008721/chinese-ar-start-develops-smart-glasses-help-police-catch-suspects (archived at https://perma.cc/B3R8-VJM6)

Chapter 7

Andersen, M *et al* (2018) Where to profit as 'tech transforms mobility', Boston Consulting Group, 23 August [online] https://www.bcg.com/en-gb/publications/2018/profit-tech-transforms-mobility.aspx (archived at https://perma.cc/P49U-FKKP)

Bradshaw, T, (2019) Forget robo-taxis: it's e-bikes that are reshaping urban transport, *Financial Times*, 13 July [online] https://www.ft.com/content/c9f3fb3e-a1da-11e9-974c-ad1c6ab5efd1 (archived at https://perma.cc/3U9R-73RJ)

Carr, G (2019) Despite setbacks, aviation is changing fast, *The Economist*, 1 June 2019 [online] https://www.economist.com/technology-quarterly/2019/05/30/despite-setbacks-aviation-is-changing-fast (archived at https://perma.cc/JL4F-4EZA)

Connolly, K (2019) 'Polar cruise boom harming the arctic', explorer warns, *Guardian*, 13 August [online] https://www.theguardian.com/world/2019/aug/13/polar-cruise-increase-harming-the-arctic-explorer-arved-fuchs-warns (archived at https://perma.cc/TRD9-WKYZ)

Crossland, D (2019) Former VW boss Martin Winterkorn faces fresh charges in emissions scandal, *The Times*, 16 April [online] https://www.thetimes.co.uk/article/former-vw-boss-martin-winterkorn-faces-fresh-charges-in-emissions-scandal-q0kdkngth (archived at https://perma.cc/7UMR-8YWV)

Easen, N (2019) Business travel startups are transforming the industry, *Raconteur*, 5 August [online] https://www.raconteur.net/business-innovation/business-travel-startups (archived at https://perma.cc/8QYT-MJ6M)

Euromonitor (2019) 'Luxury goods in China,' *Euromonitor International*, February report [online] https://www.euromonitor.com/luxury-goods-in-china/report (archived at https://perma.cc/RD5F-T6GV)

Fortson, D, (2019) Tesla boss Elon Musk risks running out of road now his rivals have woken up, *The Times*, 26 May [online] https://www. thetimes.co.uk/article/tesla-boss-elon-musk-is-running-out-of-road-now-is-rivals-have-woken-up-q58bg978j (archived at https://perma.cc/ 24FE-NX94)

Friend, H (2019) The rise of eco-conscious luxury hotels, *LS:N Global*, 15 July [online] https://www.lsnglobal.com/big-ideas/article/24373/ the-rise-of-eco-conscious-luxury-hotels (archived at https://perma.cc/ 7NKJ-CY3A)

Heineke, K *et al* (2019) Development in the mobility technology ecosystem – how can 5G help? *McKinsey*, June [online] https://www. mckinsey.com/industries/automotive-and-assembly/our-insights/ development-in-the-mobility-technology-ecosystem-how-can-5g-help (archived at https://perma.cc/VW99-KNRU)

Mance, H (2019) Boarding soon: the five-star airship bound for the North Pole, *Financial Times*, 12 October [online] https://www.ft.com/content/ f34a3a56-e8fd-11e9-a240-3b065ef5fc55 (archived at https://perma.cc/ SQ5Y-SLGW)

McNeice, A (2019) China-made electric cars vehicles are unveiled in Geneva, *China Daily*, 7 March [online] http://www.chinadaily.com. cn/a/201903/07/WS5c801d76a3106c65c34ed2f4.html (archived at https://perma.cc/VU6H-Z6ZS)

Moor, R (2016) What happens to American myth when you take the driver out of it? *New York Magazine*, 17 October [online] http:// nymag.com/intelligencer/2016/10/is-the-self-driving-car-un-american. html (archived at https://perma.cc/VRS5-ENJP)

Neslen, A (2019) BMW, Daimler and VW charged with collusion over emissions, *Guardian*, 6 April [online] https://www.theguardian.com/ business/2019/apr/05/bmw-daimler-and-vw-charged-collusion-clean-emissions-tech (archived at https://perma.cc/DC6R-86VU)

Pfeifer, S (2019) Electric planes: the revolution has some snags, *Financial Times*, 17 June [online] https://www.ft.com/content/a9dc81d2-725e-11e9-bf5c-6eeb837566c5 (archived at https://perma.cc/N2YQ-RZRQ)

The Economist (2019a) A new age of space exploration is beginning, *The Economist*, 20 July [online] https://www.economist.com/ leaders/2019/07/18/a-new-age-of-space-exploration-is-beginning (archived at https://perma.cc/LL3T-N2M2)

The Economist (2019b) Electric-scooter startups are becoming more cautious, *The Economist*, 8 June [online] micromobility' https://www. economist.com/business/2019/06/06/electric-scooter-startups-are-becoming-more-cautious (archived at https://perma.cc/2GBB-LTWZ)

The Economist (2019c) For some in China, the aim of travel is to create 15-second videos, *The Economist*, 15 August [online] https://www. economist.com/china/2019/08/15/for-some-in-china-the-aim-of-travel-is-to-create-15-second-videos (archived at https://perma.cc/2KNQ-XWHJ)

Waters, R and Bond, S (2019) Uber IPO: the long ride to profitability, *Financial Times*, 11 May [online] https://www.ft.com/content/3de00068-7307-11e9-bf5c-6eeb837566c5 (archived at https:// perma.cc/FG9N-4BKA)

Zimmer, J (2016) The third transportation revolution, *Medium*, 18 September [online] https://medium.com/@johnzimmer/the-third-transportation-revolution-27860f05fa91#.dkmhaye92 (archived at https://perma.cc/W889-CD72)

Chapter 8

Aitkenhead, D (2018) Black Mirror exclusive: Charlie Brooker and Annabel Jones on the big reveal of the fifth series, *The Times*, 30 December [online] https://www.thetimes.co.uk/article/black-mirror-exclusive-charlie-brooker-and-annabel-jones-on-the-big-reveal-of-the-fifth-series-jfc63rf7f (archived at https://perma.cc/UW9Z-5BE3)

Bailey, J (2019) Fortnite maker wants to sell more games, and build a platfrom to do it, *New York Times*, 29 August [online] https://www. nytimes.com/2019/08/27/business/steam-epic-games-store.html (archived at https://perma.cc/6FYY-SX42)

Chiu, E (2019) 'SXSW: Bleed for the Throne' JWT Intelligence, 14 March [online] https://www.jwtintelligence.com/2019/03/sxsw-2019-bleed-for-the-throne/ (archived at https://perma.cc/4NNF-VDEW)

Kane, P (2004) *The Play Ethic: A manifesto for a different way of living*, Macmillan

Kaufman, W (ed) (1989) *Existentialism from Dostoyevsky to Sartre*, Meridian Publishing Co

Lewis, L (2019) Laser frisbees and energy bolts: high-tech sport is a whole new ballgame, *Financial Times*, 1 June [online] https://www.ft.com/content/751f7d4c-8167-11e9-b592-5fe435b57a3b (archived at https://perma.cc/243Y-WJPN)

Chapter 9

Bird, J (2019) How robots and holograms are bringing online learning to life, *Financial Times*, 5 March [online] https://www.ft.com/content/4b8a810c-1a88-11e9-b191-175523b59d1d (archived at https://perma.cc/4EPP-HU9F)

Bloxam, S (2019) Trust in tech: the future world of work – should we be worried? Edelman, 15 April [online] https://www.edelman.co.uk/insights/trust-tech-future-world-work-should-we-be-worried (archived at https://perma.cc/BWZ2-VKSG)

Canaday, S (2017) Cognitive diversity, *Psychology Today*, 18 June [online] https://www.psychologytoday.com/intl/blog/you-according-them/201706/cognitive-diversity (archived at https://perma.cc/D2N4-47M4)

Deighton, K (2018) BMW's Mini wants to become your landlord and coworking space provider, *The Drum*, 3 December [online] https://www.thedrum.com/news/2018/12/03/bmw-s-mini-wants-become-your-landlord-and-coworking-space-provider (archived at https://perma.cc/ND6L-W35D)

Easton, E and Bakhshi H (2018) Creativity and the future of work, Nesta, 27 March [online] https://www.nesta.org.uk/report/creativity-and-the-future-of-work/ (archived at https://perma.cc/U4CS-552C)

Frary, M (2018a) Rise of the digital nomad, *Raconteur*, 7 December [online] https://www.raconteur.net/business-innovation/rise-of-the-digital-nomad (archived at https://perma.cc/3EM9-E3MQ)

Frary, M (2018b) The dark side of inflexibility, *Raconteur*, 7 December [online] https://www.raconteur.net/business-innovation/the-dark-side-of-inflexibility (archived at https://perma.cc/J8KG-9E7H)

Gelles, D (2018) The WeWork manifesto: First, office space. Next, the world, *New York Times*, 17 February [online] https://www.nytimes.com/2018/02/17/business/the-wework-manifesto-first-office-space-next-the-world.html i (archived at https://perma.cc/V9AF-RS84)

Johansson, A (2017) Millennials are pushing for diversity in these 3 industries, *Forbes*, 14 November [online] https://www.forbes.com/sites/annajohansson/2017/11/14/millennials-are-pushing-for-diversity-in-these-3-industries/#7865787c6a5c (archived at https://perma.cc/R84U-EZWH)

Klein, N (2019) *On Fire* Allen Lane (interviewed by BBC Radio 4, 14 September 2019)

Lebowitz, S (2018) Our grandparents wanted security and stability at work, *Business Insider*, 31 December [online] https://amp.businessinsider.com/expectations-around-good-jobs-changed-over-time-2018-12 (archived at https://perma.cc/Q5RH-W3LM)

Lufkin, B (2018) How the youngest generation is redefining work, *BBC Bright Sparks*, 28 February [online] https://www.bbc.com/worklife/article/20180227-how-the-youngest-generation-is-redefining-work (archived at https://perma.cc/26PP-PLDB)

Mirza, M (2014) Artists' Workspace Study, Mayor of London, September [online] https://www.london.gov.uk/sites/default/files/artists_workspace_study_september2014_reva_web_0.pdf (archived at https://perma.cc/TQX2-3EJF)

Moore, R (2018) Thomas Heatherwick's Coal Drops Yard – shopping in the Instagram age, *Observer*, 3 November [online] https://www.theguardian.com/artanddesign/2018/nov/03/thomas-heatherwicks-coal-drops-yard-shopping-in-the-instagram-age (archived at https://perma.cc/E5AN-47MB)

Noto, A (2019) WeWork rebrands as The We Co., *New York Business Journal*, 8 January [online] https://www.bizjournals.com/newyork/news/2019/01/08/wework-rebrands-as-the-we-co.amp.html (archived at https://perma.cc/2DXS-GXR5)

Phillips R (2019) Message to Davos: the world demands a new kind of leadership, *Management Today*, 16 January [online] https://www.managementtoday.co.uk/message-davos-world-demands-new-kind-leadership/reputation-matters/article/1523136 (archived at https://perma.cc/3HGL-Y4MG)

Reynolds, A and Lewis, D (2017) Teams solve problems faster when they're more cognitively diverse, *Harvard Business Review*, 30 March [online] https://hbr.org/2017/03/teams-solve-problems-faster-when-theyre-more-cognitively-diverse (archived at https://perma.cc/NUY3-AP5A)

Schwartz, J, Stockton, H and Monahan, K (2017) Forces of change, *Deloitte Insights*, 9 November [online] https://www2.deloitte.com/insights/us/en/focus/technology-and-the-future-of-work/overview.html (archived at https://perma.cc/A5FW-PF2E)

Treggiden, K and Tucker, E (2019) The 12 best London coworking spaces, *The Spaces* [online] https://thespaces.com/the-best-london-coworking-spaces/ (archived at https://perma.cc/EPD9-KUTZ)

Tynan, D (2018) Brands are looking to futurists to foresee trends and anticipate disruption, *AdWeek*, 2 December [online] https://www.adweek.com/digital/brands-are-looking-to-futurists-to-foresee-trends-and-anticipate-disruption/ (archived at https://perma.cc/7GTJ-XULT)

WEF (2018) The Future of Jobs Report, World Economic Forum [online] http://www3.weforum.org/docs/WEF_Future_of_Jobs_2018.pdf (archived at https://perma.cc/FB9D-Z5ZN)

Wolff, B (2018) The future of work is creative collaboration, *Forbes*, 14 August [online] https://www.forbes.com/sites/benjaminwolff/2018/08/14/the-future-of-work-is-creative-collaboration/#5c74e1b93228 (archived at https://perma.cc/7Q2D-7QKJ)

Chapter 10

BBC (2019) Cryptoqueen: how this woman scammed the world, then vanished, 24 November [online] https://www.bbc.co.uk/news/stories-50435014 (archived at https://perma.cc/V2MW-44DN)

Catlin, T and Lorenz, J-T (2017) Insurtech – the threat that inspires, *McKinsey*, March 2017 [online] https://www.mckinsey.com/industries/financial-services/our-insights/insurtech-the-threat-that-inspires (archived at https://perma.cc/L3PR-VZM5)

Cuthbertson, A (2019) Dark Web criminals switch to popular apps to sell drugs using bots and secret graffiti messages to do business, *Independent*, 13 March [online] https://www.independent.co.uk/life-style/gadgets-and-tech/news/telegram-app-drugs-sell-channels-bots-crime-graffiti-dropgangs-dark-web-a8814671.html (archived at https://perma.cc/C5KG-SQAN)

Feiner, L (2019) Facebook's libra cryptocurrency coalition is falling apart as eBay, Visa, Mastercard and Stripe jump ship, *CNBC*, 11 October [online] https://www.cnbc.com/2019/10/11/ebay-drops-out-of-facebook-libra-cryptocurrency-one-week-after-paypal.html (archived at https://perma.cc/ZUH6-ZQZ6)

Financial Times (2019a) Facebook's Libra coin is a symptom of banks' flaws, *Financial Times*, 18 June [online] https://www.ft.com/content/fb3d7c68-910b-11e9-aea1-2b1d33ac3271 (archived at https://perma.cc/9CR8-UPRQ)

Financial Times (2019b) FT sets the agenda with new brand platform, *Financial Times*, 16 September [online] https://aboutus.ft.com/en-gb/announcements/ft-sets-the-agenda-with-new-brand-platform/ (archived at https://perma.cc/4NFW-DVL9)

Financial Times (2019c) No, Mr Putin, western liberalism in not obsolete, *Financial Times*, 30 June [online] https://www.ft.com/content/34f3edc0-9990-11e9-9573-ee5cbb98ed36 (archived at https://perma.cc/J5H5-JR2S)

Fortson, D (2019) Health giants want more than your heart-rate, *The Sunday Times*, 23 June [online] https://www.thetimes.co.uk/article/health-giants-want-more-than-your-heart-rate-rn0jdc3wq (archived at https://perma.cc/W77U-DZEC)

Frost, L (2019) France and Germany agree to block facebook's Libra, Reuters, 13 September [online] https://uk.reuters.com/article/uk-facebook-cryptocurrency-france-german/france-and-germany-agree-to-block-facebooks-libra-idUKKCN1VY1XV (archived at https://perma.cc/TN69-AHBD)

Hickey, S (2019) Crypto is coming: get ready to spend Facebook's money, *Observer*, 16 June [online] https://www.theguardian.com/technology/2019/jun/16/facebook-cryptocurrency-get-ready-to-spend-money (archived at https://perma.cc/WFS9-YS4M)

Hughes, C (2019) Facebook co-founder: Libra coin would shift power into the wrong hands, *Financial Times*, 23 June [online] https://www.ft.com/content/aa97ad20-91a0-11e9-8ff4-699df1c62544 (archived at https://perma.cc/QAQ3-M9AJ)

Jefferies, D (2019) What AI can do for the insurance industry, *The Times*, 28 March [online] https://www.raconteur.net/risk-management/ai-insurance (archived at https://perma.cc/3YNN-BDD4)

Joyce, H (2019) Young people and their phones are shaking up banking, *The Economist*, 2 May [online] https://www.economist.com/special-report/2019/05/02/young-people-and-their-phones-are-shaking-up-banking (archived at https://perma.cc/4WJ8-QTGN)

KPMG (2019) Insurtech Trends 10: Trends for 2019, KPMG [online] https://assets.kpmg/content/dam/kpmg/xx/pdf/2019/02/insurtech-10-trends-for-2019.pdf (archived at https://perma.cc/38HK-WXJR)

Long, J, Roark, C and Theofilou, B (2018) The bottom line on trust, Accenture, 30 October [online] https://www.accenture.com/us-en/insights/strategy/trust-in-business?c=strat_competitiveagilmediarelation s_10394050&n=mrl_1018 (archived at https://perma.cc/ES2Q-RSND)

Maulia, E (2018) Go-Jek sparks an Indonesian banking revolution, *Nikkei Asian Review*, 29 August [online] https://asia.nikkei.com/Spotlight/Cover-Story/Go-Jek-sparks-an-Indonesian-banking-revolution (archived at https://perma.cc/L3QU-W3TL)

Paul, K (2019) Libra: Facebook launches cryptocurrency in bid to shake up global finance, *Guardian*, 18 June [online] https://www.theguardian.com/technology/2019/jun/18/libra-facebook-cryptocurrency-new-digital-money-transactions (archived at https://perma.cc/L8G9-EGND)

Popper, N (2018) After 147 years, Goldman Sachs hangs a shingle on Main Street, *New York Times*, 18 June [online] https://www.nytimes.com/2016/06/19/business/dealbook/after-147-years-goldman-sachs-hangs-a-shingle-on-main-street.html?module=inline (archived at https://perma.cc/G6RN-8CA9)

Ralph, O (2019) Lemonade takes its digital fizz to Germany, *Financial Times*, 12 June [online] https://www.ft.com/content/6533b0ce-8c39-11e9-a1c1-51bf8f989972 (archived at https://perma.cc/3MPW-KZ59)

Rinne, A (2019) Four big trends for the sharing economy, World Economic Forum, 4 January [online] https://www.weforum.org/agenda/2019/01/sharing-economy/ (archived at https://perma.cc/H535-MMZG)

Schürmann, J et al (2015) Pricing across borders: how smart manufacturers maximize value, Boston Consulting Group, 24 June [online] www.bcg.com/en-gb/publications/2015/marketing-pricing-across-borders-how-smart-manufacturers-maximize-value.aspx (archived at https://perma.cc/U2UK-3VSQ)

Tesfaye, M (2019) The evolution of the US neobank market, *Business Insider*, 16 January [online] https://www.businessinsider.com/evolution-of-the-us-neobank-market?r=US&IR=T (archived at https://perma.cc/PV6Y-L9RE)

The Economist (2019) Facebook wants to create a global currency, *The Economist*, 22 June [online] https://www.economist.com/leaders/2019/06/22/facebook-wants-to-create-a-global-currency (archived at https://perma.cc/G6WA-7CNH)

Warwick-Ching, L (2019) Open banking: the quiet digital revolution one year on, *Financial Times*, 12 January [online] https://www.ft.com/content/a5f0af78-133e-11e9-a581-4ff78404524e (archived at https://perma.cc/L7SE-VH47)

Wiseman, O (2019) The moral of the story, *CapX*, 29 June [online] https://capx.co/the-moral-of-the-story/ (archived at https://perma.cc/HBY5-6GLX)

Summary

Carrington, D (2019) Firms ignoring climate crisis will go bankrupt, *Guardian*, 13 October [online] https://www.theguardian.com/environment/2019/oct/13/firms-ignoring-climate-crisis-bankrupt-mark-carney-bank-england-governor (archived at https://perma.cc/44FS-SQTG)

Ings, S (2019) Apocalypse soon? *Financial Times*, 14 September [online] https://www.ft.com/content/aa9589e6-d42b-11e9-8367-807ebd53ab77 (archived at https://perma.cc/Q4PC-M5QH)

Index

THE POST-TRUTH BUSINESS

HOW TO REBUILD BRAND AUTHENTICITY IN A DISTRUSTING WORLD

Sean Pillot de Chenecey

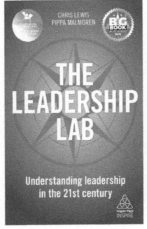

CHRIS LEWIS
PIPPA MALMGREN

THE LEADERSHIP LAB

Understanding leadership in the 21st century

HUMANITY WORKS

MERGING TECHNOLOGIES AND PEOPLE FOR THE WORKFORCE OF THE FUTURE

ALEXANDRA LEVIT

DANIEL NEWMAN/
OLIVIER BLANCHARD

HUMAN/MACHINE

THE FUTURE OF OUR PARTNERSHIP WITH MACHINES

HOW TO FUTURE

LEADING AND SENSE-MAKING IN AN AGE OF HYPERCHANGE

SCOTT SMITH
WITH MADELINE ASHBY

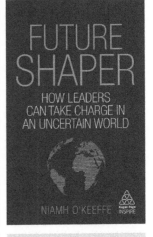

FUTURE SHAPER

HOW LEADERS CAN TAKE CHARGE IN AN UNCERTAIN WORLD

NIAMH O'KEEFFE

SUPERHUMAN INNOVATION

Transforming businesses with artificial intelligence

CHRIS DUFFEY

TOM GOODWIN

DIGITAL DARWINISM

SURVIVAL OF THE FITTEST IN THE AGE OF BUSINESS DISRUPTION

CUTTING EDGE THINKING

www.koganpage.com/inspire

Kogan Page Inspire